SOCIAL INSECURITY

SOCIAL INSECURITY

HV95
.S82

The Politics of Welfare

GILBERT Y. STEINER

84295

RAND MCNALLY & COMPANY
Chicago, Illinois

AMERICAN POLITICS RESEARCH SERIES

Aaron Wildavsky, Series Editor

BARBER, *Power in Committees: An Experiment in the Governmental Process*

DYE, *Politics, Economics, and the Public: Policy Outcomes in the American States*

SCHLESINGER, *Ambition and Politics: Political Careers in the United States*

STEINER, *Social Insecurity: The Politics of Welfare*

Copyright © 1966 by Rand McNally & Company
All Rights Reserved
Printed in U.S.A. by Rand McNally & Company
Library of Congress Catalog Card Number 66:10805

To

My Children

CHARLES, DANIEL, PAULA

PREFACE

THIS BOOK HAS been written because I could not find one like it when I was involved in the events described in Chapter VIII. As a temporary special assistant to the Governor of Illinois, I happened on the scene when public assistance policy became a critical issue. It was not possible, however, to understand public assistance in a political context from the existing literature. The issues that produced conflict — financing, federal-state relations, confidentiality, birth control, race — have been dealt with by economists and social workers interested in public relief. But the problem of what political circumstances produce particular welfare policy remained. The selection of many of the points of emphasis in the book thus resulted from the realities of political experience. It should be understood that I did not participate in the making of public assistance policy, only in the briefing of those who made the decisions. One major purpose of the book is to make it possible for people with comparable roles to be able to evaluate for other governors and other legislators the likelihood, say, of losing federal funds for noncompliance with federal requirements.

Another purpose of the book is to consider whether, in the case of public welfare clients, there has been a solution to the problem once posed by Pendleton Herring: how to provide a voice for groups that may be socially useful but politically weak. By virtue of brief early experience as a sometime employee (nonprofessional) of a private welfare agency, and by virtue of close personal relationships with social workers, I had assumed through the years that professional social work provided that voice. In the course of examining the reasonableness of the assumption, the question of the relevance of professional social work to public assistance became part of my problem.

Finally, I am concerned with trying to find some determinants of change in public assistance policy. Is publicly supported birth control information for relief clients likely? Where is the stimulus for periodic improvement in benefits? Has public assistance policy changed as much as American society has changed since the adoption of the Social Security Act in 1935? Does the way in which relief policy is made have anything to do with the adequacy of the rate of change?

The opportunity to become a participant-observer in state politics and the opportunity to indulge my interest in welfare politics both stem from my association with the Institute of Government and Public Affairs at the University of Illinois. Several of my colleagues there — Professors Thomas Anton, Glenn Fisher, and Samuel Gove — and Professor Murray Edelman of the Political Science Department of the University of Illinois have read parts of the manuscript and made useful comments. Many helpful suggestions were made by Professor Aaron Wildavsky of the University of California (Berkeley), Martha Derthick of Harvard University, and my wife, Louise K. Steiner, all of whom read the entire manuscript.

In the course of researching the book, I interviewed politicians, past and present administrators, social work practitioners, social work students, and social work faculty. Some, but not all, of these people are Wilbur Cohen, Elizabeth Wickenden, Loula Dunn, Virgil Martin, Arnold Maremont, Arthur Altmeyer, James Dumpson, and Frank Bane. Each of them made important contributions. Dawn Clark Netsch and Richard Thorne continued to provide help long after our association in Springfield ended. I have had energetic and competent research help from Myra Clark Lynch. Jean Baker typed several drafts of the manuscript. The interpretations and any mistakes are my responsibility alone.

Gilbert Y. Steiner

Berkeley, California
June, 1965

TABLE OF CONTENTS

SOCIAL INSECURITY

CHAPTER I

Introduction:
Welfare as a Political Problem

NO ONE KNOWS precisely how many Americans are in constant danger of becoming public charges. "This is a generally prosperous country," said John F. Kennedy in November, 1963, "but there is a stream of poverty that runs across the United States which is not exposed to the lives of a good many of us and, therefore, we are relatively unaware of it except statistically."[1] Even statistically there are uncertainties. Eight million persons are actual recipients of public assistance, but about four times that number belong to family groups with money incomes under $3,000 annually or are individuals with money incomes under $1,500. Not all members of this low-income group live in the shadow of the relief rolls. Some are students with a good potential for future earnings; others are confident of family or other support if necessary. Some are two-person families—but some are six-person families. Some families with incomes well in excess of the poverty-dependency level nevertheless lack resources to carry them through a prolonged emergency. From data reported to the Bureau of the Census, it has been inferred that one in seven of all family groups and almost half of all persons living alone or with nonrelatives had incomes too low in 1963 "to enable them to eat even the minimal diet that could be expected to provide adequate nutrition and still have enough left over to pay for all other living essentials."[2] The President's Council of Economic Advi-

[1]Address before the Protestant Council of the City of New York, November 8, 1963. The text is in *Congressional Quarterly,* November 15, 1963, p. 2005.
[2]Mollie Orshansky, "Counting the Poor: Another Look at the Poverty Profile," *Social Security Bulletin,* XXVIII (January, 1965), 4.

sers estimated in 1965 that 15 million children—one-fourth of all those in the country—live in poverty. However difficult it may be to fix a precise figure, it seems clear that at least one-sixth of the whole population has an actual or potential recipient interest in public relief policy.[3]

If the Great Society's antipoverty program is successful, it may make a deep cut in the size of the potential public relief case load by providing some subsidized jobs, and by training the untrained who would otherwise become dependent adults. Long overdue, the poverty program is nevertheless principally designed to help those who can take advantage of economic opportunity, even specially created economic opportunity. There remain the categorical assistance cases— the aged, the blind, the totally and permanently disabled, the dependent child in a fatherless home—for most of whom economic opportunity in the sense of a job or job training is irrelevant. The poverty war is not yet geared to help those groups.

I. GROUPS AND ISSUES

Since the expiration of the Townsend movement,[4] no important fraction of the population has organized politically in support of the cause of public relief, but there are both national policies and state policies governing relief. National policy has two faces—monetary and nonmonetary—which sometimes seem to evolve independent of each other. Nonmonetary national policy has been developed chiefly by the public assistance bureaucracy and its professional colleagues in the social work field. The critical element of that policy at this time is to provide a maximum of services to lead to self-help, self-care, or

[3]A convenient statistical analysis of the poverty problem was produced by the Conference on Economic Progress, *Poverty and Deprivation in the U.S.* (Washington, 1962). See also U.S. Department of Commerce, Bureau of the Census, "Low Income Families: 1960," *Supplementary Reports, 1960 Census of the Population* (Washington: Government Printing Office, 1964). Dwight Macdonald, in a brilliant essay, "Our Invisible Poor," *The New Yorker,* January 19, 1963, pp. 82-132, reviewed some of the literature, including Michael Harrington, *The Other America* (New York: Macmillan, 1962). On public assistance particularly, see Edgar May, *The Wasted Americans* (New York: Harper and Row, 1964).

[4]Dr. Francis Townsend's Old Age Revolving Pensions, Limited, proposed to pay a pension of $200 a month to every citizen over 60 on condition that the recipient retire from all gainful work and promise to spend the sum within one month in the United States. The pension would have been financed by a 2 per cent tax on business transactions. Townsend claimed 1200 clubs by the end of 1934. See William E. Leuchtenburg, *Franklin D. Roosevelt and the New Deal* (New York: Harper and Row, 1963), pp. 103ff. For a full study of the Townsend Plan movement, see Abraham Holtzman, *The Townsend Movement* (New York: Bookman Associates, 1963).

rehabilitation. National policy on the monetary side does not seem to command equal concern from the welfare professionals, but it is of high importance to state politicians and to congressmen. Since no state can now afford to care for all its public charges without federal help, state officials put a constant pressure on Congress to relieve the squeeze on state funds by increasing the size of the federal grant. As long as the grant-in-aid does not have obnoxious conditions tied to it, most congressmen have been responsive to suggestions for increasing federal contributions in public assistance. Congress has shown no parallel interest in problems of eligibility or of adequacy of support; these problems are matters of state policy.

State policies in public assistance have evolved out of clashes between groups primarily concerned with low taxes and groups with a political or intellectual interest in the plight of the indigent. With rare exceptions, the indigent themselves are not organized to participate in the battles. Results of the clashes vary with the dominant public image of the character of the recipients. The low-tax cause rarely wins when the image is that of a respectable, aged, white, literate citizen in his "golden years." A rigorous eligibility line designed to restrict admission to relief rolls is more common when the image of the recipient changes to that of an uneducated, unmarried, Negro mother and her offspring. Most recently, a kind of happy marriage has taken place between state groups concerned with low taxes and those who consider themselves "welfare-oriented." Noneconomic services appeal to both groups as a way to overcome economic dependency.

The new emphasis on noneconomic services satisfies many of the organized groups in the relief picture. Tax-conscious chambers of commerce see the dawn of a bright new day that will turn dependents into independents; welfare professionals see formal approval to practice "Social Work: A Problem-Solving Process" rather than "social work: relief of the poor"; state and local politicians see an easing of fiscal pressures so that schools and highways and hospitals can be financed. There is no comparable concern for the economic problems of recipients. But public assistance recipients are the personification of the captive group. They cannot decline to participate on principle. They cannot shop around for a better deal. There are no other deals because the federal-state categorical assistance programs have acquired a near-monopoly of the relief business.

The idea of public grants to the indigent is settled policy now because it was learned 30 years ago that private charity cannot meet a major economic crisis. Rather than allow itself to be trapped in a position where it provided economic aid to a relatively few people in prosperous periods and wrung its hands in depression periods, private charity has discreetly withdrawn from activity on the economic side of dependency and focused its attention on the emotional side. Public welfare, having once provided the kind of money that only the coercive power of government can command, found itself filling a vacuum. And save for some congressional gestures in 1956 and 1962, which may have been more illusory than real, this distribution of responsibility between public and private welfare in the care of the dependent poor remains substantially unchanged.

On the public side, the distribution of responsibility between levels of government has become more static than would appear from a casual look. Most of the bill is paid at the national level; much of the policy is made at the state level. Federal grants to the states for public assistance are established policy because state charity, like private charity, has been found inadequate to meet a modern economic crisis. The states have had neither the disposition nor the ability of private welfare to turn to nonfiscal therapy as a way of servicing their poorly adjusted citizens. Still, states have continued to pay just enough to the piper of public aid to have an important role in calling the tunes.

Five billion dollars were spent in 1964 by federal, state, and local governments to support eight million recipients of public aid. About 30 per cent of all federal grants to the states are for public assistance purposes, making this the second largest federal grant program. Only highway grants are larger. Unlike the situation in highway policy, however, public assistance introduces problems of race, of sex, of religion, and of family relationships. It is hard to think of four areas most American politicians would rather avoid. But the conclusion reached in 1935, that the poor are a matter of national public concern, is not reversible. The public assistance titles of the Social Security Act make it necessary for public decisions to be made about people in need where previously decisions were made by a generous daughter of the rich or a parish priest or a sympathetic school teacher.

The allocation of public money to persons unable or unwilling to support themselves involves difficult, complicated decisions. Shall those who need support because of their own incontinence be sustained at the same level as the victims of acts of God, or should public policy demand adherence to generally accepted moral standards as a condition for public aid? What level of support is appropriate? Should government provide more dollars for some it supports as a matter of charity than for some it employs? Indeed, should government provide dollars at all or should it underwrite the costs of necessary goods and services and thereby eliminate mismanagement as a possible cause of dependency? How do public policy-makers locate the line that represents marginal support—the line that will maintain the needy but will not discourage a drive for self-support? Should recipients of public aid be treated confidentially or does the paying public have a right to know whom it is supporting? Where, in a federal system, shall these decisions be made? Because no resolution of any of these questions is necessarily permanent, the battles over the appropriate level of government to make public assistance policy are themselves important. As with most American policy issues, today's state losers can be tomorrow's national winners, and today's legislative losers can be tomorrow's administrative winners.

Since 1935, it has been a matter of national policy to provide some federal support to any state that adopts a plan for old age assistance or for aid to dependent children or for aid to the blind. These so-called categories were extended in 1950 by the addition of aid to the permanently and totally disabled, and in 1960 by extension of the old age category to cover aid to the medically indigent aged. No federal contribution is made to support general assistance, *i.e.,* relief of persons who fall outside these categories. Thus, until 1961, when Congress first enacted temporary legislation to qualify children of unemployed parents under the aid to dependent children program, no federal funds were involved in aiding indigent children whose parents were without the physical handicap of old age or blindness or disability, or without the emotional handicap of widowhood, desertion, or separation. The public assistance rule of thumb applicable here provided that, in the long run, relief would not come from Washington for people physically able to work, unless a responsibility to care for children negated the physical advantages of youth, vision, and locomotion. This long-run principle was formulated in part at least as a reaction to the short-run arrangements then in effect.

In 1935, as an emergency matter, relief was coming from Washington only for the able-bodied unemployed. The Federal Emergency Relief Administration was flourishing; to encourage work relief, the Works Progress Administration was about to move into gear. These agencies spent federal funds to provide relief for the unemployed and jobs on white-collar or blue-collar public works projects for those who could work. Having been authorized to federalize relief in the states, the Federal Emergency Relief Administration did so in six states between February, 1934, and April, 1935: Oklahoma, North Dakota, Massachusetts, Ohio, Louisiana, Georgia. But even the distress of the depression did not discourage strong opposition to federal participation in "this business of relief." The 1932 Republican platform had observed that "True to American traditions and principles of government, the administration has regarded the relief problem as one of State and local responsibility."[5] Four years later Republican platform-makers narrowed in on relief administration, calling for "return of responsibility for relief administration to nonpolitical local agencies familiar with community problems."[6] Federal grants, "while the need exists," were supported contingent, however, upon contributions of "a fair proportion of the total relief burden" from state and local governments. Thus, the 1936 Republican statement was compatible with the scheme of public assistance passed by the Democratic Congress the previous year. That scheme, by not including a provision for federal grants in support of general relief and by not including direct federal relief, limited the area of disagreement. The parties were agreed on the principle of some federal grants-in-aid on some kind of matching basis. What the Republicans supported in 1936, the Democrats had passed in 1935 for the aged, for dependent children, and for the blind. Disagreement continued over direct federal relief to the needy who did not fall into one of these categories.

In the thirties, Democrats passed over the idea of a federal-state, cooperative, general assistance program to accompany the categorical programs, preferring not to tamper with the direct federal approach already in operation on an emergency basis. Republicans, whose 1936 platform statement was clearly broad enough to cover support for a federal-state general assistance program, opposed direct federal action. When the federal government got out of the business of direct relief — and it was not until June, 1943, that all federal emergency public aid begun in the thirties was terminated — it did not seem necessary or timely to develop a federal-state general assistance program. Unemployment was minimized by wartime production demands, and state and local revenues were quite adequate to support general assistance programs. Since that time, there has been no meeting of the political minds on a cooperative financing of general assistance. Nor has there been any serious kind of a push for such a program from either side.

The basic policy outline for public assistance drafted in the 1930's is unchanged in the 1960's. A federal matching grant is offered to any state enacting a program of assistance in any or all of the categories covered by the federal act: old age; dependent children; the blind; since 1950, the disabled; and, since 1960, as a part of the old age

[5]Kirk H. Porter and Donald Bruce Johnson (eds.), *National Party Platforms 1840-1956* (Urbana: University of Illinois Press, 1956), p. 341.
[6]*Ibid.*, p. 366.

category, the medically indigent aged. The matching formula varies from category to category, but it has always been more generous in the adult categories than in aid to dependent children. As a condition of receipt of federal funds, a state must file a plan which may not impose eligibility requirements more stringent than those authorized in the federal act and which must be statewide in operation. The Bureau of Family Services, whatever its location in the federal administrative system and whether it goes by its new name of Bureau of Family Services or its old name of Bureau of Public Assistance, has been responsible for the administration of all categories, with superior administrative authority vested variously in a Social Security Board, a Social Security Administrator, a Federal Security Administrator, and a Secretary of Health, Education, and Welfare, through a Social Security Administrator or a Welfare Administrator. Since 1961, the bureau has been named the Bureau of Family Services, and, since 1963, it has been split off from the Social Security Administration and made part of a new Welfare Administration in the Department of Health, Education, and Welfare. The bureau, by whatever name, keeps a close eye on state law and administration and is armed with a single ultimate sanction: power to recommend that federal funds be withheld from a state for noncompliance with the plan filed or with the federal act.

If the outlines of the formal program have remained stable since the beginning, there have been a good many changes in all other aspects of the public aid problem. The popular image of the chief beneficiaries has changed from that of old, respectable, white people to that of young, immoral, Negro men and women. The benefit pattern has changed from monthly grants of $10 or $15 to dramatic instances of several hundreds of dollars being paid to a single family. Perhaps most significant, the professionalization of social work that has taken place since 1935 has succeeded in conveying to some of the recipients of public aid and to part of the public a conviction that, in a well-ordered system, public welfare is a matter of right. But the appeal of *laissez faire* is still great enough for many Americans to resent supporting those who can't make their own way. In campaigning for the 1964 Republican presidential nomination, Barry Goldwater verbalized this resentment:

> I do not believe that the mere fact of having little money entitles everybody, regardless of circumstance, to be permanently maintained by the taxpayers at an average or comfortable standard of living.[7]

[7]Address before the Economic Club of New York, January 15, 1964. The text is in the *New York Times,* January 16, 1964, p. 21.

The idea of "toughening up" is forever popular. Toughening up, it is argued, will drive the cheaters out, the slackers to work, the unwed mothers into chastity; and it will save money. It is this clash between the ideas of public aid as a right and public aid as a matter of sufferance, to be granted with suspicion, with strings, and with restraints, that is reflected in public policy debates and political action.

II. DIVISION OF THE WELFARE MARKET

Public assistance under the Social Security Act has its competitors but they have been forced out of, or to a declining share of, the market principally because of lack of capital. Administrative inadequacies in state and locally run relief programs, and changes in family spending patterns that throw more poor people onto charity rolls are additional, if less important, explanations of the dominance of categorical assistance in the relief business. Private competitors include responsible relatives, nonsectarian, voluntary charities, and church-supported welfare. Public competitors—in the sense of tax-supported alternatives to the federal-state program for providing assistance to the indigent—are local and state governments acting independently of Washington. While the federal-state program now in operation has practically monopolized the market, the monopoly has not been accomplished without a good deal of soul-searching by the several competitors, and without close self-analysis of their views as to how the program should be managed.

Private charity, whether family, institutional, or church, lacks the capital necessary to meet the costs of relief. No one can seriously contend that if public relief were abandoned, family units could or would now assume a substantial part of the responsibility. In the first place, aside from the accepted view that it is a parent's responsibility to support an infant child, there is no agreement regarding the scope of a family's legal or moral responsibility for an indigent relative. The problem becomes especially complicated when it is a matter of choosing between support for an aged relative, say, and providing a more adequate standard of living for one's children. In addition, the family with a member or members in need of relief is itself unlikely to be in a strong enough financial position to meet the need. Dramatic tales of prosperous persons permitting aged mothers or fathers to draw old age assistance benefits make good newspaper copy once in a while—the late A. J. Liebling called such stories "Mink Swaddled in Horsefeathers"—but, for all the much reported breakdown in family ties, there is no evidence that this kind of crassness is a common situation.

One bit of evidence does exist that seems explicitly to deny the hypothesis that a diminution in public relief would mean a resurgence of family responsibility for the very poor. Clermont County, Ohio, a rural community just east of Cincinnati, with a population of 87,000, is believed to be the first county in the country to have cut off all general relief because of financial difficulties. Relief was terminated there in April, 1961, when the voters rejected a proposed tax levy. Clients did not magically become self-sufficient nor did responsible relatives come out of the woodwork when the pressure became intense. Instead, the burden of support was shifted from the public fisc to landlords, grocers, physicians, churches, schools, and other civic groups. A study of the aftermath of terminating relief showed a 54 per cent increase in money owed to landlords, grocers, physicians, and hospitals during a 15-month period.[8] The sheriff's office reported an increase in the number of evictions, and voluntary agencies such as the Salvation Army reported a rise in requests for aid. Recipients were not newcomers, adrift in a strange place without the likelihood of family attachments in the vicinity. Most of the 162 cases on the county welfare lists were long-time or native-born residents of the county. At least one of the normally accepted necessities of life in twentieth-century America was not provided: of the 250 children involved, only 18 were reported to have received smallpox, diphtheria, and tetanus immunization; only 15 had received all of their polio inoculations.

Relative support legislation in old age assistance exists now in 40 states although there is doubt about the effectiveness with which such legislation can be enforced in perhaps one-third of those states.[9] Relative responsibliity is not even always pushed in aid to dependent children cases. Absence of a firm enforcement policy is frequently related to a belief that such a policy is economically unsound, since the costs of tracking down a deserting father are often reported to be greater than the support contribution that can be secured from him. If this is true in father and infant-child situations, where there is no question of primary responsibility, it is even more likely to be so when the reluctant relative can validly claim competing responsibilities. In sum, the possibility of a family gathering needy relatives to its bosom as an alternative to public assistance is unrealistic. Not only are the means to provide support not present, as the Clermont County study

[8]Community Health and Welfare Council, "Effect on Families and Individuals in a Rural Community Where Poor Relief Was Exhausted" (Cincinnati, November 1, 1963, process duplicated).

[9]U.S. Advisory Commission on Intergovernmental Relations, *Statutory and Administrative Controls Associated with Federal Grants for Public Assistance* (Washington: author, May, 1964), p. 54.

shows, but the culture is becoming less rather than more family-centered.

Voluntary social welfare, originating in America in 1845 with the formation of the Society of St. Vincent de Paul, had its golden age in the period preceding and immediately following World War I. During the quarter century between the Presidents Roosevelt, there was a steady increase in welfare expenditures from private as well as public funds. But discussions of public versus private responsibility for relief really became academic in 1929 when it was shown that, in the previous year, 71.6 per cent of all relief in 15 important cities was from public funds. The last year in which private welfare carried any large part of the unemployment relief burden was 1932. Josephine Brown describes the shift from private to public welfare during the first years of the depression decade:

> . . . bit by bit, the doubts and fears regarding public relief had diminished under new and powerful pressure probably because the inability of private agencies to meet these increasing needs had become more and more apparent. People stopped talking about the relative merits of public and private administration and the demoralizing effects of indiscriminate relief giving, because it was so obvious that unemployment relief had to be public.[10]

Although total welfare costs grew, private welfare leveled off after World War II. The Social Security Administration estimated that expenditures from philanthropic contributions for private, secularly administered, adult institutional care and for family and child welfare services and care were substantially unchanged in comparing totals for 1945, 1950, and 1955. An estimated total of $385 million in 1945 dropped to $350 million in 1950 before climbing slightly to $360 million in 1955.[11] Today, the big voluntary expenditures are in health rather than welfare.

The early depression years compelled private welfare agencies both to make sharp changes in function and to explain, rationalize, and publicize their new direction. The Federal Emergency Relief Administration insisted on a policy of public responsibility for the spending of relief funds. Subsidies to private agencies and the resulting confusion between public and private controls were not countenanced. Without public subsidy and without adequate philanthropic support, it became necessary for private welfare to adjust to a new kind of function based on noneconomic services and activities. This adjustment has been so successfully made that voluntary agencies today provide relatively little cash assistance. Any payments made are

[10]Josephine Brown, *Public Relief 1929-1939* (New York: Henry Holt, 1940), p. 80.
[11]U.S. Congress, House, Committee on Ways and Means, Hearings, "Public Welfare Amendments of 1962," 87th Cong., 2d Sess., 1962, p. 183.

usually for special, nonrecurring purposes, while the principal emphasis is on providing a broad range of services regardless of the applicant's financial status. Anyone, it is argued, may be faced with problems beyond his capacity to resolve alone, and it is to the resolution of emotional problems brought about by death, mental illness, old age, or marital discord that voluntary welfare has turned.[12]

Private welfare's withdrawal from competition with public welfare when the need for capital is acute, and the private group's willingness to find a product other than money and a market other than the indigent is exemplified by the contrast between private and public agencies in a community like Rochester, New York. The total annual budget of the Family Service of Rochester, Inc., a private, nonsectarian agency, could not keep the County Welfare Department in operation for more than half a week, while the total public welfare budget is twice as large as the total amount spent by all Community Chest agencies in a year. Family Service has a fee scale of $1 to $12 per interview and a considerable number of clients pay fees. Most of the case load is self-supporting; most of the case load is self-referred; most interviews take place in the office. The Family Service agency has settled into serving a lower middle-class group that has become convinced that it is sensible to get counseling help for marital, family, and individual problems. In Rochester, at least, there has been no effort by the private agency to change the public-private distribution of responsibility, to carry economic assistance cases, or even to have much to do with public welfare in a professional sense. Reflecting on relationships with the County Welfare Department, Family Service's General Secretary says "there is no real interchange of experience and ideas on the practice level.... Our relations are cordial but we never really get down to talking about casework with one another."[13]

The approach of organized, private welfare agencies to public assistance is typified by caution and by an apparent determination to maintain a suitable distance. The Director of the Family Service Association of America, a federation of over 300 voluntary family agencies, gave the association's support to the Public Welfare Amendments of 1962, but he did it by letter to Chairman Mills of the House Ways and Means Committee rather than by the more forceful alternative of a personal appearance at the public hearing. The Council of Jewish Federations and Welfare Funds, a national association of 215 Jewish federations and welfare funds embracing 800 communities,

[12]*Ibid.*, p. 181.
[13]James Hunt, "Shifts in the Partnership of Public and Voluntary Agencies Serving Families and Children" (paper prepared for the New York State Welfare Conference, New York City, November, 1962, process duplicated), pp. 2, 3, 6.

also found it adequate to comment by mail, and so did the United Community Funds and Councils of America. It would be misleading to suggest that these national associations of private agencies were unconcerned about the development of the highly publicized 1962 amendments. Private welfare does care about the direction and character of the public welfare program, but its interest is more intellectual than direct. Private agencies have carefully built up a separate clientele with which they are content. Public assistance for the indigent belongs to another world.

Church charities — especially the welfare units of the Catholic Church — maintain a close watch on public assistance policy although they too have accepted the idea of public responsibility for relief. Like the secular agencies, church welfare suffered from a lack of capital when the chance for expansion was at hand. Expenditures for church welfare purposes from philanthropic contributions declined from $80 million to $45 million between 1930 and 1935. Unlike the private, secular welfare picture, church welfare expenditures increased sharply from $115 million to $290 million between 1945 and 1955 for reasons that will soon become obvious.[14] Again unlike the secular agencies, church counseling units are not ordinarily on a fee basis. In the main, however, the churches have gone out of the business of financing direct outdoor relief, and instead have a dual emphasis on problem-solving through counseling and on providing certain institutional services like child care homes.

The latter are frequently financed by public funds made available through purchase of church welfare services by public units, a factor that accounts for the high level of church welfare payments. Of $47 million spent in 1962 by 186 Lutheran social service agencies, excluding hospitals, only $7.5 million came from church sources. Most of the remainder came from government sources through channels ranging from vendor payments under old age assistance to benefits for retarded children and for homeless children. For example, the Lutherans operate facilities for emotionally disturbed children in which per-case costs run as high as $15,000 a year. It is a matter of concern to the director of the National Lutheran Council's Division of Welfare that the result of the inability of the church to support its own welfare services is to shift the emphasis "more and more to the clients able to pay for the service offered, as well as to public funds without which the service would be terminated."[15] Like other church welfare

[14]Ways and Means, Hearings, 1962, p. 183.

[15]Rev. G. S. Thompson, Executive Director, National Lutheran Council Division of Welfare, quoted in *New York Times,* February 11, 1965.

workers, however, he can see no solution. Welfare has become too great a luxury for churches to afford unless they emphasize a subsidized program or provide service to a self-supporting group.

Spokesmen for Catholic Charities, the most active and effective lobbyists for the cause of categorical assistance, have nevertheless carefully guarded their share of the market. Any efforts to expand federal participation in public assistance beyond the originally established categories have been viewed with alarm. This is especially true in the children's program. Msgr. John O'Grady, long-time secretary of the National Conference of Catholic Charities, and his associates carried on a continuing battle with national and state welfare administrators who sought federal funds for child welfare centers in urban areas. Edwin E. Witte's explanation of the initial Catholic objection to this proposal makes it understandable:

Their objection was first put in terms of a fear that this plan would involve federal and state control of church and other private charitable institutions concerned with child welfare. Soon it developed that there was another factor, namely, that public (local) money is paid in certain metropolitan centers (New York, Chicago, Philadelphia, Pittsburgh, and perhaps others) to charitable institutions conducted by religious groups for the care in these institutions of children committed to their custody by courts. It was feared that either the state or federal authorities might object to these arrangements....[16]

Largely unconcerned with the adult categories, Msgr. O'Grady later saw federal child welfare money as an effort "that undermines the great work of our religious organizations and institutions engaged in the care of orphans and neglected children," and "a serious threat to all the best traditions of American social welfare." "They want to turn the children back to the poorhouse," he complained of the American Public Welfare Association in 1949, when that group supported extending federal matching in child welfare payments to areas not predominantly rural. As for the federal administrative agency, it was advised to put its existing program in order. "Among the ordinary citizens," said the monsignor, "I found great dissatisfactions with the administration of the program. . . . We had always expected that aid to dependent children would solve many of the problems of child dependency and delinquency, but we have been disillusioned."[17] Although he claimed authorship of the aid to dependent children title ("I have studied this thing carefully from the beginning. I happened to write the original title IV of

[16]Reprinted with permission of the copyright owners, the Regents of the University of Wisconsin, from Edwin E. Witte, *The Development of the Social Security Act* (Madison: University of Wisconsin Press, 1962), p. 168.
[17]U.S. Congress, House, Committee on Ways and Means, Hearings, "Social Security Act Amendments of 1949," 81st Cong., 1st Sess., 1949, pp. 534, 539, 543.

the act. . . ."[18]), Msgr. O'Grady later appeared to regret the whole thing when it opened the way to the child welfare problem: "I would gradually withdraw the Federal Government from the entire field of assistance,"[19] and "I feel that the farther away we get from the present public assistance philosophy in serving the needs of American families the better it will be for all concerned."[20]

Similar proposals in 1956 brought an even tougher reaction. The aim of the child welfare grant provisions, claimed Msgr. O'Grady, was to make it impossible for judges to commit children to voluntary agencies operated by religious groups. Federal bureaucrats might well worry about the high rate of illegitimacy in aid to dependent children, he argued, before they moved in to destroy voluntary agencies.[21] By 1958, the ideological battle between the American Public Welfare Association and the National Association of Social Workers, on the one hand, and the National Conference of Catholic Charities, on the other hand, was described as involving the very maintenance of religion: "When the proponents of the new public welfare reach their utopia there will no longer be a place for religion in the American community," warned Msgr. O'Grady.[22]

The case was overstated, perhaps, but Msgr. O'Grady was posing a critical public policy question: should public welfare be encouraged to compete with private, secular or church-supported welfare programs where the superior fiscal capacity of the national government is not clearly needed? The problem continues to bother Catholic welfare now. Its answer is still "no." An editorial in the journal *Catholic Charities,* commenting on the provision of the 1962 Public Welfare Amendments authorizing public social services to persons not requiring financial assistance, insisted that problems of family structure and personal emotional balance where financial need is not involved are in the exclusive province of the voluntary agency.[23]

Protestant church welfare people seem uncertain on this question. Thus, the National Council of Churches of Christ in America worries about the possibility that some of the 4,000 Protestant church-related health and welfare agencies may undertake social services in commu-

[18]U.S. Congress, House, Committee on Ways and Means, Hearings, "Public Assistance Titles of the Social Security Act," 84th Cong., 2d Sess., 1956, p. 112.
[19]U.S. Congress, Senate, Committee on Finance, Hearings, "Social Security Revision," 81st Cong., 2d Sess., 1950, p. 598.
[20]Ways and Means, Hearings, 1949, p. 543.
[21]Ways and Means, Hearings, 1956, pp. 98-106.
[22]U.S. Congress, House, Committee on Ways and Means, Hearings, "Social Security Legislation," 85th Cong., 2d Sess., 1958, p. 828.
[23]"Who Has the Answer?," *Catholic Charities,* XLVI (June, 1962), 2.

nities where the job could really better be done by public agencies.[24] On the other hand, there is a gap between some Protestant clergymen and all organized social welfare, whether public or church-sponsored. A recent study of 132 Protestant ministers, including 38 Negroes, in the Washington metropolitan area concluded that ministers' knowledge of both church- and community-sponsored agencies is limited, and that ministers' use of these agencies is almost nonexistent.[25] "The state may well squeeze the church out of its traditional role in welfare," acknowledges a Lutheran spokesman. "Perhaps there is no solution to this increasing problem. But in the meantime, that which is unique about church-related welfare must be recognized and strengthened." The unique character of church welfare, this official holds, "is the capacity to recognize deeper needs [than visible economic need] and to minister understandingly to them because the love of Christ constrains us."[26]

An arrangement in the original draft bill offered by the administration in 1962 would have specifically authorized state and local welfare departments to use federal funds in the purchase of social services from nonprofit private agencies. This was approved by both Catholic Charities and the National Council, with suggestions from the latter for minimum standards that private agencies be required to meet. Authorization to purchase from private agencies was watered down in the final bill, but the assumption was that the long-existing common practice of selling church services to state welfare departments would not be affected.

Catholic Charities now recognizes that public programs are doing much of what Catholic Charities has done historically, and also recognizes that private welfare is not likely to survive without financial aid. However, argues Father Bernard Coughlin, a Jesuit social worker, government would be well advised not to squeeze private agencies from the field; rather, it should aid and strengthen those agencies which perform a public community service.[27] The Catholic Church will not compete with public agencies in providing financial assistance; neither is it prepared to stand aside in any nonmonetary aspect of welfare. "Any inference that private effort has failed and therefore public welfare alone is equal to the task is basically incorrect," said Msgr. Raymond Gallagher, Msgr. O'Grady's successor, in 1962. "The only

[24]Ways and Means, Hearings, 1962, p. 574.
[25]L. D. Bollinger, "The Minister and Social Work," *Lutheran Social Welfare Quarterly,* III (March, 1963), 11.
[26]Rev. G. S. Thompson, quoted in *New York Times,* February 11, 1965.
[27]Bernard Coughlin, S. J., "Private Welfare in a Public Welfare Bureaucracy," *Social Service Review,* XXXV (June, 1961), 192.

ingredient in which there is any superiority is in the availability of money."[28]

There can be no dispute about public welfare's superior access to money. Within public welfare, moreover, it has become increasingly obvious that most of the money may be spent by the states but that it must be raised by the federal government. To be sure, public relief independent of federal participation continues to exist in the form of general assistance to cover some cases that will not fit in the categorical assistance program. States, however, are constantly seeking ways to transfer cases to a federally aided program rather than carry the full costs on the state or local level.

Local, and then local combined with state, responsibility was the traditional American arrangement for public relief before the New Deal. Lack of capital and management failings were both present in this arrangement. Studies of the administration of poor relief in the period when local responsibility was dominant found inefficiency, political favoritism, and occasional fraud to be characteristic elements. State participation, which did not begin in earnest until just before World War I, helped to overcome some of these defects; one that it did not overcome was the problem of inadequate money for support. By January 1, 1935, only 28 states and 2 territories had enacted old age pension laws, and, within these jurisdictions, one-third of the counties did not in fact provide assistance to the aged. Six states' programs were barely functioning; four were just getting under way. Where assistance was provided, long residence requirements, provisions for divestment of property, and responsible-relative features disqualified large numbers of persons, while others had to take their turn on a waiting list made necessary by shortages of funds. Cash grants to the needy blind were paid by 27 states. Maximum annual amounts ranged from $150 to $600, but more than one-third of the states paid less than half the maximum allowed.

Although most states subscribed to the principle that children deprived of parental support or care because of the death, absence from the home, or mental incapacity of a parent should be aided by public authorities, and all but three had enacted legislation to that effect before 1935, the effectiveness of state programs in this area was no greater than that of measures for the aged. In 1931, only 55 per cent of the counties authorized to give child aid were doing so, while three years later this proportion fell below 50 per cent. As few as 16 states provided for state participation in financing grants for aid to dependent

[28]Ways and Means, Hearings, 1962, p. 581.

children; yet even in some of these no money was being provided.[29]

Entry of the federal government into the relief field on a continuing basis did not have the same kind of effect on preexisting public welfare agencies as it did on private secular and church charity. In dealing with the latter, federal action served to displace existing activity. The overwhelming fiscal superiority of the federal government was put to work under conditions that left no room for the relatively puny private efforts. Private welfare, to stay in business, turned to noneconomic services as we have seen. Passage of the public assistance titles of the Social Security Act, however, created an intergovernmental program which actually nourished and supplemented the inadequately financed state programs rather than supplanting those programs. State welfare did not have to find a new role for itself as did private welfare. State programs had been designed to provide economic aid, and now they could do so. The job for the states was to go about their business, serving both their old clients and needy new clients who could now be accommodated thanks to the expansion made possible by federal funds.

The welfare market was thus stabilized for about 25 years: money was public; counseling services were private. The groups involved found their roles. State governments sought increasing federal grants; secular, private agencies found new clients and abandoned participation in poor relief; Catholic Charities became the defender of the inviolability of private welfare's exclusive right to provide services unrelated to economic need; federal administrators, seeking something more than a watchdog function, pushed the expansion of services by the public agency. Welfare clients—a group that has difficulty in communicating with the more successful elements in society, as Frank Pinner and his colleagues have pointed out[30]—take what they are allotted and do not themselves become active participants in the struggle over who gets what assistance, when, and how much. It might all work out very nicely if only there were not a seemingly ever growing number of poor people dependent on public relief.

[29]U.S. Committee on Economic Security, *Social Security in America* (Washington: Social Security Board, 1937), *passim*.

[30]Frank Pinner, Paul Jacobs, and Philip Selznick, *Old Age and Political Behavior* (Berkeley and Los Angeles: University of California Press, 1959), p. 265.

17

CHAPTER II

The Withering-Away Fallacy

THE PARTICULAR INTERESTS of the two groups directly involved in the development of the Social Security Act of 1935 were not identical. For the policy-making group—Congress and the political leaders in the states pushing the Congress—a program of federal aid for old age assistance was the key question. Under pressure from the Townsend Plan supporters and from Huey Long, there were signs that Congress would enact an old age program as a separate measure. The Dill-Connery bill[1] to provide grants to the states equal to one-third the costs of state old age pensions had passed the House, was over the committee hurdle in the Senate. For the second group—the nonpolitical specialists in social security—a system of unemployment insurance was the most important goal to be pursued at the time. An unemployment insurance scheme, embodied in the Wagner-Lewis bill,[2] was receiving serious congressional attention, although it had not made progress comparable to the old age pension legislation. As it developed, both old age assistance and unemployment insurance were achieved; as an incidental aspect, programs of aid to dependent children and aid to the blind under a federal-state grant system were added. The views of contemporary observers and participants suggest, however, that old age assistance carried the entire program.[3]

If the realities of the times accounted for its original popularity, the subsequent popularity of old age assistance (OAA) as finally written

[1]H. R. 8451 and S. 493, 74th Cong., 1st Sess., 1935.
[2]H. R. 7659, 73d Cong., 2d Sess., 1934.
[3]Edwin E. Witte, *The Development of the Social Security Act* (Madison: Univeristy of Wisconsin Press, 1962), pp. 78-79.

into the Social Security Act can be traced to a gradual understanding that, expensive as it appeared to be at the outset, and notwithstanding its violation of the tradition of state responsibility for the poor, OAA in the context of the Social Security Act had a most attractive feature: it was programmed to wither away in favor of an ultimately almost universal system of old age insurance. The stubborn failure of public assistance to wither away has become a matter of concern to a few congressmen and some others who remember the assurances with which the original withering-away thesis was advanced. Professional specialists in welfare have responded with a shift of ground: public assistance will wither away, it is now argued, if relief clients can be provided psychosocial services by trained workers. The latter thesis is embodied in the Public Welfare Amendments of 1962 which are generally regarded as the most important changes ever made in the public assistance titles of the Social Security Act. Both theses, as well as the political climate within which each was advanced, and the policy-making process which contributed to their easy acceptance, merit examination.

I. A RESIDUAL PROGRAM

President Roosevelt's decision to delay action in 1934 on piece-meal old age assistance and unemployment insurance proposals in order to achieve a more comprehensive social security program in 1935 has been widely reported.[4] By May, 1934, Roosevelt was telling supporters that this was his position, and on June 29, 1934, he created by executive order a Committee on Economic Security with the Secretary of Labor as Chairman, and as members the Secretaries of the Treasury and of Agriculture, the Attorney-General, and the Federal Emergency Relief Administrator. The committee's function was to study the problems relating to the economic security of individuals and to make recommendations which would promote greater economic security. The executive order also created an Advisory Council on Economic Security, "the original members of which shall be appointed by the President and additional members of which may be appointed from time to time by the Committee." The committee was directed by the order to appoint a Technical Board on Economic Security from within federal departments and agencies and an Executive Director to have charge of studies under the direction of the Technical Board.

We know now that as it developed the major architects of the

[4]*Ibid.,* pp. 5-7.

Social Security Act proposed to Congress were Edwin E. Witte who was named Executive Director; Thomas Eliot, then Assistant Solicitor of the Department of Labor; Arthur J. Altmeyer, then Second Assistant Secretary of Labor; and Secretary of Labor Frances Perkins. Staff reports of the Committee on Economic Security were lengthy, able, and, in general, without significance as far as subsequent policy recommendations are concerned. Only the reports dealing with child welfare, employment opportunities, and the economic risks of illness were actually completed before December 24, 1934, when the committee reported orally to the President. All of the major reports were subsequently turned in, but the committee felt that it could not wait on the more leisurely academic and scholarly pace. The completed research reports did not serve as the basis of committee recommendations. Actually, neither committee members nor congressmen showed much interest in the staff reports: none of the members of the congressional committees involved even asked for a copy of any of the reports; members of the Committee on Economic Security probably never read any of them very thoroughly.[5]

The comparative political strength of the old age assistance proposal in the federal legislation has been evaluated by Witte who acknowledges that there was criticism over the omnibus character of the bill. He reports, however, that Roosevelt felt that an omnibus bill offered the best chance to carry the entire program:

> As the situation developed, I doubt whether any part of the social security program other than the old age assistance title would have been enacted into law but for the fact that the President throughout insisted that the entire program must be kept together. Had the measure been presented in separate bills, it is quite possible that the old age assistance title might have become law much earlier. I doubt whether anything else would have gone through at all.[6]

Even the order of the various titles of the Social Security Act was designed with the popularity of OAA in mind. Thomas Eliot, draftsman of the act, placed OAA first because he conceived it to be the most popular title. This was a correct estimate and Eliot's action had the effect of drawing opposition away from the less popular titles. One of these apparently was old age insurance which almost went down the drain in executive session of the House Ways and Means Committee. Administration members of the committee went to Roosevelt at one point during executive session consideration and told him that the old age insurance titles could not be passed. The President insisted that all

[5]*Ibid.,* pp. 39-41.
[6]Reprinted with permission of the copyright owners, the Regents of the University of Wisconsin, from Witte, pp. 78-79.

essential features of the bill be preserved, including the insurance title, and his congressional friends went away and counted again. OAA never ran into trouble in either the House Ways and Means Committee or the Senate Finance Committee, or on the floor of either chamber.

The special political appeal of the aged, combined with a belief that the aged would continue to represent the major drain on public assistance, made it inviting to accept the idea that in the long run things would get cheaper. Obviously, destitute old people could not be expected to make back contributions to a newly created insurance system and thus become immediately eligible for benefits. Nor could many classes of business and industry be expected suddenly to be able to contribute to a new social security trust fund. As the elderly poor died, however, they could be replaced in part by a not so poor group whose members had the advantage of social security pensions. As the economic condition of the country permitted, the latter group could be expanded by gradual inclusion of more businesses and perhaps finally of the professions in the insured class. The broader the insurance coverage, the lesser the expected public assistance demand, and when the OAA demand was finally minimized by this process, it would be possible for the states to take up the burdens of dependent children and the blind.

With the inclusion of survivors' insurance as part of the old age insurance package in 1939, the model looked very sound. The gospel spread through the ranks and was not easily shaken. In 1939, the Chairman of the Social Security Board predicted to the Senate Finance Committee that "As this insurance system gets into operation . . . it ought to remove a large proportion of these dependent children from the State mother's pension rolls."[7] Fifteen years later when there were 400,000 more OAA recipients than there had been in 1939, and when the number of aid to dependent children (ADC) recipients was growing past the two-and-a-half million mark, another welfare specialist still alleged that, with the amendments of the 1950's, the goal of primary reliance upon social insurance had come much closer to realization.[8] The earlier statement was understandably speculative. The later statement simply ignored reality in favor of myth. In the course of the years between these statements, there was no shortage of similar affirmations from a wide variety of sources. One of them was President Harry Truman's statement that "the basic purpose of public assistance . . . is

[7]U.S. Congress, Senate, Committee on Finance, Hearings, "Social Security Act Amendments," 76th Cong., 1st Sess., 1939, p. 14.

[8]U.S. Congress, House, Subcommittee of the Committee on Appropriations, Hearings, "Departments of Labor and Health, Education, and Welfare Appropriations for 1955," 83d Cong., 2d Sess., 1954, p. 274.

and has always been to supplement our social-insurance system. Our aim has been to expand coverage of social insurance and gradually reduce the need for supplementary public-assistance programs."[9]

Before the fifteenth anniversary of the Social Security Act, business, labor, and government spokesmen were all envisioning a more and more limited role for public assistance in the social welfare picture and both business and government were looking forward to federal withdrawal. "We think it is especially important to treat public assistance as residual," said James Carey for the Social Security Committee of the CIO in 1946.[10] And in 1950, a representative of the Illinois State Chamber of Commerce told the Senate Finance Committee that "once the old-age and survivors' insurance program is extended the Federal Government can and should begin an orderly withdrawal from the field of providing assistance to the needy."[11] The Social Security Administrator seemed to be of a similar mind only a year earlier, although he would very likely not have agreed with the Illinois Chamber of Commerce man about timing:

. . . this public assistance is a residual program to help needy persons who are not adequately protected by the various forms of contributory social insurance. . . .

. . . If we have a comprehensive contributory social-insurance system covering all of these economic hazards to which the people are exposed, I believe that in time the residual load of public assistance would become so small in this country that the States and the localities could reasonably be expected to assume that load without Federal financial participation . . . the major element is the aged, the load of the aged, and that takes time.[12]

Arguing in favor of expansion of the old age and survivors' insurance (OASI) program to cover an additional ten million persons, Welfare Secretary Oveta Hobby was officially predicting the seesaw effect in 1954. "It really happens much faster than you think," she said; "as the Federal old-age and survivors' insurance system really begins to do its job, the need for public assistance would deteriorate."[13]

Even those who were not sanguine about a diminishing public assistance load — and there were a few — could not have anticipated all the real reasons why public assistance would not wither away. Who

[9]*Congressional Record*, July 18, 1951, p. 8347.

[10]U.S. Congress, House, Committee on Ways and Means, Hearings, "Amendments to Social Security Act," 79th Cong., 2d Sess., 1946, p. 961.

[11]U.S. Congress, Senate, Committee on Finance, Hearings, "Social Security Revision," 81st Cong., 2d Sess., 1950, p. 830.

[12]U.S. Congress, House, Committee on Ways and Means, Hearings, "Social Security Act Amendments of 1949," 81st Cong., 1st Sess., 1949, p. 103.

[13]House Appropriations, Hearings, 1954, pp. 13-14.

could anticipate in the late 1930's that inflation would make social insurance inadequate for those depending on it; that death of the father would be replaced by illegitimacy and desertion as the real hard-core ADC problems—risks for which there is no public social insurance; that unemployment compensation designed to protect against temporary unemployment would not be able to protect a worker rendered permanently obsolete by a machine; that southern Negroes would move in waves to the northern industrial states and find the combination of technology and discrimination to be overpowering; and that the failure of social insurance to give protection against the catastrophes of prolonged and expensive illness or permanent disability would add to the costs of public assistance? Perhaps the closest approach by a politician to suggesting that, for whatever reason, public assistance burdens would grow came from Eugene Millikin who was ranking Republican member of the Senate Finance Committee in the early postwar period. "It has always been our theory," said Millikin, "that as we increase the benefits under the contributory system we could decrease the amount of public assistance. Personally, I think that is sheer theory. I do not think it will happen much because the States are building up large public assistance pensions and there will be all sorts of pressures to continue the system and personally I believe it will be continued."[14]

What has actually happened in public assistance is that the number of OAA recipients has declined significantly relative to the growth in population of persons aged 65 and over, but the growth in the ADC recipient rate among children under 18 has increased significantly.[15] Public assistance doesn't wither because the present character of the ADC rolls was never included as a part of the withering-away theory. Yet, from 1935 to as late as 1950, little attention was paid to ADC.

If OAA originally ranked at one end of a congressional enthusiasm-indifference continuum, it appears that ADC was at the other end. Witte reports that even when members of the House Committee acknowledged that the disparity between OAA and ADC payments was illogical, "there was so little interest on the part of any of the members in the aid to dependent children that no one thereafter made a motion to strike out the restriction."[16] In exccutive session of the Senate Finance Committee, Secretary of Labor Perkins urged the

[14]Finance, Hearings, 1950, p. 48.
[15]U.S. Department of Health, Education, and Welfare, Bureau of Family Services, *Trend Report, Public Assistance and Related Data, 1962* (Washington, May, 1963), pp. 60-61.
[16]Reprinted with permission of the copyright owners, the Regents of the University of Wisconsin, from Witte, p. 164.

striking of the inequity between the old age and children's programs, but no action was forthcoming, again apparently as much because of lack of interest as because of real opposition. The grant pattern set at that time, however, has prevailed throughout the history of the program, including the present period when interest in ADC has been maximized and that in OAA minimized. Grants for children have never caught up to grants at the adult level.

Increases in federal funds for OAA, for the blind, and for the disabled have been more generous and easier to accomplish than the increases in the ADC category. Even if the original judgment of the Committee on Economic Security was that assistance for the blind was not a critical problem for federal action because the states tended to provide better for the blind than for the aged, the Senate Finance Committee emphatically disagreed. At the same time that Congress could not be interested in the level of ADC support even when it was especially highlighted, Congress was insisting on initiating an aid to the blind program. The cynical explanation that adults vote, and that children do not, is too pat. It will be remembered that, in the first place, the ADC program began at a comparative disadvantage because of the pressing nature of the old age problem in 1935. Equity between the child and adult categories was not considered and rejected but rather was never considered in those terms. Although the Social Security Act has come to be considered a comprehensive package approach to the problems of economic security, the legislative and political histories of its origin suggest that the approach was more a collection of separate specifics for problems separately considered than a big comprehensive approach to interrelated problems. The background work and the initial plan for administration of the dependent children's program both involved the Children's Bureau in the Department of Labor. This was taken for granted in all discussion of the recommendations by the technical board and by the Committee on Economic Security. The background work in OAA, on the other hand, was done by economists as part of the general question of old age security, and the initial plan would have had the OAA program administered by the Federal Emergency Relief Administration. In short, unlike OAA and old age insurance which were tied together by the withering-away concept, the ADC and OAA categories tended to be separately compartmentalized from the outset. Levels of support were separately developed.

Because the level of support for ADC was tied by the Children's Bureau to the level of support provided for orphans of war veterans, while the level of support for OAA was tied by Witte's staff to the level of support envisioned by the Townsend Plan, there was a basic historical disparity. The disparity was emphasized by an original failure to note that the Veterans' Pension Act allowed a separate grant for the adult caretaker, but the ADC title did not. When ultimately noted, this factor failed to stir up enough concern to effect a change. The seemingly accidental failure to consider the separate caretaker grant in fixing a maximum compounded the original establishment of the federal matching share at one-third to parallel the one-third matching provided for in the Dill-Connery old age assistance grants bill. When the Dill-Connery measure was scrapped and the OAA title of the Social Security Act was written to provide for a one-half matching grant, the ADC formula was not changed to correspond. The one-third figure had originally been proposed by the Children's Bureau, but no maximum grant was involved. A combination of factors resulted in putting dependent children in a least favored category, but the combination seems to have been a combination of accidents rather than a combination of planned moves.

When a caretaker grant was finally approved after 15 years of Social Security, it provoked no more interest in Congress than had its original exclusion. In 1950, the House bill amending the Social Security Act carried a caretaker grant provision; the Senate Finance Committee bill did not. With the support of the child welfare division of the American Legion, Scott Lucas, then Senate Democratic leader, successfully amended the Senate bill on the floor to carry the House provision. In a low-pressure announcement, Lucas stated that the chairman and members of the Finance Committee "this morning" agreed to the addition as a matter of equity. Senator Taft's perfunctory complaint that the effect was to compel the Committee on Appropriations to make available an additional $75 million annually to pay for the program was the sole comment. Taft himself made it plain that his disapproval was limited to the "wisdom at this time of what amounts to appropriating money" and that he had no substantive objection to the program.[17] A conference committee struck provisions for an increase in federal matching, yet retained the caretaker grant. The tantalizing question is whether it could not have been included 15 years earlier if someone had pushed it — or even nudged it along.

Using the first postwar year, 1946, as a bench mark, the OAA recipient rate has dropped one-third, but the ADC recipient rate has doubled. Far from leaving the field to the states, federal grants for public assistance are up from $439 million in 1946 to over $1 billion in 1950, and to $3 billion now. Starting in 1946 at a little over half a billion dollars, state public aid costs have increased to one-and-a-half billion,

[17]*Congressional Record*, June 20, 1950, p. 8887.

and local units now contribute half a billion dollars against a 1946 bill of $127 million. The total dollar cost of public assistance has "withered away" to about $5 billion, and the number of people dependent on public aid "withered away" to eight million in 1965!

In the 1960's, members of congressional appropriations subcommittees faced with requests for several billions of dollars for federal grants to the states for public assistance, were speaking wistfully of the old idea of public assistance as a residual program that would wither away. "We were hopeful, I know, at one time," said Democratic Representative Winfield Denton of Evansville, Indiana, "that social security would take the place of most of the welfare. It doesn't seem to be doing that, does it?"[18] Having been told that OAA had indeed declined regularly between 1950 and 1960, the congressman returned to his theme: "Of course, this would be disputed now, but ... we were told that this public assistance was a stopgap. . . . I recognize there is not much we can do." In the Senate Appropriations subcommittee, Chairman Lister Hill, who had been around at the beginning, also spoke more in sadness than in anger: "I remember when we passed the act in 1935 the thinking was that the public assistance grants were being only for more or less of a temporary period, that soon everybody would be under OASI and you would not have any need for public assistance grants."[19]

II. AN ECONOMIC PARADOX?

Social insurance is not about to destroy the need for public assistance. Full employment, however, has become an alternate solution to the relief problem that seems logical to many people. In his annual message to the 1965 New York state legislature, Governor Nelson Rockefeller, who had budget troubles, called sharply rising welfare costs, during a year when employment and the national income were at an all time high, "the most serious economic paradox of our times." New York's problem was not unique. In California around the same time, Governor Edmund Brown reported a 1964 welfare deficiency of over $16 million. Nationally, costs of public relief in the boom month of December, 1963, were more than six times larger than in the grim depression month of December, 1936. (Even using constant

[18]U.S. Congress, House, Subcommittee of the Committee on Appropriations, Hearings, "Departments of Labor and Health, Education, and Welfare Appropriations for 1962," 87th Cong., 1st Sess., 1961, p. 654.

[19]U.S. Congress, Senate, Subcommittee of the Committee on Appropriations, Hearings, "Labor – Health, Education, and Welfare Appropriations for 1962," 87th Cong., 1st Sess., 1961, p. 400.

dollars, payments were three times larger in the later period than in the earlier.) Still, Rockefeller had good cause to be disturbed. In 1964, two years after the self-help, self-care, rehabilitation amendments had been enacted, New York State's welfare costs increased 14.2 per cent. The Governor was going to have to find for public assistance almost $90 million more in state funds than had been provided during the previous year. One-third of the amount was needed just to make up the welfare budget deficit.

In New York City, the Department of Welfare asked for a 1966 fiscal-year budget of half a billion dollars, 90 per cent of it for the public assistance division. During October, 1964, there were 455,000 persons on relief in the city, with the numbers constantly increasing. By March, 1965, the count exceeded 498,000. At the time when half of New York City's welfare workers went on strike in January, 1965, demanding both higher pay and smaller case loads, applications were pouring in at the rate of 13,000 a month, and 5,850 persons were being added to the assistance rolls every month. Mayor Wagner termed the welfare burden "really too great for the city."

A most perplexing aspect was that big-city slum problems were not the sole cause of the fiscal drain as had been commonly assumed. The wealthy New York suburban counties of Nassau, Suffolk, and Westchester had big additional welfare costs. Population increases and higher standards were the explanations for higher welfare costs that were most commonly offered. However, in Nassau County the number of public assistance recipients more than doubled between 1960 and 1964 while the population rose only 6.5 per cent. In Suffolk the population increase during the same period was 30 per cent, but relief cases increased by 87 per cent; Westchester County had a 30 per cent increase in assistance cases with a 9 per cent population rise. Admittedly, two new programs had been inaugurated during the four years — medical aid to the indigent aged (Kerr-Mills) and aid to dependent children of the unemployed (ADC-U). New programs, nevertheless, did not account for all of the increased relief load which would still have been a problem without Kerr-Mills and without ADC-U. The former was expensive; the latter, however, acted to move many cases from state and locally supported general assistance over to the federally aided categorical program rather than to provoke entirely new cases.

To term rising welfare costs during a period of full employment a paradox assumes some direct relationship between job availability and the dependency status of public assistance clients. But the great bulk of relief costs goes to support people who cannot work under any conditions. Neither is the existence of a growing relief burden in spite of an almost universal system of social insurance a paradox, because again the most rapidly growing relief program is largely unaffected by social insurance. Full employment conditions benefit only the employable. Expanded social insurance coverage benefits only the insurable. All social insurance is predicated on sometime employment of an identifiable head of a household. Yet in both Westchester County and in New York City, three out of four assistance recipients were mothers and their children, almost all of them without a male member of the family who could work. There are 1,200 children born every month to families already on the relief rolls in New York City. Of the more than 700,000 clients in the entire state—supported at a total annual cost of $814 million—only 4 per cent are considered employable.

The single most important program fact in public assistance is that since 1957 there have been more recipients of ADC than of any other category of assistance. These ADC cases are not composed of widows and orphans to any substantial extent, but rather of deserted mothers and children and of mothers and illegitimate children. Survivors' insurance is simply irrelevant in those situations, while unemployment insurance, even if the father qualifies, follows him and not his deserted dependents. One indication of the irrelevance of current social insurance legislation to the current public assistance problem is that fewer than 6 per cent of ADC cases also qualify for survivorship or disability insurance benefits.

Public assistance costs have risen sharply despite social insurance and despite almost full employment because the groups benefited by public assistance are either outside the insurance spectrum, are under-insured under present public policies, or are largely unemployable. It is a happy fact that the job market for children is bad in post-New Deal America. It is a less happy fact that it is also bad for the aged, even the healthy aged, and for the unskilled worker of any age. The situation is particularly difficult for the unskilled or aged Negro—"double jeopardy" is the characterization some Negro leaders have applied—but it is a mistake to assume that the problem can be met by crash programs of vocational training. Insufficient educational background to acquire specialized skills in a specialized economy, automation, inadequate social insurance benefits or the inapplicability of social insurance to chronic unemployables, and the withdrawal of private welfare from the relief field, collectively add up to the present level of public assistance costs.

Because the scale of benefits under ADC tends to be less than half that under OAA, the latter temporarily remains the most expensive single program of public assistance in dollars. There are about 2.2 million OAA cases in the country, representing 12.4 per cent of the population aged 65 and over. Notwithstanding a steady increase in the aged population, the number of recipients has declined slowly from a 1950 high of 2.8 million, a drop that is attributable to the extension of coverage under social insurance to virtually everyone who could manage to squeeze in a few quarters of covered employment. For OAA recipients, full employment and economic prosperity are significant only if they mean more readily available help from self-sufficient children. (Just one-quarter of OAA recipients having nondependent children were receiving help from their children in 1960.) Social insurance benefits were not originally designed to provide a subsistence income without supplementation, and the regularly enacted improvements in the benefit schedule have not kept pace with inflation. "We have women who were comfortably fixed when their husbands died 20 years ago," reports Louis Kurtis, Westchester Commissioner of Welfare; "now their resources are exhausted or inadequate."[20] Kurtis notes that Westchester job opportunities are plentiful, but that they do not have much bearing on the situation of the elderly widow.

Two billion dollars a year is spent on OAA, but it is spent unequally throughout the United States. Higher percentages of the aged are benefited in the predominantly rural states than in the urban industrial states, with a range from 49.8 per cent in Louisiana to 2.8 per cent in Delaware. After that, it is virtually impossible to bring order into the variations. There is no sign, for example, that low recipient rates mean relatively higher benefits, or that a high proportion of recipients to total aged population necessarily means skimpy benefits. No consistent pattern of relationships between recipient rates and benefit schedules emerges. Oklahoma, with the fourth highest recipient rate in the country, pays an average monthly cash benefit of $92, but Georgia with the fifth highest rate pays only $55. Hawaii and Alabama pay almost identical average monthly benefits of approximately $68, but Hawaii payments go to only 3.6 per cent of the aged population while Alabama payments go to 39.3 per cent of that state's aged. Relatively lower benefits are not a southern phenomenon. Louisiana pays $84 while Delaware's average is only $63. Wisconsin pays an average of $101 to 7.5 per cent of its aged population, but Michigan pays $79 to the same fraction of its old people.

The real economic paradox in public assistance is the fact that a state's wealth provides no sure clue to its likely level of support for the

[20]*New York Times,* December 14, 1964, p. 31.

indigent. Of the top quintile of states in average per capita income for 1959-1961, only two—California and New Jersey—were in the top quintile ranked according to average monthly OAA benefits. Six of the ten poorest states are also among the ten states with lowest benefits, but seven of the states in the top-benefit quintile had average per capita incomes below the national average. North Dakota, tenth poorest state in the country, aided 10 per cent of its aged with the eighth highest benefit ($91) in the country. Oklahoma, with its high recipient rate and high average payment, is fifteenth poorest in per capita income.

Simple explanations of state OAA recipient rates and benefit patterns clearly won't do. More precise and more complicated statistical techniques also yield hard-to-understand results in both OAA and ADC. Using regression analysis involving seven independent variables, Glenn Fisher has shown that income, population density, and urbanization of a state are closely correlated with per capita governmental spending for most functions—but the least satisfactory results provided by this method occur in the welfare field.[21] Even refining his techniques to analyze each program in public assistance separately, Fisher found the welfare expenditures of a state to be most highly resistant to rational economic explanation. State-to-state variations in how many get how much under the ADC program are no less hard to classify than are OAA benefit variations. Fisher did find high proportions of ADC cases to the total child population to be associated with state characteristics of urbanization, low incomes, and low levels of employment. These relationships are easy enough to understand. However, using the same methods and the same independent variables to analyze differences between states in average payments yields irregular results for which Fisher acknowledges he can suggest no satisfactory economic explanation.

Program variations in ADC are extreme. In West Virginia, 13.4 per cent of all children under 18 were aided in June, 1963, a percentage exactly double that of the next ranking state, Mississippi. With virtually identical percentages (1.5) of their child populations being aided, Texas and New Hampshire made average monthly payments as different as $19 in Texas and $40 in New Hampshire. Federal sharing stopped at $30 and so did average benefits in 23 states including Delaware and Nevada, although they have the country's highest per capita incomes. But, as in OAA, the relatively poor state of North

---

[21]Glenn W. Fisher, "Determinants of State and Local Government Expenditures: A Preliminary Analysis," *National Tax Journal,* XIV (December, 1961), 355; and "Interstate Variations in State and Local Government Expenditure," *National Tax Journal,* XVII (March, 1964), 73.

Dakota makes high ($42) ADC payments. Comparable differences abound, likely to be explained satisfactorily only after a meticulous examination of the political history of each state's public assistance program, category by category.

ADC now involves the largest number of people, and in a few years it will be the costliest categorical program. The total of public funds in ADC is 70 per cent that of the total in OAA, but the latter program helps only 55 per cent as many people as the ADC roll of four million individuals. Following a decline during World War II, the number of recipients in the dependent child category was at a peak of 2.2 million in 1950, when the program was first broadened to include a so-called caretaker, a relative with whom the dependent child lives. Even with the caretaker inclusion, however, the load then dropped during the Korean War, fell below two million during 1952 and 1953, rose again to cross the three million mark in 1960; and, with further broadening to include an unemployed parent segment, ADC spurted sharply upward beginning in 1961, hitting a total of 4.3 million recipients in 1964. The number almost exactly doubled in the decade between 1954 and 1964. There are more ADC beneficiaries now than there were general relief recipients in the middle of 1937, a fact that would still hold true if there were no unemployed parent cases in the present program.

This disturbing growth is officially charged to demographic conditions, to economic recessions, and to the social phenomenon of increased numbers of families headed by women.[22] Population increases, including a rapid growth in the child population, of course contribute to swelling ADC totals, but the New York suburban statistics have shown that this can be oversold. Economic decline can be held partly accountable for surges in 1954, 1957-1958, and again in 1960-1961, but it will not do as an explanation for the increases since then. Growth in the number of families headed by women can be made to serve as a principal explanation for the new highs of recent years, but there is more to it. In their understandable anxiety to protect ADC recipients from being stigmatized as immoral by more elegant members of American society, official spokesmen and official reports skirt or avoid the most depressing aspect of the ADC growth rate, that portion of it attributable to second-generation dependency, sometimes to second-generation illegitimacy. In ADC, the term "women-headed families" is not shorthand for widows and orphans. It is a euphemism for desertion

[22]U.S. Department of Health, Education, and Welfare, Welfare Administration, "Aid to Families with Dependent Children" (Washington, February, 1963, process duplicated), p. 2.

and illegitimacy, problems that are so far resistant to solution, and that those responsible for administering the program prefer not to discuss in public. Multiple illegitimacies in a single family "leaves a public image that no one applauds," acknowledged Social Security Commissioner John Tramburg in 1961, but he would not agree with inquiring Congressman Thomas Curtis that immorality could be assumed under these conditions.[23]

Of the dozens of witnesses testifying on the Public Welfare Amendments of 1962, none of the professional leaders raised the possibility of the need for a special attack on illegitimacy and second-generation illegitimacy particularly. One practicing caseworker appeared, however, and his voice from the field injected a troublesome note into the record that was otherwise stuffed with assurances to legislators that job training, rehabilitation, self-help, and self-care were the big things. "The central problem of public assistance today is not the able-bodied man who won't work," asserted Julius Horwitz on the basis of six years of experience as a social investigator for New York City's Department of Welfare, "but the production of children within the welfare system, children born of second and third generation mothers on public assistance." Horwitz, who used the opportunity to plug his novel based on public assistance in New York City, appeared not as a rugged individualist calling for a return to the old-fashioned virtues of sacrifice and hard work to replace government grants, but as a participant-observer outraged by the unreported realities:

In New York City I became aware that tens of thousands of people on public assistance were living in a nightmare world of drug addiction, alcoholism, violence, packed together in buildings unfit for human habitation, at rentals that were and still are scandalous, that children were being bred with no thought to their place in the world and that the birth of a child was beginning to emerge as the means for guaranteeing financial security and recognition to a growing group of young girls who themselves had grown up in dependency and who were unprepared, by their environment or training, to enter into the productive life of their communities.[24]

Illegitimacy in ADC has a political significance that is often obscured by the magnitude of the social problem it creates. The Health, Education, and Welfare statistics report wide differences in

[23]U.S. Congress, House, Committee on Ways and Means, Hearings, "Temporary Unemployment Compensation and Aid to Dependent Children of Unemployed Parents," 87th Cong., 1st Sess., 1961, p. 239.
[24]U.S. Congress, Senate, Committee on Finance, Hearings, "Public Assistance Act of 1962," 87th Cong., 2d Sess., 1962, p. 436. The Horwitz novel is *The Inhabitants* (Cleveland: World Publishing, 1960).

benefits paid under the ADC program. Accompanying explanations do not take into account differences in state legislative attitudes towards moral standards different from those commonly accepted. Governors and state legislators who are conscientious with budgets and finances have found that their plans often go astray because of unanticipated welfare costs, and that large deficiency appropriations become necessary. Abraham Ribicoff says that, in his six years as Governor of Connecticut, he found "very few problems that were as frustrating and as bothersome as the whole problem of welfare costs."[25] It can be predicted that this hard-to-find deficiency money will only be sought out with reluctance by some politicians who feel that the need for funds is related to immoral behavior that somehow should have been avoided. Whether governors and legislators view illegitimacy as a failure of society or whether they view it as individual sin is likely to be an important determinant of the levels of ADC support.

Political attitudes of this sort cannot be measured as precisely as can economic data. It is certain, however, that one factor contributing to legislative insistence, in 1963, on ceilings for Illinois ADC payments was data showing that 59 per cent of the state's ADC cases involved illegitimate children. Forty per cent of the cases involved two or more illegitimate children, 12 per cent involved four or more illegitimacies in a single family. Illegitimacy and second-generation dependency in ADC may not yet be massive crises, but, in the words of Henry Heald, society expects its most talented minds to be able to detect faint murmurs before they become massive crises. An explicit acknowledgment of the problem by the talented minds in public welfare is overdue, and so is a search for a specific plan to deal with it more effectively than it has been dealt with under the present policy of ignoring the reality of its existence. To continue to let statistics like those in Illinois be "revealed" during a search for welfare money does a disservice to the recipients.

ADC money is now going to recipients with very different characteristics from the recipient group of the depression. As a matter of fact, the whole public relief program now deals with recipients with different characteristics from those of recipients of the depression period. There is no economic paradox. There is a policy lag in public assistance that can be traced to an erroneous assumption about the continuing need for the original categories, to the inability of the client group to organize in support of its own interests, and to impediments to innovation that are built into the welfare policy-making process.

[25]Ways and Means, Hearings, 1961, p. 103.

III. A POUND OF CURE-ALL

It took 27 years for the great reexamination of public assistance to occur. When that reexamination took place in 1962, it tended to concentrate on ways to achieve long-run reductions in cost, although it has yet to be demonstrated either that there is any adequate substitute for money in relief or that money payments in relief have ever been adequate. Important changes between 1935 and 1962 in federal legislation were, with very limited exceptions, restricted to changes in benefit formulae involving the federal share of costs. Evolution of these changes and their significance will be considered subsequently. At this point, it is useful to look at the Public Welfare Amendments of 1962 with a view to considering the change in emphases when the extremes — 1935 and 1962 — are viewed in close succession.

By 1962, it was evident that there would be no withering away of public assistance. A series of conclusions reached in 1938 by William Haber finally seemed self-evident by 1962. Haber had characterized relief as "a permanent program," predicted that probably three-quarters of all public assistance cases in 1937 represented long-time public relief cases, and observed that "the nation is committed to care for the aged and other dependent persons and the cost of such care must be considered as a continuing claim on the public budget."[26] Specifically, Haber concluded that the major part of the relief problem was not due to unemployment; that relief was not an emergency problem, but a permanent one; that state and local resources were inadequate to meet relief costs; that social security insurance provisions would have little effect on dependency and relief; and that a long-range federal program was needed covering work projects and general relief. Assertions as to the permanency of public assistance as a major federal obligation were infrequent during the period up to 1953. Jane Hoey, of the Bureau of Public Assistance, did tell the House Ways and Means Committee in 1949 that public assistance remained a major item through periods of prosperity because "the people we have on the list are unemployable people. They are too old or too young to work, or they are handicapped physically or a mother is needed in the home where there are young children. This is not an employable group we are now taking care of, by and large."[27] It will be recalled that Social Security Administrator Arthur Altmeyer, Miss Hoey's boss, was telling that same committee at the same time that "this public assist-

[26]William Haber, "Relief: A Permanent Program," *Survey Graphic,* XXVII (December, 1938), 591-94.
[27]Ways and Means, Hearings, 1949, p. 415.

ance is a residual program to help needy persons who are not adequately protected by the various forms of contributory social insurance. . . .If we have a comprehensive contributory social insurance system . . . in time the residual load of public assistance would become so small in this country that the States and the localities could reasonably be expected to assume that load without Federal financial participation. . . ."[28]

Somehow, the time has never come when public assistance has been residual. Haber and Hoey, running against the tide with their prophecies of gloom, have turned out to be a good deal more right than their professional colleagues who foresaw a dropping-off of the aged, but who did not anticipate the growth of the dependent child class, and who did not anticipate that social insurance would, in the manner of insurance, provide benefits more closely related to premiums than to need. If there was hope until 1953 that the insurance-assistance fulcrum would behave as expected, that hope was not part of the official policy line during the Eisenhower years when the idea of maximizing state and local responsibility for public assistance was emphasized.[29] From 1953 through 1960, increases in federal funds were forthcoming over administration opposition that was based on an expressed concern that support would mean control, and that federal control was inconsistent with the administration's political philosophy. Thus, an earlier administration's faith that good social insurance would drive out bad public assistance was replaced by a later administration's belief that bad federal support would drive out good state responsibility.

This was the history that faced the New Frontier group elected in November, 1960. It was hardly in a position to maintain the Eisenhower preoccupation with maximizing state responsibility as a way towards a balanced budget. But a return to the proposition that public assistance was a residual program—and therefore one that need only be sustained rather than improved—was not tenable. Admittedly, the OAA recipient rate per 1,000 population had declined from 190 in 1953 to 141 in 1960; the comparable rate of persons receiving both OAA and old age insurance had increased over that same period from 32 to 41. The ADC figures carried a more depressing message. The number of families receiving ADC increased from 573,000 in 1953 to 784,000 in 1960, and the number of families receiving both ADC and OASDI (old age, survivors', and disability insurance) child's benefits

[28]*Ibid.,* p. 103.
[29]President Eisenhower's Budget Message for fiscal 1959, for example, spoke of "modernizing the formulas for public assistance with a view to gradually reducing Federal participation in its financing." See *Congressional Record,* 85th Cong., 2d Sess., 1958, p. 397.

increased from 30,600 to 41,000 over that same time span. Whatever else it was doing, after 25 years social insurance was not making an important dent in the public assistance totals. Nor could it be alleged that it was still a problem of limited coverage. In 1950, coverage had been extended to most urban self-employed persons, to regularly employed agricultural and domestic workers, and on a voluntary group basis to employees of nonprofit organizations and those of state and local governments. In 1954, a Republican Congress further amended the Social Security Act making it possible for coverage to be extended to some 10 million persons who, at some time during a year, have earnings as farmers or in previously excluded jobs in agriculture, or in domestic service, and to additional groups of state and local government employees. In 1956, military service was covered and 850,000 other jobs were included. It was thus possible in the year of John Kennedy's election to the presidency for his principal social security advisor to write that "with these major extensions, coverage of sub-stantially all gainful work in the United States is within sight — a goal that seemed politically and administratively unattainable twenty-five years ago."[30]

If the curtain had to be lowered on the extend-social-insurance-so-that-the-public-assistance-load-will-fall-away performance, it also had to be lowered on the *status quo*. Besides involving ever increasing national and state costs, the program was faced with the consequences of allegations by critics that public assistance was fostering illegit-imacy. Denial of continued support to some 20,000 Negro children in Louisiana on the basis of a state finding that their homes were unsuit-able was one such consequence. The Louisiana action brought world-wide condemnation.[31] Arthur Flemming, Eisenhower's Secretary of Health, Education, and Welfare at the time, found himself in an awkward position in seeking to limit an obviously discriminatory state practice in a program that his department and his president insisted must be state controlled.

The new Democratic administration determined to have its sup-porters in the welfare field come up with a fresh approach. A reap-praisal which, according to the new Health, Education, and Welfare Secretary, Abraham Ribicoff, was "possibly unprecedented in its scope and depth" was the first order.[32] There is considerable doubt that

[30]Wilbur J. Cohen, "Twenty-Five Years of Progress in Social Security," in William Haber and Wilbur J. Cohen, eds., *Social Security: Programs, Problems, and Policies* (Homewood, Ill.: Richard D. Irwin, 1960), p. 84.

[31]The Louisiana case is reviewed and pertinent documents are reprinted in *Social Service Review*, XXXV (June, 1961), 203-14.

[32]U.S. Congress, House, Committee on Ways and Means, Hearings, "Public Welfare Amendments of 1962," 87th Cong., 2d Sess., 1962, p. 158.

the Ribicoff characterization is entirely accurate, but it is certain that no reappraisal of public assistance since 1935 was undertaken with as much enthusiasm or represented a more clear-cut case of the faithful persuading the already committed.

In the postelection, preinauguration period, John Kennedy created a task force on social welfare under the leadership of Wilbur Cohen, then of the University of Michigan. Cohen's competence in the field and the pertinence of his experience, beginning with work as Edwin Witte's assistant in the days of the Committee on Economic Security, were generally acknowledged. The task force report was confined to the need for stopgap measures to meet the problem of recession. Temporary legislation was proposed, particularly a program of aid to dependent children of the unemployed and a federal extension of unemployment compensation benefit periods. Testifying before the House Ways and Means Committee in support of these proposals, Ribicoff promised a thorough review and investigation of federal welfare law. He started with a meeting with representatives of the National Association of Social Workers on May 2, 1961, and achieved at least an offer of cooperation. Shortly thereafter, a somewhat larger group representing public agencies, private agencies, and the schools of social work was constituted as an Ad Hoc Committee on Public Welfare.

Ribicoff followed this by announcing the appointment of George Wyman as a consultant to offer recommendations and suggestions for administrative and program actions relating to procedures and operations in the Children's Bureau and in the Bureau of Public Assistance. The consultant had excellent credentials as Director of the Los Angeles Welfare Department, former California Welfare Director, and Director-Designate of the New York State Department of Welfare. Among other reports developed at the same time, a document prepared by Elizabeth Wickenden, Consultant on Technical Social Policy for the National Social Welfare Assembly, seems to have had some significance. Miss Wickenden's *Public Welfare — Time for a Change* was sponsored by the New York School of Social Work, under a grant from the Field Foundation which also provided support for the Ad Hoc Committee and for Wyman.

Given the composition of the various committees, consultant staffs, and advisory groups, there was never any danger of honest differences of opinion. Admittedly, no claim was made that any of the groups was broadly representative of anything other than the professionals in social welfare. Seven of the nine members of Miss Wickenden's advisory group and two of its four consultants were members of the Ad Hoc Committee on Public Welfare. Of the 23 members of the

Ad Hoc Committee, only Justice Josephine Wise Polier of the New York City Domestic Relations Court did not have an attachment to a school of social work or a welfare agency.

The various reports noted the changes in social and economic conditions since passage of the Social Security Act, and tacitly acknowledged that public assistance had not proved to be residual. Unlike the staff reports of the Committee on Economic Security a quarter century earlier, the 1962 reports included no data, only findings and conclusions and recommendations. They called for retention of the temporary ADC-U program, closer coordination of ADC and child welfare programs, the elimination (or drastic reduction) of residence requirements, a stepped-up program of grants for the training of social workers, and, above all, a positive approach in terms of prevention, rehabilitation, and services. In listing the principles basic to all the proposals of its report, the Ad Hoc Committee begins:

Rehabilitative Services by Professionally Trained Personnel

Financial assistance to meet people's basic needs for food, shelter, and clothing is essential, but alone is not enough. Expenditures for assistance not accompanied by rehabilitative services may actually increase dependency and eventual costs to the community. The very essence of a vital program should be full use of all rehabilitative services including, but not confined to, provision of financial assistance. The ultimate aim is to help families become self-supporting and independent by strengthening all their own resources. Achieving this requires the special knowledge and skill of social workers with graduate training and other well-trained specialists.[33]

With the preeminent significance of noneconomic services established, the committee proceeded to its remaining basic principles: adequate levels of financial assistance to needy persons and families; efficient administration and organization of welfare programs; improvement through continuing research; and state backing for local welfare programs.

George Wyman's opening legislative recommendation called for a new category of the Social Security Act to combine ADC and Aid to the Disabled as Family Aid and Services, to "emphasize the necessity for State plans to include diagnostic, preventive, protective, rehabilitative, and consultative services for families and individuals." His second proposal in the legislative area called for a change in the name of the Bureau of Public Assistance to Bureau of Social Welfare to show that money assistance is not the sole concern of the Bureau. Only with

[33]Ad Hoc Committee on Public Welfare, *Report to the Secretary of Health, Education, and Welfare* (Washington, September, 1961), p. 13.

these two matters out of the way did Wyman turn to extension of ADC-U and to "Principles for Financial Formulae."[34] Like the Ad Hoc Committee, he made no specific comments on the level of benefit payments to recipients. Where the old Committee on Economic Security had its technical people concentrating on economic need, the Ribicoff Reappraisal people concentrated on noneconomic need. Money needs of a dependent group had become old hat.

Ribicoff came to the House Ways and Means Committee on February 7, 1962, with the bill endorsed by President Kennedy in his special message to Congress on public welfare a week earlier. In case there was any doubt about the Secretary's conviction that he brought a new look, his language emphasized the point:

This landmark bill will bring a new spirit in our public welfare program.

We have arrived at the moment when only comprehensive changes will suffice. The bill now before you embodies such changes.

We have here a realistic program which will pay dividends on every dollar invested. It can move some persons off the assistance rolls entirely, enable others to attain a higher degree of self-confidence and independence, encourage children to grow strong in mind and body, train welfare workers in the skills which will help make these achievements possible, and simplify and improve welfare administration.

As the nature of this bill indicates, we are at a crossroads in public welfare. We cannot afford to continue our present methods.

I believe that H.R. 10032 spells the way for a long overdue change in the direction and philosophy of our welfare programs.[35]

Ribicoff was telling the House Appropriations subcommittee about his plans around the same time, and in no less tentative language:

And I do believe that we finally will have reform in the operation of our welfare laws that will have meaning for this country, including the Federal Government and the States.

It has been a completely new philosophy of anything that has gone on in the last 25 years.

I don't think what we are asking Congress to do is to appropriate funds for a stale old policy that everybody was unhappy with. Now we are saying—we have turned around and finally brought in a new change and a new philosophy in welfare.[36]

[34]George K. Wyman, *A Report for the Secretary of Health, Education, and Welfare* (Washington, August, 1961).
[35]Ways and Means, Hearings, 1962, pp. 63, 165, 166, 174.
[36]U.S. Congress, House, Subcommittee of the Committee on Appropriations, Hearings, "Departments of Labor and Health, Education, and Welfare Appropriations for 1963," 87th Cong., 2d Sess., 1962, pp. 96, 163, 173.

Miss Wickenden subsequently endorsed the Secretary's views about the freshness of the approach. "I feel," she told the House Ways and Means Committee, "that this bill which is before you is a real landmark in that process of rethinking the approach of the public welfare program, especially as it affects families and children." And, "I think it is a major forward step, and I have been in this business since 1933. I came to work with Harry Hopkins in the Relief Administration. This, I think, represents a major forward step." Superlatives were contagious. Miss Wickenden's colleague, Robert Bondy, Director of the National Social Welfare Assembly, announced that "this is a momentous piece of legislation" and compared it to the original Social Security Act. A somewhat more controlled evaluation of just how much might be expected from the bill was offered by Ellen Winston, then Commissioner of Public Welfare of North Carolina, speaking for the American Public Welfare Association. Dr. Winston acknowledged that the proposal would "bring about some rather substantial changes in the content and administration of these programs." However, "they would not constitute a major departure from the major outlines of the public welfare system as it is now established. . . ."[37]

With an apparently sympathetic new administration in Washington, with a mandate to go forth and produce a program, with a defensiveness born of attacks at the state level on some shibboleths of public assistance — notably money payments and the irrelevance of illegitimacy — and with a closed group consisting only of members of the fraternity, it is not surprising that the welfare professionals responsible for developing the 1962 legislative proposals were convinced that a new day had dawned. Of course, the ideas being pushed as comprehensive changes and as landmarks were not new. The 1956 amendments had explicitly placed increased emphasis on state responsibility for services to help recipients achieve increased self-care, self-support, and a stronger family life. The declarations of purpose of the various titles had been appropriately amended then. In OAA, for example, there was added to the statement of purpose, "and [for the purpose] of encouraging each State, as far as practicable under such conditions, to help such individuals attain self-care." A state plan was required by the 1956 act to "provide a description of the services (if any) which the State agency makes available to applicants for and recipients of old-age assistance to help them attain self-care." Moreover, the 1956 amendments authorized federal sharing on a 50-50

---

[37]Ways and Means, Hearings, 1962, pp. 408, 337, 331, 440. Several months thereafter, Dr. Winston was appointed Commissioner of Welfare in the newly created Welfare Administration.

basis of "services which are provided by the staff of the State agency...."[38]

The ADC language of 1956 was in line with advanced professional thinking. It authorized services "to help maintain and strengthen family life and to help such parents or relatives to attain the maximum self-support and personal independence consistent with the maintenance of continuing parental care and protection." For the programs for the blind and disabled, the key words were "self support and self-care." In all cases, the dollar-for-dollar sharing of costs of services was stipulated. It should be noted that these costs fell within the open-end authorization established in 1935. They became part of the total item of grants to the states for public assistance, and the subsequent appropriation of federal funds caused no special problems in those cases where state services were provided.

The "landmark" amendments of 1962 added the furnishing of "rehabilitation" as a major purpose. The spokesman for the American Public Welfare Association considered this critically important: "What is most urgently needed is a clear declaration of policy, set forth in Federal statute, which places a major emphasis on prevention and rehabilitation. The public welfare agencies then have a solid platform upon which to develop services and facilities necessary to accomplish that objective." Ribicoff echoed the idea: "The byword of our new program is prevention — and where it is too late — rehabilitation, a fresh start."[39] One would hardly expect welfare practitioners to argue that the failure to write "rehabilitation" next to "self-help" and "self-care" and "maintenance of family life" in 1956 spelled the difference between six fruitful years and six years without progress. Yet this is precisely the impression that they gave.

It was in dealing with federal support for training of public assistance personnel that the optimism of proponents seems most difficult to understand. The 1956 amendments had included a five-year program for specialized training of welfare workers under an 80-20 federal-state grant program. For fiscal 1958, the Appropriations Committees declined to appropriate funds for the purpose. No request was made for 1959. Appropriations again refused money in 1960, and no funds were voted for fiscal 1961. Against this background of total congressional disinclination to provide money for training under the 80-20 formula, the Senate Finance Committee amended the 1961 ADC-U legislation to increase the federal share of training grants to 100 per cent and extended the life of the paralyzed program an additional year. It was

[38]Title III, Part II, Public Law 880, 84th Cong., 1956.
[39]Ways and Means, Hearings, 1962, pp. 441, 165.

not surprising that the Appropriations Committees seemed no more eager to make funds available for a 100 per cent grant program than they had for an 80 per cent grant. No money for training was appropriated in fiscal 1962. Despite this gloomy record, the American Public Welfare Association attached "great importance to the authorization of funds for the training of persons who would provide services" and the National Social Welfare Assembly found no provisions of the bill more important than those dealing with training grants.[40] Admittedly, these comments were directed towards the provisions of the original administration bill which authorized direct grants to institutions of higher education for training of ADC and child welfare workers. The House Ways and Means Committee amended this provision to restore the rather faded, never implemented, federal grant to the states program for training. Given the importance attached to the direct grant by professional spokesmen not only in the House but later in the Senate Committee where a return to the original administration proposal was urged, the historic unwillingness of either house to implement any training grant program in this field seems a much more realistic indicator of the level of political confidence (or nonconfidence) in the professional welfare approach to public assistance than does continuing authorization of a program that was never allowed to get off the ground in the first place.

When he signed the Public Welfare Amendments of 1962, President Kennedy characterized them as "the most far reaching revision of our public-welfare program since it was enacted in 1935," and said that enactment of the amendments "marks a turning point in this nation's efforts to cope realistically and helpfully with these pressing problems."[41] As finally adopted, the law authorized federal payment of 75 per cent of the costs of rehabilitative or preventive services prescribed by the Secretary of Health, Education, and Welfare, and retained the preexisting provision for payment of 50 per cent of the costs of other noneconomic services provided by a state. The "comprehensive change" in the matter of prevention and rehabilitation then involved payment of an additional one-quarter of state costs if a state chose to adopt the Secretary's notions of rehabilitative services. A state which does not so choose can carry on business as usual and get its old 50 per cent. Service funds are now also authorized for use to prevent potential clients from becoming actual cases, a kind of back-door way of authorizing public assistance agencies to take on a limited family service agency role. By the professionals' own sensible case load standards,

[40]*Ibid.*, pp. 441, 336.
[41]*New York Times,* July 27, 1962, p. 1.

however, the public assistance worker is already tremendously over-loaded and undereducated. The client who does not require money is thus ill advised to take his problem to the public assistance agency, and no state can afford to encourage such activity in order to collect half or even three-quarters of the costs.

Federal funds are authorized to be used in community work projects or on-the-job training. This is the principle of work relief, adopted by Harry Hopkins and the Works Progress Administration, which performed a useful function in the 1930's, but which was subsequently set aside as expensive and likely to produce problems involving makeshift projects, poor planning and supervision, improper matching of worker and job, low efficiency, and lax discipline. Prior to adoption of the ADC-U program in 1961 (which was extended for five years by the 1962 act), work relief in federally aided public assistance categories was academic. Children, the aged, the blind, and the dis-abled were not in the labor market and hence not involved in questions of work relief. General assistance programs supported entirely by state and local funds were not subject to restraints on work relief and had the additional advantage, for this purpose, of dealing with presumably employable clients. Nevertheless, even in those seven states in which work relief was concentrated — California, Illinois, Michigan, Ohio, Pennsylvania, West Virginia, and Wisconsin — each had only a small proportion of the general assistance case load on work relief.[42] While the "momentous" amendments of 1962 were moving through Con-gress, the Bureau of Family Services was preparing its own evaluation of work relief. The conclusions are not such as to make the work relief authorization part of the "turning point in this nation's efforts to cope realistically and helpfully with these pressing problems." The bureau found:

1. Properly administered work relief projects can help recipients become better able to compete for jobs in the regular labor market. But according to the inquiry, few projects are doing so. The Bureau believes that this is because many welfare agencies were not equipped to classify recipients according to their work capacities and did not offer enough different kinds of work.
2. As currently administered, work relief by itself is not significantly reducing the assistance rolls. In the Bureau's view, it can do so only if the economy produces additional regular jobs to which people with constructive work relief experience can be referred.
3. Work relief costs more in public funds than does an assistance program without work relief. The better programs all showed evidence of consid-

[42]U.S. Department of Health, Education, and Welfare, Bureau of Family Services, *Work Relief . . . a current look* (Public Assistance Report No. 52; Washington, March, 1962), p. 7.

erable expenditure for administration and supervision, and some increase in assistance payments to cover work expenses.

4. The problem that earlier work relief administrators faced in selecting projects still exists: Projects that are useful to the community are more likely to interfere with regular employment, and hence are difficult to justify as work relief.[43]

The new legislation authorized $5 million for day care centers for children of working mothers for fiscal 1963 and $10 million annually thereafter. The provision reflected concern about the estimated 400,000 children under 12 who already had to care for themselves while their mothers worked. It was also important to the new-look idea of permitting more able-bodied ADC mothers to park their children in such centers and go to work. A corollary hope was that some other ADC mothers could be trained to qualify as day care center operators. The latter idea was not so new, and it is not at all certain that it is even very good. Grace Abbott once summed up her views of an earlier practice of work relief for mothers of young children. "WPA paid women to take care of other women's children," noted Miss Abbott. "It would have been much more useful to pay them to take care of their own children."[44]

Fiscal implementation of the day care provision has been disappointing. Appropriations for the day care program for 1963 were lost when the 87th Congress adjourned without enacting the first supplemental appropriations bill for 1963. Loss of the supplemental funds bill as an aftermath of the long dispute between House and Senate Appropriations Committee chairmen over the respective rights of the houses eliminated new programs that would have been financed by the bill. Although it carried the full $5 million authorized for the year, Clarence Cannon, chairman of House Appropriations, said of the bill in explaining his decision to block its consideration, that "there was nothing in the bill of immediate urgency."[45] By the following year, the whole day care idea seemed to lose its steam in Congress. The House appropriated $8 million for fiscal 1964 for the purpose; the Senate cut that amount in half, and the cut was sustained in conference. Moreover, the Senate came very close to sustaining an amendment proposed by Appropriations subcommittee chairman, Lister Hill, that would have required state matching of day care funds. In acting on the 1965 budget, the House subcommittee cut the proposed $8 million to $6

[43]*Ibid.*, p. 15.
[44]Grace Abbott, *From Relief to Social Security* (Chicago: University of Chicago Press, 1941), p. 275.
[45]*Congressional Quarterly,* October 19, 1962, p. 1962.

million, while the Senate this time did add a requirement for matching state funds in day care. Although there was an encouraging note in the removal of the matching provision a year later, the program that might have boomed along with $25 million over its first three years wound up with $10 million.

Among the remaining major changes made by the 1962 amendments, one authorized protective payments in a limited number of cases where the recipient is incapable of managing money, a principle that had long been recognized in social insurance benefits, but heretofore opposed for public assistance by the welfare professionals who surely could have had it at almost any time since 1935. Another change was designed to encourage OAA recipients to contribute to their own self-support by authorizing states to exempt from the assistance budget as much as $30 a month in earnings. This provision did not appear in the original administration proposal, and was successfully maneuvered through the Senate by Paul Douglas who had been trying to achieve it since 1956.

Whatever may have been Secretary Ribicoff's views as to the comparative importance of various parts of the legislation, many state governments and probably most recipients found the most important feature to be the one not recommended by the administration in the first place and actually opposed by the administration when it was adopted in the House. The measure as passed carried an increase in the federal share of the adult categories of $4.20 a month over the figure in effect on a temporary basis since 1961. On the ADC side, the administration proposal—to make caretaker payments to both parents of ADC children who are needy because of unemployment or disability of the parent—was adopted. As it developed, Ways and Means Chairman Wilbur Mills ultimately used the second caretaker provision as a lever to push his committee's improvement in the adult formula: "...if this amendment is stricken, these people [adult categories] will not have anything in the way of an increase in this bill. But bear in mind that there will remain an increase in the bill for aid to the dependent children program.... I always try to be fair between the groups and the four categories."[46] President Kennedy later made it clear that he expected the states to pass on the increase, observing that it "would truly be a miscarriage of justice and a frustration of the legislative intent if these new Federal funds merely replaced existing state funds...."[47]

Congressional interest in the amendments was not intense. Seven of the 25 members of the House Ways and Means Committee took an

[46]*Congressional Record,* March 15, 1962, p. 4269.
[47]*Congressional Quarterly,* August 3, 1962, p. 1314.

active part in the hearings; only four members of the Senate Finance Committee took enough obvious interest to question more than one witness. The only unhappiness in the House arose over the usual closed rule which made it impossible to vote separately on the increase in the federal share of costs for services and the increase in the federal share of benefits. But neither sound nor fury was very intense. In the Senate, the atmosphere was full of good will once an amendment to include medical insurance was lost. Douglas' amendment to exempt some of the earned income of OAA recipients started at $25 and under amiable prodding by Robert Kerr was increased to $50 (later cut back to $30 by the House-Senate conference committee), and adopted without dissent. The same amendment had been lost in conference in 1956 because of administration opposition and lost again in 1958. "Never in my wildest dreams did I think that such an amendment as this would be accepted unanimously by the Senate," said Douglas, whose confession of surprise was followed by "[Laughter]."[48]

So the "long overdue change in the direction and philosophy of our welfare program" seems upon close look to be not so much of a change in either direction or philosophy. The dominant philosophy up to 1962 had been a states' rights philosophy, a policy of providing federal support for categorical programs drawn by and tailored to the interests of the individual states with an absolute minimum of insistence upon uniformity. The 1962 amendments changed neither the tendency to provide generous federal support to state programs nor the willingness of Congress to let the states write their own programs within the limits of the original Social Security Act. The great thrust on behalf of prevention and rehabilitation seems more gimmicky than substantive. With respect to prevention, Jacobus tenBroek has properly noted that these measures are not new or different from the existing provisions of the law. "For all its sweeping promises and glittering rhetoric the program presented to us by the federal administrators may accurately be described as an ounce of prevention—and a pound of cure-all."[49] The measures adopted in 1962, in short, are unobjectionable, but they are not what they are cracked up to be.

Against this background, the significance of the Public Welfare Amendments of 1962 is not in their new approach to the problem of public assistance—for the approach is really not new—but in the need of the proponents of the legislation to assert that a new approach was

[48]*Congressional Record,* July 6, 1962, p. 12838.
[49]Jacobus tenBroek, "An Ounce of Prevention—And a Pound of Cure-All" (address before the California Association of Health and Welfare, Oakland, Calif., May 2, 1962, process duplicated), p. 1.

being offered. The public assistance program was in more serious trouble than ever before in its history. No danger existed of Congress cutting off funds. Real congressional control of public assistance appropriations is virtually nonexistent. More realistic was the possibility that Congress would wipe out the restraints on the states adopted in 1935 and 1939. Save for the 1950 adoption of a program of aid to the permanently and totally disabled (APTD) and 1961 passage of ADC-U, few liberalizations in eligibility or techniques have been accomplished on the federal level since the 1939 amendments; but welfare groups have been successful in limiting major formal unshackling of the states to the single area of confidentiality of assistance records.

In November, 1960, the incoming administration gave reason for high hopes that the days of sympathetic political interest in the problem of dependency had returned. But by November, 1962, public assistance spokesmen were in an unsatisfactory position. They hoped at first for a law that emphasized legislative and presidential blessing for more intensive and extensive servicing of public relief clients. They got the law, but before it was finished it was a law that many legislators read as a way to eliminate relief clients. For two or three or perhaps four years, it would be possible to tell politicians that it takes time for a new approach to become effective. After that, it would be expected that prevention and rehabilitation show results. It would be expected that illegitimacy, immorality, fraud, and costs diminish dramatically. And, right on schedule, the House Appropriations Committee said in April, 1964, that costs should not continue to rise "especially in view of the 1962 amendments which were supposed to reduce these costs...."[50] Unfortunately, the proponents of the new welfare program do not know how to accomplish this miracle, nor did they really mean to let the impression get abroad that this was to be expected. Somehow the 1962 amendments got oversold somewhere along the line. Their proponents did not go out of their way to deny that the new look would mean a cheaper program and a more respectable clientele. To have done so might have endangered the amendments, because the political mood and the goals of the professionals in welfare did not coincide.

[50]*Congressional Quarterly,* April 17, 1964, p. 719.

CHAPTER III

The Two Faces of Policy

THERE ARE INCONSISTENCIES in congressional behavior in the public assistance field. The formula governing grants to the states for benefit payments is constantly being liberalized, the federal share constantly being increased. Accompanying requests for funds to train professional social workers are regularly denied. If there are no outright opponents of public assistance, no voices calling for repeal of the program, there are no enthusiastic supporters either. Legislative proponents talk about ways to overcome the need for the public assistance program, and its detractors suggest that the bureaucracy of public assistance will not allow the program to fade. Yet, efforts to write medical assistance for the aged into social insurance rather than into public assistance were long resisted by some of those congressmen who are most skeptical about public assistance really being permitted to wither away.

Although there is almost as much federal money involved now in public assistance as there is in foreign aid, appropriations hearings in public assistance remain relatively perfunctory. Costs are constantly increasing, and doubts are expressed about the efficiency and the values of some of those responsible for administration of the program, but Congress has taken no steps to provide itself with independent, specialized assistance in this field. Neither the Senate Finance Committee nor the House Ways and Means Committee has a public assistance staff specialist. Official data are forthcoming from the administration in great profusion, nongovernmental data and reports are offered by the professional welfare associations, and occasional exposés are produced by newspapermen in search of scandal; Congress itself has created no mechanism for the collection and evaluation of these materials. In congressional interest, public assistance has become the tail attached to social security—a reversal of the situation in 1935—and social security itself ranks behind both taxation and reciprocal trade as major concerns of the Senate Finance Committee and the House Ways and Means Committee. Whatever the reason for the absence of analyses of public assistance prepared for Congress by its own staff people, the result is a primary dependence on the administrative agency for information and an erratic pattern of legislative attention to federal relief policy. Long periods of inattention to anything other than the size of the federal grant contrast with sporadic bursts of interest in the program which result in policies that are either sharply restrictive or expansive.

I. GROWTH OF THE GRANT-IN-AID

A generous outpouring of federal funds by a series of Congresses is one side of the national public assistance policy picture. Whatever else may be said of national relief policy under the Social Security Act, it may not be said that the federal share of benefits has lagged behind the states' share. The skeptics among welfare professionals who have deplored the politicians' presumed greater interest in highways than in the poor are now finding that federal public assistance expenditures are closing in on highway expenditures. Nor has the policy of fiscal generosity been abandoned or even modified by Congress in the face of a dropping-off of state and local welfare expenditures as a percentage of total governmental outlays for support of the needy.

By the early 1960's, public assistance had become the second most expensive of the programs of federal grants-in-aid to the states, the most expensive among programs not supported by trust fund revenues. In 17 states, principally in the south, but also including New York, Pennsylvania, Massachusetts, Rhode Island, and Colorado, more federal money was spent in 1962 for public assistance than for highways. Federal highway money that year was less than 7 per cent more than federal public assistance money out of a combined pot of almost five-and-a-quarter billions for highways and relief. At the end of World War II, state and local governments were paying 60 per cent of all public assistance costs, but by 1953 they were paying only half, and since then the state and local share has dropped below half. When general assistance is excluded, the state and local share of public assistance costs is down to less than 43 per cent.[1]

[1] U.S. Department of Health, Education, and Welfare, *Health, Education, and Welfare Trends* (Washington, 1962), p. 91.

Since the first year of the operation of public assistance under the Social Security Act, the sum of federal payments to recipients has increased steadily. This is not true either of state payments or of local payments. Maximum monthly amounts subject to federal participation have been increased from $30 to $75 in the old age, blind, and disabled categories, and medical payments have been added. Maximum monthly amounts subject to federal participation in the dependent children category have been increased from $18 for the first child, plus $12 for each additional child, to $32 for each recipient, including adult caretakers. The federal share of each individual payment within these maxima has been increased in the adult categories from one-half of $30 to $31 of the first $37, plus at least half (but not more than 65 per cent) of the next $38, depending on the relationship between the individual state's per capita income and the national per capita income. In the dependent children category, the federal share of the maximum has been increased from one-third of $18 or $12 to $15 of the first $18, plus between 50 and 65 per cent of the balance up to $32. In the program of aid for the medically indigent aged, the Kerr-Mills program, federal participation extends to a state's total expenditures, and federal sharing is graduated between 55 and 83 per cent of state costs, depending again on the state's relative per capita income.

Under what conditions have these changes occurred? What kind of strategy is the proponent of improved public assistance benefits best advised to follow? Does the drive for improvement come through the administrative agency into a sympathetic White House and then get pushed through a reluctant Congress, or does the fiscal policy-making process in welfare have different characteristics?

Congressional Leadership Established

An initial generalization is that the spur for increases in federal expenditures for public assistance has come from Congress rather than from the White House. Consistently since the war the lead has been taken particularly by the Senate to increase the relative share of federal costs in the public assistance program. So-called fractional formula amendments of 1946, 1948, and 1952 set a pattern for congressional adoption, sometimes via unorthodox procedures, and often over administration objections, of a series of public assistance benefit increases. Benefits were improved five times in the decade beginning with 1952, always on the initiative of Congress. Both before and after that year, the Senate was the starting point. The procedures have frequently been unorthodox because they have involved adoption of substantial increases by floor amendment rather than in committee, because in some instances the increases have been carried without the approval of the chairman of the Senate Finance Committee, and because they have been consistently accepted by the House after originating in the Senate.

Few members of either the Senate or the House are in a position to oppose increases in the federal share of assistance. The increment is not great in any single instance, but the benefit to both the states and the recipients can have political and humanitarian advantages all at once. Normally, the sole disadvantage for a congressman is the need to buck a President straining to keep the budget under control. Less interest in benefit levels has been shown by Presidents than by congressmen. When the former take strong opposition stands, legislators are squeezed — and usually they abandon the President.

The extent of congressional support for benefit increases was demonstrated in 1948 when it was great enough to override a veto, while the style developed then — amendment from the Senate floor of a bill dealing with other aspects of social security — was to be repeated often. An amendment from the floor keeps the issue of increased spending for relief out of the Senate Finance Committee. In turn, when budget-minded Harry Byrd was chairman, he did not usually take a strong opposition stand. No bill carrying a public assistance benefit increase has been vetoed since 1948 despite regular administration opposition to such increases and at least one veto threat. Passage over a presidential veto is always impressive, and the ease with which this was accomplished in 1948 may have given pause to Presidents in later years who were faced with benefit increase bills they had opposed.

The vehicle for action in 1948 was legislation to overturn the consequences of a 1947 Supreme Court decision that had the effect of permitting administrative extension of social security coverage.[2] By changing the interpretation of the employer-employee relationship from preexisting common law rules, the Court allowed the Treasury Department to announce a plan for collecting social security taxes from door-to-door salesmen, life insurance agents, certain piece workers in the home, and newspaper vendors. It was estimated that perhaps 625,000 persons would be covered by the ruling, all accomplished without benefit of action by Congress. Only a few days after the second session of the 80th Congress convened, Representative Bertrand Gearhart, a California Republican, offered a joint resolution to overturn the Supreme Court ruling.[3] The Ways and Means Committee promptly held executive hearings, listened to the objections of the

[2]*United States* v. *Silk,* 331 U.S. 704 (1947); *Bartels* v. *Birmingham,* 332 U.S. 126 (1947).
[3]*H. Jt. Res. 296,* 80th Cong., 2d Sess., 1948.

Treasury Department and of the Federal Security Agency, and reported the resolution out. Asserting itself against both the Court and the administration, the House approved the resolution before the end of February by 275 – 52, with support from a majority on each side of the aisle. In May, the same month that President Truman recommended liberalization amendments in social security to a Congress that was not responsive, the Senate Finance Committee reported the Gearhart resolution.

This set the stage for Arizona's Ernest McFarland to offer an amendment to raise the public assistance maximum amounts subject to federal sharing by $5 monthly in the adult categories and $3 in the ADC category.[4] The federal fraction within the maximums was similarly changed. McFarland had obviously concluded that the benefit increase would be impregnable if it were added to the Gearhart proposal. Gearhart supporters could be expected to feel more intensely about passing the basic resolution than they might feel about holding the line on benefits, while Gearhart opponents – including President Truman – could be expected to swallow the resolution (which after all would only return the situation to the *status quo* before the Supreme Court decision) in order to achieve the positive benefits of increased federal financial help. The calculation was correct in its projection of congressional behavior. Ultimate passage of the resolution came by a 74 – 6 vote after the McFarland amendment had been adopted 77 – 2. Even the handful opposing its final passage admitted that they were, as Alben Barkley, then Majority Leader, put it at the time, "in a hell of a fix."[5] Without debate, the House concurred in the McFarland amendment the same afternoon it passed the Senate.

Ten days later, the resolution was back on Capitol Hill with a veto message from the President expressing his objection to the elimination of door-to-door salesmen from coverage under the Social Security Act. Truman also attempted to force the reluctant Congress to record itself on the benefit question separately. Expressing strong support of the increase in public assistance benefits, the President suggested legislation embodying this feature of the disapproved resolution. "Speedy action on public assistance legislation is clearly possible," he argued. "I note that section 3 [the McFarland amendment] was adopted as an amendment on the floor of the Senate, and passed by both houses in a single afternoon. Accordingly, I am placing this matter before the Congress in adequate time so that the public assistance program will not suffer because of my disapproval of this resolution."[6]

[4]*Congressional Record,* June 3, 1948, p. 7035.
[5]*Ibid.,* June 4, 1948, p. 7124.
[6]*H. Doc. 211,* 80th Cong., 2d Sess., 1948

But there were few door-to-door salesmen in McFarland's Arizona, and there were probably even fewer congressmen who were much worried about President Truman's opinions in June, 1948. A brave little band of loyalists in the House echoed the Truman line that public assistance increases were indeed needed and could and should be enacted on their own merits. But passage over the veto came by a fabulous majority of 223 votes (298 – 75), coincidentally exactly the same majority that was secured for the Gearhart resolution in the House in the first place. McFarland laid it on the line to the Senate: "If we disagree as to the first part of the resolution, our point of view depends upon what we consider most important. I say it is far more important to increase assistance for the aged, blind, and dependent children. They need this assistance now.... After Congress adjourns we cannot tell them that we can put an amendment on another bill . . . if we want to give assistance to those persons, it is my humble opinion that we had better vote for it at this time."[7] Democratic leader Barkley, reflecting on the fact that he was still in a fix, made only a perfunctory observation that he would vote to sustain the veto. The amended resolution was passed in the Senate over the veto by a strong 65 – 12.

The new level of federal participation was to hold for four years except for the addition of direct payment to vendors for medical or remedial care beginning in 1950. Also in the 1950 amendments, Congress finally took cognizance of the fact that a dependent child case usually involves a needy mother or other relative. This was the point "overlooked" in 1935, when the ADC program was modeled after the Veterans' Orphans program. Federal participation was now extended to one needy relative. The great battle in 1950 was fought over the principle of disability assistance versus disability insurance, however, rather than over the benefit levels in any of the categorical programs.

Benefits came back as an issue in 1952 without the complications of a Gearhart resolution, but again through the back door, in legislation improving social insurance benefits.[8] When the social security amendments of 1952 came to the Senate, they carried no provision for an increase in public assistance sharing. Rushed through the House with bipartisan support and without hearings, ostensibly because all the recommended changes were within areas that had been studied during the hearings and executive sessions prior to adoption of the 1950 amendments, the bill increased social security benefit payments by 12.5 per cent. The Senate Finance Committee also waived hearings, but it deleted the insurance premium waiver for the disabled without prejudging its merits, explaining that the bill was so urgently needed

[7]*Congressional Record,* June 14, 1948, p. 8092.
[8]H. R. 7800, 82d Cong., 2d Sess., 1952.

that it did not wish to delay action with hearings or to take the time for full consideration of the insurance premium waiver provision.[9] No mention of public assistance was made up to this point.

Another McFarland amendment was then proposed from the floor, like its 1948 counterpart. Adopted by a standing vote, this was the first overt sign in the 1950's of interest in increasing public assistance allowances along with the "urgently needed" social insurance increases. It increased the federal share of grants for OAA, the blind, and the disabled by $5 a month, and the ADC grants by $3 a month. The House concurred in conference but won agreement on restricting the increases to a two-year period.

When that period expired in 1954, Eisenhower unsuccessfully sought to cut back the federal share. By 1956 he was willing to settle for an extension of the McFarland formula until 1959; instead, he had to take an increase that originated on the Senate floor. Led now by Russell Long, Senate Finance gave Eisenhower another increase he did not want in 1958, and it gave President Kennedy an increase he did not ask for in 1961. A year later there was another raise that the administration opposed, but this time it originated in the House, in order, as Wilbur Mills admits, to forestall the embarrassment of House members who were determined not to let the Senate act first again.[10]

The concern of members of Congress, particularly in the Senate, for the fiscal problems of their state governments sometimes leads to a policy of provide-money-now-and-worry-about-controls-later. Senator Russell Long's activity on the Senate floor in 1958, in connection with his efforts to obtain a cost-of-living increase of $5 per month for recipients of blind, disabled, and aged assistance, is a case in point.[11] Indeed, the 1958 legislation is a reasonable illustration of legislative-executive relations in public assistance issues during the Eisenhower Congresses. With 33 cosponsors, Senator Long offered an amendment to a pending bill dealing with extending unemployment compensation support to provide the cost of living increase in the adult assistance categories. His concern was dramatically expressed: "the least of those in our society are not provided for any better here than in Communist Russia." Emphasizing the seeming paradox by which foreign aid was more generously provided than domestic public assistance, Long noted that American aid to Laos in 1957 was $17 per person "in contrast to the niggardliness of our assistance to some of our citizens. . . . " The Senator found other things to be compelling two

[9]*Senate Report 1806,* 82d Cong., 2d Sess., 1952, p. 2.
[10]*Congressional Record,* March 15, 1962, p. 4269.
[11]*Congressional Record,* May 26, 1958, pp. 9458ff.

days later, when the question of the niggardliness of assistance to dependent children was raised by the late Senator Richard Neuberger of Oregon. Neuberger, acknowledging that as a cosponsor he was "surprised and chagrined" to find that ADC was not included in the Long package, sought to amend the amendment to include that category.[12] Its absence, said Neuberger, "was called to my attention only a few moments ago by some of those who likewise are interested in the program for the needy dependent children." But Long made it clear that there had been no oversight, and equally clear that the Senate was divided between those who were well versed in Senate affairs and those who were only well intentioned. Responding to Neuberger's admission that his information about the amendment was so recent that he had not had time to draft his suggested addition, Long stated, "I have a great mass of information on that subject . . . and I shall be glad to show it to the Senator . . . but I do not believe we have time to get into it." By way of clinching his point that the whole subject had been carefully explored, that a count had been made, and that the ADC category was being sacrificed, Long met the question directly. He did not think that an ADC increase should be included in his amendment "for several reasons. First, I do not think the amendment would receive any more votes if it contained a provision for dependent children." With such a first reason, there was no need for a second, and none was offered.

As it developed, Neuberger could have been accommodated since the Long amendment lost anyway on a tie vote, 40 − 40. The amendment may have been a ploy designed to convince a reluctant administration that an upward adjustment in federal public assistance costs was inevitable. Two months after the loss of the Long proposal, the House Ways and Means Committee reported out a social security bill that increased from $60 to $66 the maximum benefit payment in the adult assistance categories in which the federal government would share. In addition, the House committee bill increased payments to dependent children in which there would be federal sharing up to a maximum monthly benefit of $33. The increases, somewhat modified, became part of the Social Security Amendments of 1958.

Presidential Resistance

If Senate leadership in public assistance benefit improvements is clear, so is presidential reluctance. Throughout his tenure, President Eisenhower fought a losing battle to avoid the shifting of public

---

[12]*Congressional Record*, May 28, 1958, pp. 9694ff. All of the statements which follow are from this source.

assistance costs to the federal level. In a special message to Congress on social security in January, 1954, Eisenhower talked of a basic revision in the public assistance matching provisions to establish its financing on a "sounder" basis.[13] Increases in the federal share of payments were adopted in 1956 when the President's budget message had asked that the existing formula, originally adopted in 1952, be temporarily extended "to allow time to reappraise the need for the present high level of the Federal contribution to public assistance."[14] Administration-sponsored draft bills would have extended the formula to June 30, 1959.[15] By 1958, the administration was moving hard on a policy that was not "hold the line," but rather "realign the distribution of costs." The budget message that year stated that "proposals will be sent to the Congress for modernizing the formulas for public assistance with a view to gradually reducing Federal participation in its financing."[16]

In one of his last appearances as Secretary of Health, Education, and Welfare, Marion Folsom urged the House Ways and Means Committee not to report the 1958 benefit increase because "a further general expansion of the Federal Government's financial share in the present [public assistance] programs, and particularly any further expansion under the present formula for Federal matching is undesirable."[17] Thereafter, Arthur Flemming, in one of his first appearances as the new Secretary of Health, Education, and Welfare, came before the Senate Finance Committee and said he would recommend an Eisenhower veto if the House-passed increases in the public assistance formula were retained. "We assume it is possible for the States to participate to a greater extent in the public assistance program than is now the case."[18] And again, "in this country we have regarded these programs as State programs, and the thing we are objecting to is a further increase in the percentage of Federal participation in the program."[19] And finally, the iron fist: "if this percentage of Federal participation continues to go up, I am sure of the fact that Federal controls will continue to increase."[20]

[13]*Congressional Record,* January 14, 1954, p. 257.

[14]*Congressional Record,* January 16, 1956, pp. 561, 574.

[15]H. R. 9091 and H. R. 9120, 84th Cong., 2d Sess. Representative Wilbur Mills suggested that 1959 was chosen because it was not an election year.

[16]*Congressional Record,* January 13, 1958, pp. 388, 397.

[17]U.S. Congress, House, Committee on Ways and Means, Hearings, "Social Security Legislation," 85th Cong., 2d Sess., 1958, p. 6.

[18]U.S. Congress, Senate, Committee on Finance, Hearings, "Social Security," 85th Cong., 2d Sess., 1958, p. 130.

[19]*Ibid.,* p. 141.

[20]*Ibid.,* p. 145.

In the unlikely event that the administration position was not clear, Maurice Stans, Director of the Bureau of the Budget, wrote Chairman Harry Byrd of the Senate Finance Committee, expressing opposition to the public assistance provisions of the then pending social security amendments. Pointing out that the President had stated his belief that states and localities should assume a larger share of the public assistance burden, Stans concluded that "we do not believe that a further increase in the already disproportionate overall Federal share in this program can be justified."[21]

During the same week that the Stans letter was put into the record of the committee, Republican leader William Knowland came out of a conference with the President and cited a Flemming statement to the effect that the public assistance features of the pending legislation were so obnoxious that a veto of the whole bill, which included important social security improvements to which the administration did not object, would result.[22] But some adroit footwork by Senator Robert Kerr who managed the bill in the Senate resulted in a compromise that Eisenhower decided to buy. Kerr fenced with Flemming about conditions for presidential approval, then offered amendments to make the bill more palatable, *i.e.,* cheaper, insofar as federal public assistance costs were concerned. The Kerr amendments reduced the federal sharing maximum in the adult categories from $66 to $65 and in the ADC category from $33 to $30. Subsequently, a floor amendment by George Smathers of Florida reduced the basic federal share of ADC costs to the preexisting $14 of the first $17, rather than the $15 of the first $18 approved by the House and by Senate Finance.

By the time the bill found its way to the President's desk, then, it made two important changes in public assistance financing: it instituted the principle of variable matching grants in accordance with the relative fiscal capacity of the states, and it increased the federal matching maximum in the adult categories. The proponents of public assistance liberalization found that Long's earlier effort was the decisive element in assuring inclusion of the equalization formula for public assistance in the House-passed bill, its retention in the Senate bill, and the strong support for final adoption of a bill over White House opposition. "Throughout all the days and weeks of discussion, there was general awareness that if a desirable and satisfactory substitute in public assistance was not worked out, the Long amendment would be adopted sometime, somehow, and perhaps without inclusion of ADC."[23]

[21]*Ibid.,* p. 110.

[22]*Ibid.,* p. 418.

[23]Wilbur J. Cohen and Fedele F. Fauri, "The Social Security Amendments of 1958: Another Significant Step Forward," *Public Welfare,* XVII (January, 1959), 5.

It is not clear who threatened whom with exclusion of ADC from liberalization. Public welfare spokesmen make it appear that opponents of change were being haunted by the chance of change in line with the Long amendment and thus without ADC.[24] But there was no sign that members of either house were manning the barricades for ADC formula improvements. Indeed, Senator Neuberger who, on May 28, 1958, announced he would press the case for ADC increases whenever the Senate considered increasing other welfare payments apparently was talked out of it by August 16. California's Senator Thomas Kuchel did offer an amendment that day which would have increased the federal matching maximum from the Senate Finance Committee's $65 to $70—for the adult categories. Perhaps persuaded that it had gone as far as it could go without a veto, the Senate voted down the Kuchel proposal.

When Eisenhower signed the bill, he took advantage of the opportunity for the last word by noting that the increase in federal public assistance participation was not with his blessing: "I believe deeply in the concept that the States and communities can best determine the actual needs of individuals and best administer programs of assistance to them—and that the State and local financial responsibility in these programs should be strengthened, not weakened."[25]

Although the line was held in 1960, there was no disposition to achieve the Eisenhower objective of increasing state and local responsibility. Then, when the New Frontier bustled in with emergency repairs to the social security and public assistance programs in 1961, its major interest was in extending the ADC program to cover dependency by reason of unemployment of one or both parents. In effect, this created a kind of federal support for general assistance, and it was anticipated that there would be some significant shifting from the general assistance to the ADC category and thereby some increase in federal costs, as the program subject to federal participation swelled and that supported only by state and local funds shrank. Perhaps for that reason, there was no concurrent formal request for an increase in the totals subject to sharing nor for an increase in the percentage of federal sharing.

The Senate Finance Committee, however, reported out a social security bill with an increase in federal participation in public assistance. Eventually, it resulted in a temporary, insignificant increase in the maxima subject to federal sharing—$1 in the adult categories only. The likelihood that the new administration did not consider a mere

[24]*Ibid.*
[25]Quoted in *ibid.*

change in money grants to be a sufficiently vigorous approach to the problem seems great. It seems equally likely that it was not about to take up as its own the line that the Eisenhower administration had been using about keeping federal participation down.

John Byrnes, now ranking Republican member of the House Ways and Means Committee, offers some comments on the Democratic administration's discomfort. Noting first that there had been no administration request for a public assistance increase, Byrnes stated flatly that the amendment was approved against the administration's position, a contention that was not denied. His picture of conference committee activity by department personnel is that of professionals with their loyalties divided between a cause they felt they understood and a leader who was still studying the issues. Byrnes explained that "a very interesting thing happened in the conference. The administration spokesmen said they opposed this amendment. They said, in fact, that they did not want any amendment to any existing public assistance program until they were able to review the whole program. But while they took that position, they constantly were giving suggestions as to how we could sweeten the thing up so that we could get it out of conference. . . . The doubletalk from the Department of Health, Education, and Welfare as to whether this was a good or bad amendment and whether or not it should be adopted was unbelievable."[26] No member of the committee felt impelled to explain the behavior of the Health, Education, and Welfare people, and the conference report was approved without opposition.

The new look in welfare programs proposed by the Kennedy administration as the Public Welfare Amendments of 1962 emphasized rehabilitation, retraining, and experimentation. Although the legislation ultimately adopted carried a $4 increase in federal sharing for the adult categories, it was not an increase requested by the administration. Rather, the administration supported making permanent only the $1 increase enacted against its will in 1961, and opposed the larger amount.[27] The $4 figure was retained by House and Senate, nonetheless, thus allowing Kennedy to join Eisenhower on the list of chief executives unable to keep control of public assistance costs. The big change was that the House finally got to initiate the benefit increase — but only in anticipation of Senate action.

During the first full year of the Great Society, no effort was made to improve relief benefits. A relatively small increase was included as part of the Medicare legislation of 1965.

[26]*Congressional Record,* June 29, 1961, p. 11791.
[27]*Congressional Record,* March 15, 1962, p. 4281; *Congressional Quarterly,* June 22, 1962, p. 1060.

II. SIGNS OF CONGRESSIONAL DISCONTENT

Despite the pattern of congressional willingness to improve the formulae for public assistance grants, there is another side to national policy. It would be a mistake to assume that Congress has cheerfully embraced the public assistance program as a continuing affair. There have been outbursts of discontent on the part of congressmen about one or another part of the program since its origin. Nevertheless, it has been shown that Congress has regularly been more generous in providing public assistance money than several Presidents would have liked and that Congress has actually been the leader in increasing benefit amounts. How can the apparent contradiction between attitude and appropriation be explained?

Even without a reluctant administration, the appropriations process is usually a difficult one. The personality of the appropriations subcommittee chairman is part of the luck of the draw in any particular case, while the need to run a series of obstacle courses — to secure approval first for an authorization and then for the actual appropriation from different committees in each house — is a normal part of the established congressional procedure. With most appropriations bills, it has come to be expected that the authorization will be below the administration request, that the House appropriation will be below the authorization, that the Senate appropriation will come somewhat closer to the authorized figure, and that a conference committee will agree on a figure below the Senate's figure but above that of the House. For example, to use the history of foreign aid funds as a bench mark, the pattern just described has been repeated continuously since 1948. Although the 1964 appropriation battle was unusually bloody and the consequent 33 per cent cut in the original request was the largest ever made in that field, a 20 per cent cut was by no means unusual during the 1950's, and in both fiscal 1962 and 1963, the request had been cut by 18 per cent. Congress has never authorized all the money requested by the administration for foreign aid, and Congress has never appropriated all the money authorized. The evident determination of legislators to look at the program very carefully makes it necessary for the defense to be sharp, an added advantage of the two-stage process as it is usually followed.

A Protected Appropriation

Public assistance grants-in-aid fall outside the grim picture spelled out above. Public assistance enjoys the sweetest life of any appropriations bill in Congress—no annual authorization is required, and the appropriations committees have only a *pro forma* control over the amount of money to be made available. Moreover, committee members seem to have no illusions about the limits of their freedom. They accept the fact that they must vote all the money requested, that there is a preexisting protection for public assistance grant funds. The adequacy of the defense of the request for funds thus becomes academic because there is neither a penalty for fuzziness nor a premium for precision. Because of these special arrangements, the results of the appropriations process cannot readily reflect legislators' attitudes.

This is not to suggest that there is a plot to delude the Congress. There is congressional control of the relief purse through the establishment of the formula for federal sharing in state categorical assistance costs. An economy-minded Congress is at liberty in fact as well as in constitutional law to lower the federal share of OAA or ADC payments. It is at liberty to lower the maximum amount to which federal contributions will apply. President Eisenhower urged Congress to move in this direction in order to impose a greater proportionate financial responsibility upon the states. When Congress chooses to move in the opposite direction, there is foreknowledge that more money will be required. The sharing formula established by Congress acts as an authorization to appropriate. However, once the formula is adopted, Congress has really contracted to appropriate whatever funds are required to meet the formula. Under the several public assistance titles of the Social Security Act, the Treasury is directed to disburse to the various states whatever amounts are certified by the federal administrative agency. The amounts to be disbursed are, in turn, a function of the size of the respective state case loads and the imposition of the appropriate federal sharing formula for each category. Deficiencies or excesses are adjusted at the time of the next quarterly disbursement. Although an amount inadequate to meet these obligations technically may be voted, it is unlikely that the national government is about to default on a self-imposed obligation to the states. Public assistance appropriations thus take a place with the interest on the national debt as a fixed charge.

For most appropriations, the legislative committees involved fix the authorizations for expenditures on the basis of formulae which, while in some cases less precise than those governing public assistance payments, presumably have some systematic underpinning. Actions of the legislative committees may be thought of as a refinement of the formula proposed by the administration. The appropriations subcommittees further refine the formula. But public assistance grants do not receive the same treatment as most other appropriations. Once the public assistance formula is fixed by the House Ways and Means Committee and the Senate Finance Committee and adopted by Congress in the form of amendments to the Social Security Act, no further refinement of that formula is practical. Representative John Fogarty, Chairman of the House Appropriations subcommittee, made the situation very explicit in the course of the hearings on the 1957 public assistance appropriations:

As I understand this program, these grants to States for assistance and administration are based upon the plans submitted by the States, and when they meet the requirements of the Social Security Act and are approved by you, we just have to appropriate that money, do we not? There is no other way around it, according to law?[28]

Replied the witness, Director Jay Roney of the Bureau of Public Assistance, "That seems to be correct."

Again, in favorably reporting a supplementary appropriation of $159,600,000 for public assistance in May, 1964, the House Appropriations Committee acknowledged its helplessness. "While it is distressing," the report said, "to see this program costing more every year, there is practically no control that can be exercised via appropriations."[29] That point became evident again in the early months of 1965 when a supplementary appropriation of $407 million was requested and voted.

In view of this background, one cannot examine congressional actions in providing appropriations for public assistance grants and expect by that means alone to test congressional sentiment about the program. It would be misleading to argue that because Congress has always provided all the money requested by the administration to make assistance payments that Congress is satisfied with the program. The absence of an annual or even an occasional dispute over appropriations should more realistically be credited to the planned or fortuitous wisdom of the draftsmen of the Social Security Act in providing for an open-end, permanent authorization, and in making no reference to the possibility of scaling down the grants to meet available appropriations. The presumption was that appropriations would be forthcoming as needed. In the absence of other arrangements, this has become a self-fulfilling prophecy.

If the multi-billion dollar appropriation for assistance payments is

[28]U.S. Congress, House, Subcommittee of the Committee on Appropriations, Hearings, "Departments of Labor and Health, Education, and Welfare Appropriations for 1957," 84th Cong., 2d Sess., 1956, p. 845.
[29]*House Report 1386,* 88th Cong., 2d Sess., 1964.

a formality, what are the really critical points in congressional activity? Appropriations will come easily only as long as the basic law is unchanged. The congressmen most directly concerned with the basic law are members of the House Ways and Means Committee and the Senate Finance Committee, and the members of the respective appropriations subcommittees for the Departments of Labor and of Health, Education, and Welfare. The latter are involved less through formal control over assistance funds and more through actual control over funds for tangential programs like training grants and through their responsibility to hear the presentation of the agency and to make an evaluative report. Congressmen less directly involved sit on the District of Columbia appropriations subcommittees where they are asked to pass on the welfare budget of the District. This is the only occasion on which congressmen get a look at the operation of a particular welfare program.

Storm warnings have recently issued from all of these points along the critical path. In reporting the 1962 "landmark amendments" to the House, Wilbur Mills spoke of the "increasing number of comments which are critical of the public assistance program."[30] While commending then Secretary Ribicoff and the efforts of his department to make some improvements, Mills emphasized the House Ways and Means Committee's decision to grant new latitude to the states to deal with public assistance problems. This latitude took the form of a committee- and House-approved provision authorizing states to take any action permitted under state law to insure that ADC payments are made in the best interests of the child involved. Particularly repugnant to welfare groups was the possibility that this would open the way to voucher payments. The provision was wiped out in the Senate Finance Committee. But Mills made it clear that the House Ways and Means Committee was acting deliberately: "Thus a State could pass legislation authorizing voucher payments in lieu of cash payments.... The committee recognized that this gives the States broad discretion or broader discretion than they have had in all the years of the operation of this program."[31]

A reading of the *Congressional Record* at the time of House passage of the 1962 amendments is illuminating. Where one might reasonably expect rank-and-file congressmen to take pains to record themselves in favor of help for the widows and orphans and senior citizens, only a single member spoke or even bothered to insert unuttered remarks along these lines. William Fitts Ryan, representing a New York

[30]*Congressional Record,* March 15, 1962, p. 4267.
[31]*Ibid.,* p. 4268.

City district, commended increased federal support for rehabilitative services, for training, for foster care, and for extension of the ADC program, but his was a lone voice. Most House members were saying nothing. In view of the enthusiasm of the administration and of the welfare professionals, silence, coupled with approval of increased state control over ADC payments, could not be considered a commendation.

Byrd of West Virginia

Only a few months after the 1962 amendments had been enacted, Robert Byrd of West Virginia dropped his bomb on the District of Columbia welfare appropriation by reporting to the Senate the results of his subcommittee hearing and the reports of the General Accounting Office investigations into ADC eligibility in the District.[32] A statistically valid sampling of 280 cases, or 5 per cent of the 5,601 cases in the ADC category, as of September 1, 1961, was selected for the investigation. There were 236 cases actually investigated, 42 of the remainder having been closed prior to the review, and the other 2 eliminated for technical reasons. Of the 236 cases, 133 cases were found to be ineligible on the basis of the investigative findings and 8 cases on the basis of events occurring subsequent to the investigation, making a total of 141 cases found ineligible out of the 236 cases. The percentage of ineligibility was 59.7. Ninety-five cases, or 40.3 per cent of the total, were found eligible. Of the cases found eligible, only 23 cases, or 9.7 per cent, were considered absolutely clean and without any infractions. In view of the findings, the Comptroller General recommended to the subcommittee that there be an investigation of the entire District of Columbia ADC case load.

Whatever the validity of the results of the investigation cited by Byrd — and in fairness it should be noted that some professionals argued that an important distinction should be drawn between temporary technical ineligibility and wilful cheating — the impact of his report on the Senate is of great importance. Byrd's performance drew an outburst of laudatory comment from all across the floor. Even making allowances for the rhetorical style of the Senate, it was an outburst over and beyond the usual words of commendation for an appropriations subcommittee chairman who reports on efforts to save money.[33] Hubert Humphrey, who qualifies as a Senator sympathetic to the professional welfare position on public assistance, characterized

---

[32]*Congressional Record,* September 28, 1962, pp. 21190ff.
[33]*Ibid.,* pp. 21202ff. All of the statements which follow are from this source.

Byrd's report as "a factual, objective, lucid, detailed report, such as I have never heard presented by any other Senator during my service in the Senate." Nor was the welfare section excepted. Humphrey specifically commended Byrd for his investigation in the field of public welfare. "I agree with him," said the then Democratic Whip. "I think these programs are endangered when abuse develops and is not corrected or when there is a lack of proper accounting." Compliments came, too, from liberal Republican John Sherman Cooper:

> Not only has the Senator found some defects in the District of Columbia and exposed them to public view, but also he has worked hard to correct the defects in a constructive way.

> I admire everything the Senator has done.

For John Stennis, the work of Senator Byrd showed "senatorial statesmanship of the highest order." Byrd showed in a fair and impartial way, said Stennis, that the programs could not continue unless they were cleaned up. The work he did was called a challenge to every state government which has to do with the administration of welfare programs. Republican Senators Gordon Allott of Colorado and Roman Hruska of Nebraska joined in the praise, and Majority Leader Mansfield characterized Byrd's performance in reporting, without benefit of notes, on the District budget, including the report on welfare, as "a presentation which I believe is unparalleled in the history of the Senate."

A year later, Senator Byrd returned with another District of Columbia appropriation bill and the emphasis was again on the operation and costs of the welfare program in the District.[34] The hearings he conducted had not been any gentler than his 1962 hearings. A less vulnerable agency than the District of Columbia Welfare Department might have responded more vigorously to some overt cases of browbeating of witnesses. But Byrd's presentation to the Senate was as complete as had been the case in 1962 and the admiration of his colleagues was undiminished. No general public assistance legislation came before the Senate in 1963. By his work on the District welfare budget, the Senator from West Virginia established himself as a specialist on both District affairs and welfare policy and administration generally.

One new element in 1963 was the presence of Abraham Ribicoff as the new junior Senator from Connecticut and as possible heir to Robert Kerr's unofficial job as principal Senate Democratic specialist in welfare legislation. Senator Kerr had carried the Democratic ball in

[34]*Congressional Record,* November 18, 1963, pp. 22088ff.

the Senate for public assistance legislation throughout most of the Eisenhower years and for the first two years of the Kennedy administration. With his counterpart in the House, Wilbur Mills of Arkansas, Kerr opposed social security financing of medical care for the aged but otherwise supported most of the goals enunciated by public welfare professionals. Kerr, in the opinion of the professionals, had an excellent understanding of welfare issues. Where Russell Long tended to confine himself to increasing federal grants to the aged, Kerr was willing to cover the whole public assistance spectrum. In view of the reluctance or lack of interest of the Senate Finance Committee Chairman, Harry Byrd, it was Kerr who handled public assistance legislation for the committee on the Senate floor.

In political terms, Kerr's death, on January 1, 1963, improved the prospects at that time for social security coverage of medical care for the aged but weakened interest in public assistance legislation. Long, with whom welfare lobbyists had not been able to establish a close relationship, became ranking Democratic member of the Senate Finance Committee; this did not necessarily mean that he would rate a leading position in the public assistance field. Ribicoff's election to the Senate when he was fresh from his service as Secretary of the Department of Health, Education, and Welfare and major administration proponent of the 1962 Public Welfare Amendments seemed to make him a natural successor to Kerr. His close ties to the leadership won him appointment to Kerr's seat on the Finance Committee despite his very junior status. (At the time of his appointment by the Democratic Steering Committee, Ribicoff stood 53rd in seniority of 58 Democratic Senators. Two other contenders for the appointment, William Proxmire of Wisconsin and Edward Long of Missouri, ranked 34th and 48th respectively, thus underscoring the point that seniority only controls when all other things are equal – and they rarely are.)

The stage was set for an initial showdown on welfare philosophy and on leadership when Byrd opposed extension of the ADC-U program to the District and declined to recommend funds for that purpose in the budget for fiscal 1964. His position was sustained by the full Appropriations Committee, 19-7. Ribicoff took up the challenge as chief sponsor of a floor amendment to extend ADC-U to the District. Most of the stops were pulled on both sides. Ribicoff made the appropriate observations about Byrd's sincerity and his hard work. The emphasis, though, was on his own experience as Governor of Committee, Ribicoff stood 53rd in seniority of 58 Democratic Senaarchitect of "a fresh, new approach to all the problems of welfare in the Nation." The autobiographical saga of how Ribicoff recognized the absence of imagination and change in the public assistance program and proceeded to breathe new freshness and vitality into it was detailed down to the moment when there was presented to Congress a new program in the entire field of welfare, and both houses voted a new approach in welfare.[35] Implicit in the presentation was the argument that the pending amendment was a logical outgrowth of the program in which Ribicoff was an expert, that to deny ADC-U to the District was to deny the applicability of the general principle to the specific case, and that Congress had committed itself to the general principle.

A public assistance debate is not considered complete without presentation of case material on both sides. The welfare-oriented group can be expected to produce cases showing God-fearing, honest, clean-living, family-centered unfortunates trapped by seemingly absurd residence requirements or whatever the subject of study may be. Opponents are equally capable of loading the record with unpleasant pictures of ne'er do wells, unmarried mothers blithely using ADC payments to support paramours and to buy liquor, and relief recipients arriving in Chryslers to pick up their checks. Senator Ribicoff followed the pattern, but this was an occasion when he would have done better to use a fresh, new approach to welfare policy debates as well as to welfare policy. The morning of the Senate vote on the ADC-U issue, the *Washington Daily News* (November 18, 1963), carried a story about Sonny Cooper, a 33-year-old Negro father of 11 children who had drowned himself:

With Sonny at home the family got his wages, $35 a week, $70 a week or nothing a week.

With Sonny away the family was eligible for welfare aid, $77 a week, every week.

So a couple of months ago Sonny took his clothes and left. And when he could find nowhere to put his clothes he threw them in the gutter. And when he could find nowhere to put himself he threw himself in the river.

Ribicoff read the story on the Senate floor and drew the obvious conclusion that it was irrational for 11 hungry children to become eligible for aid after their father drowned himself but to be ineligible when the father was alive. Byrd subsequently countered with a veritable flood of reports and cases to sustain his position that ineligibility was taken much too casually by the District welfare administrators.[36] More particularly, he knew the Cooper story too, and had anticipated Ribicoff's use of the timely tragedy. Byrd proceeded to read to the

[35]*Ibid.*, pp. 22069-71.
[36]*Ibid.*, pp. 22074ff.

Senate a police report disclosing that the suicide victim had been arrested 18 times on charges of drunkenness, disorderly conduct, assault with a deadly weapon. His wife was the complainant in the assault charge. He had been separated from his family for five months and his wife stated that her husband was a drunkard who refused to work.

Byrd did not let go of the advantage. He turned away with the apology that he was sorry to have had to remark on the case but that he had not brought it into the discussion. The ensuing hundred or so pages of the *Record* are filled with Byrd's reports and related documents bearing on the program. Significantly, as if to show a cosmopolitan understanding, the final entry offered by Byrd was the full text of a report of a New Jersey legislative committee that was highly critical of the incidence of fraud in the program in that state. Ribicoff never resumed the offensive. On the roll call, his amendment was defeated 35-42, one of the negative votes being supplied by Mike Mansfield, the Majority Leader. In the conflict between supporting its Appropriations Committee and supporting its own previous actions as interpreted by the administration's leading welfare spokesman, the Senate chose the former. It chose the challenger over the heir apparent. By so doing, Senators gave Robert Byrd an important boost and indicated that they were by no means persuaded by the look of the new-look welfare program.

Another recent, significant indicator of congressional attitudes is the final disposition of the District's 1964 appropriation. On the theory that a continuing field check on eligibility was necessary, Byrd, in committee, had sponsored funds for the addition of 42 more social workers and welfare case investigators than had been requested by the District Commissioners. (In addition, he had sponsored funds for 37 new positions in the Child Welfare Division.) A comparable effort on Byrd's part had been successful a year earlier. But in dealing with the 1964 appropriation, House conferees stood firm against inclusion of funds for any unbudgeted positions; all of the Byrd additions were dropped in conference. The net result of congressional action was to deny ADC-U in the District of Columbia, and also to deny added funds for what Senator Humphrey characterized as "generally improving the welfare system in the District."

Proponents of ADC-U for the District thought Byrd had called in all his outstanding vote loans in the 1963 clash with Ribicoff. That may have been the case, but it does not detract from the fact that the demonstration of expertise and its result put Byrd in a commanding position when the fight was renewed a year later. The 1964 Democratic primary ballot in the District included a straw poll on an ADC-U program. With 72,000 yeas against 1,600 nays, there were grounds for a new effort in the summer of 1964 after the District's 1965 appropriation came to the Senate floor, again without funds for ADC-U. Byrd's subcommittee deleted the ADC-U item, the Senator explained, after approximately 100 questions were asked about it so that the committee could act in an informed manner. He contrasted the extensive Senate subcommittee inquiry with the perfunctory interest of the House subcommittee, insisting that House approval of the item should be considered against its legislative history there: "only 12 questions were asked in the House subcommittee." Ribicoff's subsequent amendment, designed at least to establish the principle by appropriating only $339,000 to run an ADC-U program for six months, did not provoke the full-dress clash of the previous year. This was now Byrd's domain in the Senate, and the Senator from West Virginia knew it. He urged the Senate four times to proceed to a vote, saying that he did not wish to debate the question further. Before the vote, however, Hubert Humphrey again went out of his way to score some points for Byrd and to defend the latter as the specialist:

> ... this subcommittee, under the chairmanship of the Senator from West Virginia has not been unmindful of human needs in the District of Columbia. ... I have been aware of the efforts he has made and the hours he has spent. ... He does not need my defense ... the chairman and his subcommittee have been very considerate of the many welfare needs of this city.[37]

When the vote came, Ribicoff again lost, Byrd won, 32-39. And, with only minor variations on the theme, it was played again in June, 1965. Byrd opposed bringing the District into the ADC-U program; Ribicoff offered his amendment. On the key vote, Byrd once more had 7 more votes than Ribicoff; ADC-U was rejected.

Subsequent to adoption of the Public Welfare Amendments of 1962, then, Congress has been slow about implementing the philosophy of the legislation. The Senate has turned away from the judgment of the Health, Education, and Welfare Secretary who proposed the amendments and who is now a colleague, and on a key issue three times followed instead the leadership of a determined critic of the public assistance program as it is presently constituted.[38] Although the critic sometimes reflects the southern attitude on race, he has drawn help on this issue from some strong civil rights supporters.

---

[37]*Congressional Record,* July 31, 1964, p. 10729 (Daily Edition).
[38]For a summary of Byrd's impact on the District of Columbia welfare program, see the *New York Times,* June 12, 1963, p. 22.

The Case of Congressman Denton

There are additional indicators of congressional discontent, although there is not yet a sign that Congress is ready to demand the kind of overhaul that it demanded recently in the foreign aid program. One of these indicators is the continuing unwillingness to make new money available for the training of professional caseworkers in public assistance. Another is the frequency with which references are made now to the idea that public assistance was sold — or at least understood by legislators — as temporary.

The latter point and the apparently growing impatience with the program that accompanies it are evident from a systematic review of the kinds of questions and comments made over a ten-year period in the House Appropriations subcommittee by its now ranking Democratic member, Representative Winfield K. Denton of Indiana. Denton, a former state's attorney and former Democratic leader of the Indiana House of Representatives, is neither a flashy nor a nationally publicized legislator. Denton has a high Democratic partisan score. He makes no extended speeches on the floor. In committee, Denton is relaxed, and normally not especially persistent in his inquiries. He has served on the Labor — Health, Education, and Welfare Appropriations subcommittee continuously since 1955, and he had a period of service on the Appropriations Committee before 1953 when the change to Republican control of the House cost Denton his seat on that committee. Denton runs from a comfortably Democratic district and has wide labor and liberal group support. Only the subcommittee chairman, John Fogarty of Rhode Island, has longer service on the Labor — Health, Education, and Welfare subcommittee than Denton, and only Denton and Fogarty have served since the mid-1950's.

Denton has been interested in aid to schools in federally impacted areas, in hospital construction programs, and in medical progress generally. Recently he has offered legislation to prohibit liens on property of aid to the blind recipients. Perhaps the cause that Denton has championed most constantly is his "runaway pappys" bill, an effort to make it a federal crime to desert a family. Although Denton seems to feel that the bill, if enacted, would have an impact on the size of the ADC rolls by reducing desertion cases, the Justice Department has never been enthusiastic about involving federal agencies in domestic relations law. Welfare personnel argue that the 1950 Noleo amendment, requiring that local law enforcement officials be notified when ADC desertion cases are activated, serves much the same purpose as the "runaway pappys" proposal. Administrative officials who appear before the subcommittee try to be noncommittal about the bill, sound enough strategy in dealing with legislation that seems to have no future but to which an inquiring congressman is devoted.[39] Secretary Ribicoff, perhaps by way of emphasizing his announced desire to take a fresh look at all public assistance policies, responded to Denton's mention of the bill in 1962 with a surely unexpected expression of support, but the measure was not moved even with this high-level endorsement.

Denton's first years on the subcommittee found him raising no questions with the department spokesmen, adopting the pattern generally followed by members of easy acceptance of the need to appropriate the requested amount. By 1961, he was acknowledging that there was not much to be done, although during previous years he frequently reminded department personnel that "in 1951 your department told me . . . that the welfare problem would end." In one exchange along those lines with Secretary Marion Folsom in 1957, Denton announced that he was disturbed about increased welfare costs and Folsom offered reassurances, which turned out to be a poor prediction, based on the withering-away idea: "I don't think you will find the assistance growing to $2 billion a year. . . . As long as you have got 90 percent [of the population] covered under social security, it is bound to go down."[40] The Denton of 1957 said he was "disappointed" at the persistence of public assistance because he thought that it was supposed to be a temporary program, but his questions were designed to elicit opinions and not to put bureaucrats on guard. His resigned tone in 1961 regarding the inevitability of heavy costs was reinforced by one of Denton's infrequent floor speeches in which he deplored "cumbersome, inefficient, and wasteful" methods of processing claims under permanent and total disability, but he had no criticism of the substantive program or its cost.[41]

The tone changes sharply in 1963. Apparently the combination of a series of administrators offering soft words together with the impact of the Byrd investigation in the District of Columbia stung Representative Denton into doing some digging and forming some conclusions:

. . . I am disappointed in your budget for welfare. That is almost $3 billion. It is 60 percent of this Department's appropriations. When I went on this committee in 1951 the amount was $1 billion. It has gone up 300 per cent. In

[39]U.S. Congress, House, Subcommittee of the Committee on Appropriations, Hearings, "Departments of Labor and Health, Education, and Welfare Appropriations for 1961," 86th Cong., 2d Sess., 1960, pp. 144, 642.

[40]U.S. Congress, House, Subcommittee of the Committee on Appropriations, Hearings, "Departments of Labor and Health, Education, and Welfare Appropriations for 1958," 85th Cong., 1st Sess., 1957, p. 78.

[41]*Congressional Record,* May 17, 1961, p. 8245.

the 1961 budget it was $2 billion and those three years, the budget has gone up another billion dollars.

... But Mr. Mitchell, who is the former Commissioner, told me I was wrong in saying welfare was only a stopgap. I went back and got some statements out of past hearings.[42]

There followed a reading of Arthur Altmeyer's 1947 testimony before the House Appropriations subcommittee in which Altmeyer had argued the seesaw effect of increasing social insurance coverage. Denton quoted Altmeyer:

So, if we had coverage of the old-age and survivors' insurance system which include the whole working population—farmers and farm labor particularly—we would find that our old-age-assistance rolls and our aid-to-dependent-children rolls would decline rapidly.

You will recall that the intent of the Social Security Act was that the insurance system in course of time would largely supersede this public assistance plan that is financed out of general revenues.[43]

Denton also cited exchanges from hearings in 1950 and 1952 in an effort to make it clear that he did not plan to be told again that he had misunderstood the allegations of the social security planners. Again and again, he returned to the point that after 25 years of social security and almost universal coverage, the costs of public assistance continued to increase very significantly. More important from the standpoint of the department, Denton indicated that he had an explanation of his own to replace the explanations forthcoming from the administrative agency:

I don't think that you are going to find any agency that wants to act as receiver for its Department. As one welfare lady told me, anybody who didn't try to increase their Department wasn't worth their salt. I don't think you can expect the welfare agency to ever try to get us over into the social security field.[44]

Finally, Denton turned to the District of Columbia investigation and the plan for the nationwide audit of the ADC program demanded by the Senate Appropriations Committee. He criticized the fact that 11 of the 15 members of the Advisory Committee for the audit had social work backgrounds. "I do believe that an auditor who audits his own books will very seldom find something wrong."[45] As for the impact of the Byrd investigation itself, Denton was explicit:

[42]U.S. Congress, House, Subcommittee of the Committee on Appropriations, Hearings, "Departments of Labor and Health, Education, and Welfare Appropriations for 1964," 88th Cong., 1st Sess., 1963, pp. 141-42.
[43]*Ibid.*
[44]*Ibid.*, p. 144.
[45]*Ibid.*, p. 159.

Let me put the problem this way. Put yourself in our place. Right under our nose, under our eyes, we have had an investigation in the District of Columbia that shows 50 percent fraudulent cases. We do know that there is fraud all over the country generally. You are conducting this investigation.

Now, of course, the other body undoubtedly is going to wait until they get that report from you on the investigation. Now if it is as bad over the country as it is in the District of Columbia, you don't need but half of this money you request.[46]

Some apparently heretofore suppressed frustration came out as part of Denton's comment to Wilbur Cohen about myth and reality in legislative control of welfare administration:

I am surprised to hear you say that welfare paid any attention to Congress at all. Here is one agency that we are asked to make appropriations for. Now, they are laughing at us when we say something. We suggest that they spend less; we suggest that they reduce administrative expenses. They say, "We spend so much money and you are going to have to match it."

... Here is what worries me about this agency. It's responsible to nobody.[47]

Assistant Secretary Cohen offered the textbook reply, and Denton responded like a man who had lost his faith:

Mr. Cohen. It should be responsible to the legislature.
Mr. Denton. Let me show you. Suppose we tell you to spend less money. What will you tell us? You would laugh at us, wouldn't you?
Mr. Cohen. I would not do that, sir; no.
Mr. Denton. Not to our face.

This exchange between Denton and Cohen was appreciably less amiable than one which took place early in 1958 when Cohen appeared before the subcommittee on behalf of the American Public Welfare Association. At that time, Cohen revealed to the subcommittee that an "historic moment" had been reached the previous month when for the first time the number of ADC recipients exceeded the number of OAA recipients. Denton made inquiries of Cohen, used the ADC-OAA ratio change as an excuse to make his annual short speech for the Denton "runaway pappys" bill, but did not challenge Cohen's assertion that the bill would not be useful legislation. Indeed, at the 1958 hearings Denton made a series of observations that clearly identified him as a politician likely to be sympathetic to the welfare professionals' way of formulating the public assistance problem. In a pleasant exchange with Jay Roney, then Director of the Bureau of Public Assistance, Denton inquired about reasons for high administrative costs and was told that in some cases administrative costs were high because of

[46]*Ibid.*, pp. 169-70.
[47]*Ibid.*, p. 171.

the high cost of administering eligibility requirements. The costs of tracking down responsible relatives and seeking support from them in those states with relative-responsibility laws was cited as a case in point; Denton appeared to accept the explanation easily enough.[48] Almost gratuitously, he made an observation on salary schedules for welfare workers that should have earned him an honorary membership in the American Public Welfare Association: "I do not think they get paid enough, the welfare workers." And after expressing an interest in the problem of growing rates of illegitimacy in ADC, Denton let it be known that he thought the specialists should be taking the lead, that uninformed legislators should not rush in with legislation, that he was afraid that indiscriminate legislation would do more harm than good, and that any legislation on the problem should emanate from the bureau.

Although the ADC problem continued to hold Denton's attention in 1960, every sign up to and including the "I recognize there is not much we can do" observation in 1961 indicated that Denton would go on indefinitely voting whatever was needed to meet public assistance costs and that only a somewhat tiresome preoccupation with his "runaway pappys" bill prevented a perfect welfare score. But his parting shots in 1963, after the Byrd investigation, were directed against the open-end authorization and against welfare personnel interested in organizational self-perpetuation.

The significance of Denton's apparent disaffection with the program is in his background. A northern liberal from an urban area, he has a history of friendliness to public assistance. A veteran congressman who makes fond mention of the days of the New Deal and of Franklin D. Roosevelt and who scored high in support of the Kennedy administration's domestic program, a former state legislator and former county prosecutor who talks authoritatively about experiences in intergovernmental relations in welfare, Denton should be safely in the welfare fold. For years, Denton has seemed resigned to going along with a program that is admittedly expensive but to which he has seen no alternative. Now he has been set off on a critical line that has culminated in his joining with the ranking Republican member of the subcommittee to suggest the possible desirability of changing the open-end appropriation for public assistance grants, a change that would affect the character of the entire program.[49]

[48]U.S. Congress, House, Subcommittee of the Committee on Appropriations, Hearings, "Departments of Labor and Health, Education, and Welfare Appropriations for 1959," 85th Cong., 2d Sess., 1958, pp. 389-95.
[49]House Appropriations, Hearings, 1963, pp. 172-73. I am grateful to Representative Denton for a critical reading of this section.

Denton's shift in attitude is the result of a combination of the paternalism of the administrative officers in dealing with him through the years and of the results of the Byrd investigation. The latter was the trigger because the seeming ease with which improprieties were exposed raised in the mind of this appropriations subcommittee member the question of whether the subcommittee's traditional ready acceptance of the inevitability of the public assistance appropriation was justified. The question was magnified for any member who had conscientiously participated in the process of legislative oversight over a number of years. Denton cannot be explained away as a publicity-seeker because he has no such history. Whether the Health, Education, and Welfare people concerned with legislative relations can bring Denton back into the friendly fold will be a sign of their chance of achieving acceptance of a permanent public assistance program under the rules and guidelines established three decades ago for a "residual" program.

The Elusive Training Grants

Public assistance workers perch on the bottom rungs of the social work prestige ladder. Even the top rungs of that ladder, however, where the psychiatric social workers sit, do not equal the status level available to the professional groups with which social workers would like to be identified — most particularly, psychiatrists and medical doctors, and more generally, members of the healing or helping professions. The efforts of social workers to achieve the desired higher status have taken two forms: one, an interest in the licensing of social workers that would ultimately restrict practice to persons appropriately trained and certified; two, an interest in insuring that the supply of trained persons be made more comparable to the demand, by providing grants to the states for in-service training of workers in public assistance, and by providing grants to the colleges and universities to use for fellowship support of social work students who choose public assistance work. The licensing question has a variety of facets which are considered in Chapter VII of this book. Training grants, however, are very closely related to the question of congressional attitudes.

Since the 1956 amendments to the Social Security Act, welfare professionals have been attempting to activate its provisions authorizing appropriations for a federal-state program to increase "the number of adequately trained public welfare personnel available for work in public assistance programs." The initial authorization was for $5 million for fiscal 1958, and for an open-end appropriation in the four succeeding years. After five years of complete failure in efforts to secure actual federal appropriations for the federal-state 80-20 matching grant program, proponents were rewarded in 1961 not with money, but with a one-year extension of the authorization and a change in the authorization formula to eliminate the provision requiring 20 per cent matching by the states. Given the inability to get money from Congress, it was a reasonable assumption that even the 20 per cent would be very hard to extract from state legislatures in the event a breakthrough occurred in Congress. Striking the requirement for state funds may have been sound long-run strategy; in the short run, however, the first need is still for congressional action, and the nonmatching grant idea itself promptly became a justification for opposition on the part of some members of Congress. In adopting the 1962 Public Welfare Amendments, Congress extended the 100 per cent federally financed training grant authorization indefinitely but closed the amount at $3.5 million for fiscal 1963 and $5 million thereafter. An appropriation of $3.5 million would finance 600 academic fellowships and traineeships, as well as study opportunities through short-term workshops or seminars for 800 employees of state and local agencies. It would also compel a good deal of soul-searching in some universities where social work students have not always been of competitive fellowship caliber.

During the years in which there has been authorization to appropriate for training public assistance personnel, there has not been even a near miss in actually securing funds. This is accounted for in part by federal department interpretation of state administrative costs as including short courses, in-service training, and some educational leave activity. Such an interpretation makes it possible for 75 per cent of the costs of such training to be federally assumed under the provisions of the 1962 act which increased the federal share of administrative costs where states comply with standards laid down by the secretary. Prior to 1962, educational leave was covered in some cases by the 50-50 federal-state sharing of administrative costs. For example, in fiscal 1958, 329 state or local public assistance workers were on educational leave with salary and/or other expenses paid by their states and charged to costs of administration of the program; the number grew to 577 by fiscal 1961. In 1963, the Senate Appropriations subcommittee explained its denial of federal funds under the 100 per cent federal grant section by noting that since 1,100 welfare workers were expected to get training under the 75-25 administrative costs sharing formula during fiscal 1964, it was unnecessary to appropriate other federal funds for training.[50]

More than a difference in the distribution of costs of training is involved in the relative advantages of earmarked training grants com-

[50]*Senate Report 383*, 88th Cong., 1st Sess., 1963, p. 67.

pared to back-door financing of training under the guise of administrative costs. Approval of money for training *qua* training would provide recognition of the need for the professionalization so devoutly desired by social workers. In addition, federal appropriations to Health, Education, and Welfare for training grants under the no-matching authorization would increase the volume of training. While the federal agency is sympathetic to the idea of spending for this purpose, some state agencies are reluctant to divert funds for training even though every state dollar brings three federal dollars under the administrative costs arrangement. Finally, and of prime importance, implementation of the authorization would permit direct grants to universities, so that the flow of new people into the field could be stimulated. The National Science Foundation makes such grants to increase the flow of engineers, mathematicians, and scientists, and there are comparable grants in the mental health field. To be restricted to providing training for persons already in public assistance work limits the likelihood of initially attracting highly talented people who are attentive to opportunities for fellowship support in other areas.

Appropriations for training of public assistance personnel have never gotten past the committee stage in the House. Senate Appropriations showed a sympathetic flash in 1962 and recommended that $1.5 million be appropriated for training; the accompanying report, however, was a plain expression of no confidence:

> It is difficult to believe that high caliber individuals will spend the time required for this training when the jobs for which they are preparing offer such relatively low pay.[51]

The House Appropriations Committee had previously declined to approve an appropriation, stating that, in its opinion, any training grant program should be on a matching basis of some type.[52] When this House report was filed on March 23, 1962, the Public Welfare Amendments extending the nonmatching authorization were still in committee, but Health, Education, and Welfare decision-makers did not take the clue. Apparently they concluded either that the Appropriations Committee would ultimately come around, or that there would not really be any money appropriated whether the grant was total or had a matching feature. If a matching grant was to be required, it would be more advantageous to proceed under the 75-25 costs of administration section, where the total sum authorized was open-end rather than limited to $5 million annually as under the training section. As no effort

[51]*Senate Report 1672*, 87th Cong., 2d Sess., 1962, p. 56.
[52]*House Report 1488*, 87th Cong., 2d Sess., 1962, p. 47.

to change the nonmatching feature was made, it was adopted in the 1962 amendments. It has already been noted that Senate Appropriations thereafter rejected separate training funds, claiming in 1963 that the 75-25 provision was adequate. Its House counterpart made the same point about the lack of need for a separate training program.

Despite the history of rejections, there are some distant signs of congressional acceptance of the idea of professional training as a worthy objective. As early as 1957, the House Appropriations subcommittee approved funds under the training section but the full committee struck the item. "I don't believe I had five out of fifty votes in the [Appropriations] Committee," John Fogarty subsequently explained. At various times, the training grant money, always proposed at the bureau level, was lost at the department level or at the Bureau of the Budget level. But even when all these hurdles were negotiated, it could never make it past Congress.

In the budget request for at least one year, fiscal 1961, elimination of the training money was decided upon at the department level as a matter of strategy. Secretary Flemming concluded that the failure to secure funds in previous years could be traced to the 80-20 formula which many legislators thought too high a federal share.[53] Accordingly, Flemming made no request for funds under this section but instead sought liberalized salary and expense money which could be used for training under the then prevailing 50-50 administrative costs sharing formula. James Kelly, the department budget officer who has seen several bureau chiefs and several secretaries come and go, was quite explicit about the plan to use administration funds for in-service training. "Well," he said, "there is a need for this kind of training so you examine all the authorities that you have, and see which one you think has the greatest likelihood of being supported."[54]

Abraham Ribicoff, during his tenure as Secretary, recognized that the training grant proposal was not received sympathetically by Congress; he attempted to provide an excuse for legislators to change their position. In asking for $3.5 million for training, Ribicoff explained that he wasn't asking Congress to appropriate money for a stale old policy that everyone was unhappy with and which had been frequently rejected. Things were going to be different—"we have turned around and finally brought in a new change and a new philosophy in welfare."[55]

[53]House Appropriations, Hearings, 1960, pp. 121-22.
[54]*Ibid.*, p. 631.
[55]U.S. Congress, House, Subcommittee of the Committee on Appropriations, Hearings, "Departments of Labor and Health, Education, and Welfare Appropriations for 1963," 87th Cong., 2d Sess., 1962, p. 173.

That was the year that the Senate Appropriations Committee approved $1.5 million, a high-water mark in the nonprogress of pushing training money through Congress.

When $3 billion are appropriated for public assistance grants with a minimum of whimpering, however, it seems illogical for a relatively small sum of money to be refused for financing a program to train people so that the $3 billion can be spent usefully. It is also illogical for Congress to make training funds available through a back door, while firmly denying funds for a similar purpose when the proposal is put directly. A variety of explanations may be suggested. One tenable explanation is that Congress does prefer the shared formula between federal and state governments, and that if the present training authorization were to carry a matching provision it would be used. Another explanation, equally tenable, is that there is a lack of faith in the value of professional training for public assistance as it is currently carried on. Politicians tend to have a low regard for social workers, and social workers find administrative officials — regarded as fellow professionals — more congenial than they find legislators. It is unlikely that more than a handful of congressmen have any idea of the content of a social work training program. For all of the volume of material, resolutions, and statements of principles constantly being offered for the record by welfare spokesmen, there is no sign that a legislator seeking a content analysis of graduate training in social work could find it as part of the material offered in support of training grants. Nor is there an explicit discourse by any spokesman on the subject of exactly what it is that workers should know before they are turned loose on public assistance clients. If the suspicion voiced by Representative Denton — that public assistance personnel view with alarm any possibility of the withering away of the program — is widespread, it too would reenforce a reluctance to vote training funds.

Under present arrangements, then, there is a widely utilized 75-25 matching grant for postentry training. Trained workers, however, flee from the public assistance field as soon as possible. Even if preentry training money is provided, potential social workers are more likely to avail themselves of preentry mental health and child welfare traineeship support than of public assistance traineeship support because of the usual traineeship commitment to work some predetermined period in the field of support. In terms of assessing the development of the public assistance program, however, this is less important than the fact that Congress still seems to lack sufficient faith in the trained public assistance professionals to provide directly any money that would allow the professionals to multiply in their own image.

79

CHAPTER IV

State Versus Federal Power

THE TRADITION OF local responsibility for the poor dies hard. The federal public assistance statute, provoked by the fiscal inability of the states to develop programs adequate for the depression crisis, was meant to shore up, not to replace, state old age and mothers' pension laws. Without a demonstration that relief of the poor was a problem that required a uniformity of policy, efforts by economists and social workers to impose such uniformity were resisted. Through the years, there has been some shifting of the balance between federal and state power; however, the goals of those who would move toward maximizing national policy-making authority are far from realized. Neither the minimum standards imposed on the states nor the prohibitions on state action are onerous. Moreover, they are negotiable rather than absolute, permitting the adept state to have things very much its own way.

I. A STATE CAN WIN

There are at least three ways in which state public assistance policy can be made contrary to the national program. First, although it is expensive, it is not impossible for a state to go it alone in public assistance. Unlike the unemployment insurance program, no special earmarked tax, with a forgiveness feature for complying states, is imposed to support public assistance. The state that cannot or will not comply with the federal act can go its own way and pay its own bills. It is not, of course, refunded the federal revenue that might otherwise be diverted into the state to support the program, but the connection between nonearmarked federal taxes and any specific program is hard to establish. Nevada is still without a program of aid to the permanently and totally disabled (APTD), while Alaska, Indiana, and Arizona held out until 1963. By the beginning of 1965, 18 of the states had adopted ADC-U programs; the remaining majority prefer to meet that problem through state and locally financed general assistance programs or to ignore it entirely.

Reluctance to come aboard the federal grant train can stem from a variety of causes. In the case of the APTD program in Nevada, for example, the number of potential recipients scarcely justifies the administrative machinery that would be required. The unwillingness of many states to develop ADC-U programs is traceable in part to a lack of sympathy with the aims of the program, in part to a fear that the federal connection will shoot state standards and costs upward, and in part to the inevitable lag between the creation of a new program and its general acceptance. The same factors, in unequal doses, account for the delayed adoption of the original ADC program in many states. Finally, a federal grant program may be resisted because it is presumably unnecessary or because it carries obnoxious conditions. The Kerr-Mills program of medical aid to the indigent aged has been attacked on both of these grounds. Since support in one category can be achieved without regard to other categories, the price of independence in a single area is not prohibitive.

A second way in which public assistance policy can be developed at the state level is by agreement to play a somewhat modified version of the original game. This requires either negotiation between state and federal units prior to the filing of a state plan for approval by the administrator, or congressional adoption of a specific exception protecting a state plan that would otherwise not qualify. Advance negotiation should be distinguished from a third technique for making state policy contrary to national policy: noncompliance, deliberate flouting of federal law or regulations with the expectation either that the state case is strong enough to compel the federal agency to find a way to ignore or justify the disobedience, or that the case is strong enough to result in a change in the general law.

The most difficult problems in federal-state grant relationships in public assistance occur when a state wants to utilize federal grants but tries to negotiate terms slightly different from those deemed appropriate by the federal administrative agency, or when a state which is already committed to the federal program noncomplies with its terms and is dropped for its unruly conduct. The impact of the resolution of these hard cases on policy in other states gives them importance beyond the state of origin. Michigan recently negotiated and lost in connection with its state plan for an ADC-U program. Missouri and Pennsylvania negotiated for years for approval of aid to the blind programs that did not conform to the federal act because they were too generous. A leading case in the withholding of federal funds for noncompliance is that of Indiana in 1951 when the state knowingly violated the federal statutory requirement for confidentiality of relief data. In earlier years, Illinois, Oklahoma, and Ohio had run afoul of federal law or regulations largely because of a willingness to be overly generous — and overtly political — with OAA funds.

Whatever the cause of federal withholding, attitudes on both the federal and the state sides appear to be different in the more recent period from attitudes developed up to the Indiana confidentiality dispute. In the beginning, a tough-minded Social Security Board, distrustful of state behavior, gave no quarter but asserted its authority without hesitation. Later, in part because of the approach of a different national administration to the question of federal-state relations, in part because of the growth of an interlocking federal-state bureaucracy which made communication and adjustment relatively easy, and in part because of strong congressional antipathy to withholding funds from an on-going program, the federal agency adopted a less rigid philosophy that seems to distinguish between new and existing programs. ADC-U in Michigan was new, and so was a South Dakota Kerr-Mills plan rejected in 1964. Changes in previously approved plans are given more tolerant consideration. Even when it came face to face with an extreme case — Louisiana's suitable home provisions of 1960 — which would have put earlier federal administrators behind the ramparts, the Department of Health, Education, and Welfare found a way legally to accept the state action and moved toward a compromise. Again, in 1963, when Illinois decided to pursue a system of direct payments to landlords in seeming violation of the Social Security Act's requirement for cash payments to the needy, Health, Education, and Welfare responded to what it considered intense pressure by agreeing that funds paid to recipients in excess of those matched by the federal grant were not liable to the cash requirements of the federal act.

A somewhat different position regarding the separability of federal and state funds had been taken earlier by the agency when Missouri and Pennsylvania sought to provide pensions for the blind without regard to the income and resources limits of the law. There, federal matching funds were not approved for qualified recipients as long as nonqualified recipients benefited under the same state law even though only state money was used in the latter cases. In 1922, Missouri passed legislation which provided a blind pension of $20 a month if the recipient had limited amounts of property and not more than $600 of earned income per year. Over the years, Missouri increased the amount of the exemption as the cost of living increased until, in 1961, the total exemption reached $3,000 of earned income, while the pension went up to $65 a month. Pennsylvania has had a similar aid to the blind program; by 1961 that state provided a pension of $70 if a blind individual did not have more than $5,000 of personal or real property and his earned income did not exceed $2,880. Neither the Missouri nor the Pennsylvania aid to the blind plans were ruled eligible for grant funds until 1950, when the federal government participated in the programs to recipients who qualified under the new $50 per month earned income exemption of the federal law. The Missouri and Pennsylvania plans were permitted to exist along with the federal plan by special law, but they were expected to phase out. Congress continued to reenact the special legislation periodically between 1950 and 1960, until it was made permanent in 1962. Through the years, Health, Education, and Welfare attempted to eliminate the programs. According to Missouri Representative Thomas Curtis, attempts were made by the department to force Missouri and Pennsylvania to conform to the federal program, action that Curtis characterized as "restrictiveness. . .and resistance to innovation."[1] The latter phrase hit Secretary Ribicoff on a raw nerve, and the department offered no overt objection to the 1962 amendment that made permanent the temporary dispensations previously allowed by Congress.

There is almost absolute discretion in the federal agency to accept or reject a state plan in light of judicial ruling that the grant money "belongs" to the federal government.[2] Since the confidentiality dispute of 1951, however, the state claim for funds, once the plan is approved, is more secure than it was when the federal agency was feeling its oats. Washington welfare bureaucrats are apparently not as tough as they used to be.

Timing, partisanship, local support, and congressional interest all may affect the chances of state success in policy battles with Washington:

1. Timing. In the short-run sense, the federal agency can be expected to fight harder to maintain its position shortly after a victory or a

---

[1] U.S. Congress, House, Committee on Ways and Means, Hearings, "Public Welfare Amendments of 1962," 87th Cong., 2d Sess., 1962, p. 291.
[2] *Arizona* v. *Hobby,* 221 F. 2d 489 (1954).

loss than after a protracted period of no conflict. Successive losses reduce respect for the authority of the agency. Successive victories tend to create the illusion of a powerhouse that cannot be challenged with any real hope of success.

In the long-run sense, the intensity of federal control of the public assistance program probably diminishes as the federal agency responsible for administration becomes less insecure, less of a novelty, and begins to establish quiet negotiation procedures that could serve as alternatives to noisy withdrawal of federal cooperation. In other words, as the federal agency grows older, it can be expected to be more likely to establish an accommodation with its clientele group—in this case, the state public assistance policy-makers.

2. Partisanship. The undesirability of allowing partisan politics to be involved in the problem of the relief of the destitute is widely acknowledged. A federal-state public assistance policy dispute is not likely to be resolved in favor of the state if it is apparent that there is a partisan political basis for the state deviation from the regular order.

3. Local support. A state that can show unified local support for its position from newspapers, politicians, business groups, and other influentials at the local level is more likely to have its way than is a state group that is going it alone.

4. Congressional involvement. Congress is more sympathetic to the efforts of a state to maintain an independent public assistance policy than is the administrative agency. If a state can involve Congress in the resolution of a dispute it is more likely to be successful than if it must depend on the administrative agency. Although special legislation to overturn an administrative ruling is hard to achieve, an expression of congressional interest is a useful tool. Unlike the procedures in internal revenue taxation, merely filing a bill will not produce administrative acquiescence, but such an action may provoke careful rethinking. This is especially true where the issue can be put to Congress as a state challenge to the federal bureaucratic denial of rights claimed by a state legislature. In this field, Congress acts as guardian of the prerogatives of the states.

These considerations are evident in examining the details of some major federal-state conflicts dealing with alleged political use of a state's OAA rolls, the flouting of a federal confidentiality requirement, and the classification of recipients on a basis other than need. At a later point, it becomes appropriate to consider state success in fighting the national agency's effort to reduce or wipe out the permissible residence requirement and state success in establishing some extra-legal patterns of discrimination between recipients.

II. EXPLOITING POLITICAL SCANDAL

It is indicative of the degree of freedom first accorded the states by the public assistance titles of the Social Security Act that Congress did not see fit to authorize denial of federal aid to a state that established substandard benefits. Authority, found in the original draft bill, for the board to require a state benefit schedule that met minimum standards of health and decency was stricken by the House Ways and Means Committee to meet objections of southern congressmen. This left states free to pay any amount whatever and still have the benefit of some federal matching grants. In addition, several other clauses in the draft bill relating to federal supervisory authority over state action were rewritten to tip the balance initially on the side of state rather than national decision-making power. The conditions for approval of state plans are stated negatively, so that the states are able to impose any conditions they see fit, except that age, residence, and citizenship qualifications may not be more stringent than the maxima set forth in the act. This leeway permits the imposition of income and property restrictions, lien laws, and such other qualification features as a creative state may invent. Provisions of the draft bill relating to methods of state administration were changed to free the states from federal control over the selection, tenure, and compensation of personnel working in the program. Finally, a series of procedural safeguards were inserted to restrict the power of the federal agency to withdraw approval of a state plan for violation of the federal act. Some of these state advantages were soon lost, as political scandals in relief in several states were legitimately exploited by astute federal welfare administrators who believed that the real success of the legislation depended on additional federal administrative control.

Once established, the Social Security Board was not disposed to take a mousey attitude in its relations with the states. Professionalization of relief administration had been a particularly important element in the credo of the group that developed the program, and the loss of the opportunity to insist on a merit system for state personnel was aggravating. In at least one state, the preconceptions of the federal administrative group regarding the character of the state people made federal-state cooperation virtually impossible. Anxious to avoid political intrusion, Washington saw things in blacks and whites, politically run programs versus professionalization. Claiming that the federal aim was to elevate the social workers' "professional guild" to a commanding position, the Superintendent of the Iowa Division of Old Age Assistance was outraged by the attitude of a group of visiting federal field officials who arrived shortly after the Iowa state plan was approved early in 1936:

> In fact, it seemed to them preposterous to believe that members of the commission did not even know the party affiliation of the major portion of the employees, both state and county, or that our Governor or officials generally already had waged a successful battle to prevent the inroads of those who would make the payment of old age assistance a matter of political patronage.[3]

Making allowances for the fact that the agency was new, Mark Hale still characterized its procedures in federal-state affairs as "slow, at points cumbersome, highly centralized, divorced from the operating offices of state agencies, at times obscure and often subjective."[4] The judgment is consistent with a picture of a federal unit that distrusted its state partners, avoided involving them whenever possible, and hoped for a change. The national interest required that the program be developed under whatever conditions Congress imposed; federal administrators from the beginning hoped that the conditions would be improved.

Despite the sharp reduction in the discretionary authority of the Social Security Board insisted upon by the House Ways and Means Committee, the board was still empowered to withdraw federal cooperation. It did so in Illinois in 1937, in Oklahoma in 1938, and in Ohio in 1938. Illinois was formally found to have been out of compliance with certain mandatory financial and accounting procedures, with requirements for a fair hearing for applicants whose applications had been denied, and with "other essentials of adequate administration."[5] Withdrawal came seven months after an administrative study of the Illinois OAA division had been undertaken by the board, and after Illinois spokesmen acknowledged that they were "humiliated" by the criticisms, for some of which they had "practically no defense."[6] By the end of August, 1937, Illinois' plan was reapproved tentatively, and the state suffered no loss of funds since certification for the quarterly period was accomplished. Had reapproval not been forthcoming within the quarter, the state would have lost about $1.5 million of federal funds.

[3]Byron T. Allen, "Federal-State Cooperation in Public Assistance," in *Social Security in the United States, 1938* (New York: American Association for Social Security, 1938), p. 37.

[4]Mark Hale, "The Process of Developing Policy for a Federal-State Grant-in-Aid Program as Illustrated by the Work of the Social Security Board, 1935-46," *Social Service Review*, XXXI (September, 1957), 307.

[5]Social Security Board, *Annual Report 1937* (Washington), p. 92.

[6]Arthur P. Miles, *Federal Aid and Public Assistance in Illinois* (Chicago: University of Chicago Press, 1941), "Record of the Hearing . . . ," p. 188.

Oklahoma's problems grew out of the board's exposure of the padding of OAA rolls. A random check in 46 of 77 counties showed payments of $685,000 to ineligibles. Public hearings disclosed that among the recipients were 157 corpses and 12 inmates of insane asylums. Fourteen hundred case files were missing.[7] A purification of the system was undertaken which made it possible for the board to restore Oklahoma to the approved list retroactive to the first of the month following decertification; still, one full month was lost. Whether popular confusion between OAA and the Townsend Plan was the hard core of the Oklahoma trouble or whether it was a plain case of attempted vote-buying by the state administration could not be pinned down at that point. Before the year was out the board announced that it would withhold $1.5 million from subsequent grants to Oklahoma pending submission of accurate records of eligibility.[8] The latter action took the back-door form of audit exceptions rather than the front-door form of withdrawal of certification. Audit exceptions were a favorite technique of the board in the first years of the program when accountants were easy to come by, social workers hard to find, and the strength of the board vis-à-vis state administrative agencies could be magnified by emphasizing accounting procedures. More recently, audit exceptions have become insignificant.

The most celebrated case of direct conflict between federal and state agencies in the early period of public assistance was that provoked by the activities of Martin L. Davey, Ohio's Democratic Governor, who had unexpectedly beaten New Dealer Charles Sawyer in the Democratic primary of 1934, thereby certainly starting off on the wrong foot in New Deal Washington. Although there is no evidence that Davey's success against Sawyer was the cause of his trouble with the Social Security Board, the Governor began with few friends in power to intercede for him when he needed to negotiate peace. When Oklahoma was caught in a misuse of assistance funds that same year, the intervention of Senator Elmer Thomas did not dissuade the board from action, but Thomas did serve as an intermediary who worked toward a solution. In Ohio, the public press became the intermediary; it was in the interest of the press to keep the charges flying, the conflict unresolved.

If the Social Security Board had been seeking a case on which to

[7] *Time,* March 7, 1938, p. 16.
[8] *New York Times,* November 24, 1938, p. 32. In February, 1937, Witte wrote that "it is not an easy matter to overcome the widespread confusion of old age assistance with flat pensions for all old people, which the Townsend movement has done so much to create." From Edwin E. Witte, *Social Security Perspectives* (Madison: University of Wisconsin Press, 1962), p. 119.

hang its claim for inclusion of a state merit system requirement in the federal act, it could not have found a more choice situation than that in Ohio in 1938. Ohio's Division of Aid for the Aged was characterized as "a political instrument to influence the votes of old age assistance recipients, applicants, and their relatives." The board alleged that the staff of the division had personally delivered Christmas letters informing OAA recipients of Davey's order increasing payments by 10 per cent together with his "earnest wish for a Merry Christmas and Happy New Year."[9] A printed statement, the charge continued, had been distributed to recipients over the name of the Chief of the Division of Aid to the Aged extolling the Governor as personally responsible for benefits for the aged in Ohio. Governor Davey was indignant. Asserting that he had done no more than write the OAA recipients a letter asking for their support on the basis of the many things he had tried to do for them, Davey acknowledged only that a little booklet written by the chief of the division was enclosed with his letter.

The board's charges were made public on August 6; the Democratic primary was held on August 9. Davey, who lost to Sawyer in his bid for renomination accused the board of playing "dirty politics on the eve of the primary election" by its threat to withhold federal funds.[10] The coincidence of dates underscores the fact that Davey was without a protector. It may be that, as Arthur Altmeyer said later, "you finally reach the point where final action must be taken,"[11] but no administrative agency is so politically insensitive as to take untimely punitive action against a state official who has friends in high places in Congress or the White House. Ohio was not the only state where OAA programs were involved in the 1938 primaries. The involvement in Ohio was extreme; the political leader was vulnerable.

In the play for power between the federal administrative agency and the states, the latter won the first pot when, in writing the 1935 act, Congress limited the Social Security Board's authority; in order to maintain the advantage, the states had to operate carefully. Imposition of federal standards by statute can be resisted as long as most states adopt standards for themselves that are not significantly below a level deemed reasonable by national authorities. If there had not been states that seemed deliberately to confuse the OAA program with an old age pension as a matter of right, it is unlikely that the act would have been

[9]*New York Times,* September 7, 1938.

[10]*New York Times,* September 19, 1938, p. 8.

[11]U.S. Congress, House, Committee on Ways and Means, Hearings, "Social Security Hearings Relative to the Social Security Act Amendments of 1939," 76th Cong., 1st Sess., 1939, p. 2400.

amended in 1939 to require the states to consider all income and resources in determining assistance budgets. Similarly, to forestall the imposition of a merit system requirement, the states would have had to avoid all sign of administration by political spoilsmen for political gain. It was too great a strain for a number of states, including Ohio; in 1939, the board had no trouble in having the act amended to include the merit system requirement that had been deleted in 1935.

Not only did the national agency win the second pot by the inclusion of a merit system requirement, it went on to win yet a third, in 1940, when the issue was whether Ohio was to be reimbursed by act of Congress for the loss sustained during the period of suspension in 1938. Congress was delighted to ratify what it thought was an accord between the participants. Although the Senate was told that an agreement had been worked out among the board, its general counsel, the Federal Security Administrator, and both senators from Ohio, and that all concerned were in complete accord and agreement on the matter of reimbursement, the accord was shattered after congressional action was complete. Arthur Altmeyer, finding the idea of reimbursing a state that had violated the act to be intolerable, went to the President and persuaded him to veto the bill. Roosevelt's message pointed out the danger of setting a precedent that "would mean that States no longer would be compelled to maintain the standards set up by the Congress but could violate these standards with impunity and still get their money."[12] If Ohio had been successful in its attempt to gain reimbursement, no state would consider itself seriously inhibited by the only real sanction available to the national agency — withdrawal of federal funds. The House, to which the veto message came first, was torn between pressure to squelch Altmeyer — "One little bureaucrat appointed to his office because he may have written a magazine article is more powerful than a Congress and a Senate elected by the people"[13] was one of the points made on the floor — and pressure to sustain the President and the integrity of the federal law. There were 19 more votes to override than to sustain, but nothing approaching the necessary two-thirds majority was secured. Two days after the veto was sustained, the board wrapped up loose ends by announcing that it would not reimburse Oklahoma for its loss during 1938 either.

Thus, by the beginning of 1940, the dealer was winning — the scales were tipped for federal supremacy. In its first years, the Social Security Board administered a public assistance program during a period of economic crisis. The popular mood reflected both sympathy

[12]*Congressional Record,* 76th Cong., 3d Sess., 1940, p. 650.
[13]*Ibid.,* p. 657.

for the recipients and indignation toward state politicians who were caught using relief as an instrument of partisan gain. The Washington bureaucracy abjured politics, embraced professionalism, and used accounting audits as the basis of its objections to state action. Before a wartime economy brought full employment, the national agency was in control. It had met and defeated the challenge of independent state action, had sustained its right to withhold money and to make it stick, had had the law changed to deny to the states their original rights to deal loosely with need as a requirement for assistance, to establish their own personnel policies, and to publicize relief data. At that point, says Altmeyer, who never shied away from enhancing federal authority, "we had all the authority we needed."[14]

III. CONFIDENTIALITY: A TURNING POINT

The requirement that states take action to insure the confidentiality of relief records—included in the package of restraints on state freedom adopted in 1939—was a reaction to the political excesses of the previous year. Choosing, for strategic reasons, to emphasize administrative rather than political considerations, the Social Security Board made its case for confidentiality in terms of the need to gain full cooperation from all the persons involved in an application; it also acknowledged an interest in protecting recipients from exploitation:

> The Board believes that such a provision is necessary for efficient administration, and that it is also essential in order to protect beneficiaries against humiliation and exploitation such as resulted in some States where the public has had unrestricted access to official records.[15]

Laws of most states had simply been silent on the subject of free access to the relief rolls by the general public. Where there was state legislation, it varied from California's protection of the lists, except by court order, to Colorado's provision for publication every six months in county newspapers. A relatively common statute making lien listings public—found, for example, in Kansas and Wisconsin—had the effect of opening at least part of the OAA rolls. But most of the evidence suggests that it was misuse of the records by some politicians (and some unscrupulous advertising uses), rather than any other factor, that led to congressional action.

In testimony before the House Ways and Means Committee,

[14]Personal interview.

[15]"Proposed Changes in the Social Security Act," *A Report of the Social Security Board to the President and to the Congress of the United States, December 30, 1938.* Reprinted in *Social Security Bulletin,* II (January, 1939), 17.

Arthur Altmeyer, supporting the confidentiality proposal, narrowed in on scandals associated with use of the rolls by politicians. "In a number of states, last year," he said, "the old age assistance lists were used by candidates for office, and the recipients were deluged with campaign literature and promises, counterpromises, and warnings, and counter-warnings, that created a very bad situation."[16] Altmeyer was presumably referring to the well-publicized case of Ohio, but members from Maine and Wisconsin and Kentucky were also sensitive to the question of pensions and politics in view of the 1938 campaigns in their states. Altmeyer detailed for the Ways and Means Committee in executive session some of the political uses of the rolls that the board objected to in 1938, including some cases that were not publicized.

In its report, the Ways and Means Committee noted only that "Provision is made to restrict the use of information concerning recipients of State old age assistance (particularly their names and addresses) to purposes directly connected with the administration of old age assistance. This is designed to prevent the use of such information for political and commercial purposes."[17] The amendment then adopted by the House required state plans for OAA, ADC, and assistance to the blind to provide "safeguards which restrict the use or disclosure of information concerning applicants and recipients to purposes directly connected with the administration of . . . assistance." Confidentiality was not even mentioned in hearings before the Senate Finance Committee, although the proposal to impose a merit system requirement did generate discussion there. No member of either house chose to defend the idea of free public access to public assistance lists, nor did any member suggest at this time—as many were to do a dozen years later—that publicity had a cleansing effect.

During the late 1940's, public assistance returned to the front page of the newspapers. Hanky-panky by state and local politicians was no longer the issue; now it was hanky-panky by the recipients that was the cause of trouble. State and municipal investigations of the costs and characteristics of the categorical programs and of general assistance drew press attention; press investigations in turn provoked more official state and municipal attention. In summarizing newspaper accounts and special reports, Donald Howard found that public assistance was under public attack in 16 of the 29 states studied in 1948. Six kinds of charges dominated these accounts and reports: many persons receiving public assistance should not have been doing so, either because they were really not needy or because relative responsibility should have

[16]Ways and Means, Hearings, 1939, p. 2407.
[17]*House Report 728,* 76th Cong., 1st Sess., 1939.

been enforced; social workers kept people on relief unnecessarily, policies were dictated by Washington and the states (rather than by locally developed programs); public assistance weakened people; assistance payments were too high; administration was inefficient. Press and investigative disclosures and charges of this sort were deemed to have an adverse effect on the program by undermining official, legislative, and public confidence in public assistance, and thus jeopardizing appropriations and public support. Whatever gains accrued in administrative efficiency and public concern were considered outweighed by the adverse effects.[18]

Critical examination of public assistance by press and official agencies should not have been unexpected at the time because the rolls were growing in a period of prosperity, when they were not supposed to. The program had been understandably unchallenged during the depression period, and the war years were peaceful years for relief. OAA recipients actually declined by 130,000 between 1941 and 1945, although the population aged 65 and over had increased by 1.2 million persons. In the same period, the number of children under age 18 increased by 1,020,000, but the total receiving ADC declined by 300,000. This was entirely consistent with expectations of declining relief loads in full employment and increasing loads in depression periods. But when the expected postwar depression did not set in, it became difficult for nonspecialists to understand why OAA recipients increased by as many as 750,000 from 1945 to 1950, when the aged population increased by 1.9 million. An increase of six million in the child population was accompanied by an increase of 1,010,000 children receiving ADC.[19]

Specialists found the increases troublesome enough to merit some effort at explanation. In 1951, for the first time, the Social Security Administration took formal cognizance of the fact that "questions were raised in some areas about the extent to which public assistance is needed in a period of full employment and high income levels."[20] The administration found population growth, inflation, less strict requirements of support by relatives, and increases in the divorce and illegitimacy rates to be the causes of heavy public assistance expenditures. A more detailed examination of the changes in the ten-year period

[18]Donald Howard, "Public Assistance Returns to Page One," *Social Work Journal,* XXIX (April and July, 1948), pp. 47-54, 114-20.

[19]U.S. Department of Health, Education, and Welfare, Bureau of Family Services, *Trend Report, Public Assistance and Related Data, 1962* (Washington, May, 1963), p. 60.

[20]Federal Security Agency, Social Security Administration, *Annual Report 1951* (Washington), p. 40.

1940-1950, made in the Bureau of Public Assistance, concluded, not unexpectedly, that the tripling of OAA expenditures and the quadrupling of ADC expenditures in the decade was a result "of a complex of factors."[21] Cost-of-living increases and population growth were acknowledged, but the instinctive reaction of those who claimed "not that much" was confirmed. Thirty-two per cent of the increase in OAA costs and 79 per cent of the increase in ADC costs were increases beyond the changes explained by inflation and population growth. Other factors included an increase in the proportion of the population aided (which, of course, is the real issue), an increase in the levels of assistance, and interaction between the two. With all of the social, economic, and technical factors evaluated, "the facts indicate a real growth in the number of persons covered by the programs and a true upward change in the standard of living provided assistance recipients."[22] In other words, allowing for all readily explained factors, the relief rolls and relief costs had still gone up very significantly.

Additional trial explanations for the increases in the number of relief recipients were forthcoming from the *Saturday Evening Post,* the *Detroit Free Press,* and the *Chicago Daily News,* each with a circulation somewhat in excess of that of the *Social Security Bulletin.* Each of these hypotheses cited fraud and inefficiency as causes; each of them pointed to public scrutiny of the relief rolls as the remedy. The report of the *Detroit Free Press* writer who had undertaken an investigation into public assistance in Detroit is representative of the group:

> A reading of the stories will prove conclusively, I believe, that social workers and welfare administrators have used the confidentiality of the records as a shield for their own malpractice. . . .
>
> Never once in the three years of Detroit welfare probes have social workers been able to bring forth a single recipient who has been rehabilitated as a result of social work techniques. . . .
>
> The Free Press has maintained that welfare records are public property by virtue of the fact the records are compiled by public servants who spend public funds in giving aid to persons supposedly in need.[23]

An important reason that confidentiality became a target was that it could be attacked and eliminated without really endangering the basic principle on which there was consensus: providing a minimum measure of the necessities of life for unemployables lacking these necessities. Of the particular conditions under which relief would be

[21]Ellen J. Perkins, "Old Age and Aid to Dependent Children, 1940-1950," *Social Security Bulletin,* XIV (November, 1951), 13.
[22]*Ibid.,* p. 29.
[23]*Congressional Record,* 82d Cong., 1st Sess., 1951, p. 12199.

provided, confidentiality was always one of the least secure. We have seen that its adoption came as a reaction to specific events. During the dispute over repeal, it was to be alleged that confidentiality was not even a workable remedy for the evil it was supposed to correct. Finally, vigorous attack came from the press which has a vested interest in "the public's right to know" that is comparable to the vested interest of welfare professionals in confidentiality. Under these circumstances, once press interests were reenforced by state government interests, the provision was doomed.

Confidentiality would not have been set aside if its newspaper and magazine opponents had not had assistance from the states' rights adherents. That assistance centered on Indiana's defiance of the federal act, based on the theory that the general question of secrecy of the rolls was beyond the reasonable scope of federal authority. Indiana's road to public assistance fame began accidentally rather than as a consequence of careful calculations. An Elkhart County prosecutor, suspecting that judgments against divorced fathers might be unpaid, tried to examine the ADC records to check his hunch. He was denied access, since his need was related to the efficient administration of the prosecutor's office, not to the efficient administration of the ADC program. The frustrated prosecutor, subsequently elected to the State Senate, cosponsored legislation requiring county welfare officials to provide other county officials with a quarterly roster of public assistance recipients and the amounts paid to each recipient. Amended to provide that the rosters be made available to the public, the bill was enacted over the veto of Governor Schricker. It was to become effective in July, 1951. Although comparable action was taken by the legislatures of Florida, Alabama, and Illinois, the Florida act fell under a veto, while the Illinois and Alabama statutes were made dependent on appropriate changes in the Social Security Act. Indiana, however, was uniquely and unabashedly out of conformity. After a hearing, Federal Security Administrator Oscar Ewing ordered federal funds discontinued, finding the state law to be in conflict with federal law.

Before Ewing acted, senators from Illinois and Indiana moved to support the asserted right of their states to provide for disclosure of relief rolls. Everett Dirksen of Illinois first intended to offer an appropriate amendment to the Federal Security Agency appropriation bill. A great many abuses could be traced to the fact that the rolls were not subject to public inspection, said Dirksen, adding that confidentiality "has created something of a difficulty, something of an organization, if I may use the term, among certain social workers."[24] Later

---

[24]*Ibid.*, p. 6425.

offered by William E. Jenner of Indiana in Dirksen's absence, the amendment was accepted without objection to be taken to conference. "I believe that it is necessary," said the subcommittee chairman in charge.[25] Guided by replies to a telegraphed inquiry to state governors, however, Senate conferees dropped the amendment for want of strong support from the state capitals.[26]

In light of subsequent behavior at the Governors' Conference in 1951, one may conclude that states' rights are more important to governors meeting in solemn conference than to individual governors answering telegrams alone. Jenner pushed his amendment aggressively. Adopted a second time by the Senate but lost in the House Ways and Means Committee, it was then attached to the Revenue Act of 1951. Meeting just as the congressional conferees on the Revenue Act were beginning their work, participants in the 1951 Governors' Conference forcefully attacked confidentiality in the presence of Oscar Ewing and of Arthur Altmeyer.[27] Its efficacy as a deterrent to political use of the relief rolls was explicitly denied by Governor Howard Pyle of Arizona:

> I have had the bitter experience in Arizona of discovering in the midst of a political campaign that the person against whom I was running had a very complete list provided by the old age organizations. . . .
>
> Now if a list can be available through the cooperation of the welfare people for the use of propagandizing the future of their welfare, then why shouldn't government, in its own defense, and the people, in their own defense, be given the privilege of making a list available for the contrary position?[28]

And Bracken Lee of Utah added testimony:

> . . . in 1950, in my state, the rolls were used . . . politically. . . . [Governor Edwin] Mechem, from New Mexico—tells me that they were used in 1950 for political purposes. . . .[29]

Herman Talmadge of Georgia was concerned with costs. A mandatory publication rule, he claimed, would cut down the Georgia rolls by one-third, or possibly even more. Fifty per cent of his mail, said Talmadge, was about the welfare program. Mennen Williams of Michigan pointed out that the right of the states to publish did not mean that

[25]*Ibid.*, p. 6477.
[26]Wilbur Cohen and Jules Berman, "A Chapter of Legislative History," *Social Service Review*, XXVI (June, 1952), 229-34.
[27]Glenn Brooks, *When Governors Convene* (Baltimore: Johns Hopkins University Press, 1961), pp. 68ff.
[28]*Proceedings of the Governors' Conference, 1951* (Chicago: author), p. 98.
[29]*Ibid.*, p. 115.

the states would necessarily publish data on recipients. The states' rights case was stated by Adlai Stevenson of Illinois:

> ... this is a very fundamental case of state responsibility. ... it should lie with the States to determine whether or not there should be any publicity with respect to their respective programs. ... it should lie with our individual states to determine whether or not — and to what extent, and with what suitable safeguards they choose to impose — there should be any publicity about the relief rolls.[30]

An informal resolution incorporating the Stevenson views passed unanimously. The unanimity of gubernatorial opinion was not lost on the conference committee. It reported a Revenue Act including a rider limiting the authority of the administrator of the Federal Security Agency to withhold federal funds if state legislation prohibits commercial or political use of public assistance data that may otherwise be made a matter of public record. Ewing was said to approve of the compromise arrangement involving the political and commercial usage prohibition. At the Governors' Conference, however, Ewing had stated that if Congress asked his advice, he would urge it not to enact a bill permitting the lists to be opened.[31] Some members of the House were of the same opinion. Winfield Denton, for example, did not approve of his own state putting a gun to the congressional head: "But the Indiana Legislature chose to take the State out of conformity with the Federal law, and keep it out, before Congress had an opportunity to take any kind of action. This deliberate and continued nonconformance has compelled Congress to act in haste, under the pressure of a local emergency forced upon it by a State legislature."[32] President Truman found the rider objectionable, too, but signed the bill explaining that the need for revenue outweighed his objection to a provision which "may well result in unwarranted publicity and personal indignity and unhappiness for aged people and others receiving public assistance."[33]

The effect of the Jenner amendment was more symbolic than practical. Tailored for Indiana which had the political and commercial usage prohibition in its statute, the amendment adopted ultimately had scant effect on the relief rolls there or in other states that opened their rolls.[34] Scarcely a year after passage, it was a matter of little interest. Few public inquiries were actually made in the nine states that pro-

[30]*Ibid.*, p. 95.

[31]*Ibid.*, p. 99.

[32]*Congressional Record*, 82d Cong., 1st Sess., 1951, p. 13279.

[33]*New York Times*, October 21, 1951, p. 57.

[34]Charles I. Schottland, "Social Work Issues in the Political Arena," *The Social Welfare Forum, 1953: Official Proceedings* (New York: Columbia University Press, 1953), pp. 27-28. See also Margaret Greenfield, *Confidentiality of Public Assistance Records* (Berkeley: University of California Bureau of Public Administration, 1952), p. 40.

vided access by January, 1953. There was no material effect on the case loads in those states. Hardly any so-called "cheats and chiselers" were exposed. By the same token, few otherwise eligible recipients preferred the hardship of voluntary withdrawal. For reasons more likely to be connected with the economic effects of the Korean War than any other single cause, OAA and ADC recipient rates both regularly declined in 1951, 1952, and 1953 from their highs in 1950. Nevertheless, Arthur Krock of the *New York Times* characterized the Jenner amendment as a very important piece of legislation because it represented one of the few assertions in recent years of states' rights over centralized federal bureaucracy.[35] And, by the time the 1953 state legislative sessions adjourned, 21 states had opened their rolls for public inspection. When the federal agency declared that its studies showed publicity to be ineffective in achieving withdrawals and harmful to the deserving, Governor Stevenson suggested the federal people try a restudy;[36] the President of the National Conference of Social Work reaffirmed a belief in confidentiality.[37]

The political importance of the confidentiality dispute is very great. First, it serves as a kind of turning point in the activities and authority of the federal agency in relation to state policy-makers. Before the Jenner amendment, the threat of federal withholding was real, while the likelihood of overcoming a decision of the administrator to withhold funds was not considered strong. Before the Jenner amendment, the amendments to the public assistance titles — aside from the changes in the federal sharing formula — had taken the form of corrective devices for state deficiencies in personnel standards and state political intrusion into relief. Now it appeared that a state with clean hands might achieve a desired change in federal law even if that change ran contrary to the predilections of the administrative agency. The success of the Jenner amendment suggested that in the making of categorical relief policy politicians could be no less influential than welfare professionals.

Second, the fact that the Jenner amendment actually had little impact on relief rolls and relief costs is important in view of the temporary peace that followed it. Proponents of the amendment did not try a follow-up attack on public aid as a concept. The year after passage of the amendment, Congress rushed through an increase in public assistance grants without bothering with hearings and without significant opposition. Seemingly content with their limited achievement, those who supported the repeal of the confidentiality item made no

[35] *New York Times,* October 25, 1951, p. 28.
[36] *New York Times,* May 26, 1952, p. 18.
[37] *New York Times,* May 28, 1952, p. 27.

mass attack on the whole program. Confidentiality almost seems to have been traded off for a few years of tranquility.

Third, the passage of the Jenner amendment brought added strength to those groups opposing federal liberalization of eligibility for public assistance. Welfare professionals continue to dream of amending the federal act to prohibit residence requirements as a condition of eligibility, to prohibit lien laws, narrowly to restrict relative responsibility provisions, and to eliminate categories and make need the sole determinant of eligibility. Rather than achieving success in these areas, they have sometimes seemed lucky to retain the *status quo*. Part of the explanation is that in this one great controversy that resulted in an actual test of the professionals' prediction of unhappy consequences they were wrong. That was more important than the fact that those who thought the Jenner amendment would work wonders in reducing costs were also wrong. The net conclusion must be that the amendment saved no money, but it did no demonstrable harm, and it made some taxpayers feel better.

Finally, the course of the dispute demonstrates the separate channels in which welfare professionals and politicians move. Social workers, who teach their students "to start where the client is" never considered where Congress was. The profession claimed that there was "differential treatment" involved in publicizing public assistance subsidies without publishing subsidies paid farmers and publishers. Actually, the latter are public records, but Congress was worried about public assistance, not farmers or publishers. Invoking the comparison was like telling a dependent old person that many old people work—an absurd, general nonsolution to a particular, real problem. Confidentiality was sold as a remedy for abuses by politicians; when it was repealed, however, the remedy for that evil was expressly retained. But the clientele of the *Social Work Journal* was told to view confidentiality as a professional tenet, its repeal as rejection of that previously accepted tenet. The whole structure was said to be in grave danger. "The attack [on confidentiality]," wrote a specialist in the field, ". . . is but one facet, perhaps the most immediately effective one, of a total attack on public assistance as such." And, further, the forces of light were exhorted to labor against the forces of darkness: "The success of the anti-confidentiality drive has been chiefly due to popular misconceptions. These constitute a major challenge to social workers and others whose business it is to understand the reasons people need public aid and the policies governing that aid."[38]

[38]Elizabeth Wickenden, "Confidentiality of Assistance Records," *Social Work Journal,* XXXIII (April, 1952), 91, 93.

Opponents of the Jenner amendment, resentful of Indiana's arrogant defiance of federal law, argued that Indiana could put its own house in order, if it had ineligibles on the rolls, without changing federal law. Proponents of the amendment argued the practical question of financial savings and the political question of curbing bureaucratic control. Welfare professionals argued that unorganized, underprivileged people should be protected against the possibility of a humiliation that they might or might not feel. It was a battle of the tangible against the shadowy. Many of the battles on welfare policy since that time have been of the same order; those with the tangible case usually win.

IV. CLASSIFYING THE NEEDY

Suitable Homes

Elimination of more than 20,000 children, most of whom were Negro, from the Louisiana ADC rolls in 1960 on the basis of a state decision involving suitable homes is more a part of the nationwide agitation about the ADC program than it is a question of federal-state policy differences but the latter element is abundantly present. Two months before the formal hearing on the question of the conformity of the Louisiana act to the Social Security Act, with the issue already known internationally, Health, Education, and Welfare Secretary Arthur Flemming stated that, although "the conscience of the country is aroused," there was very little room to intervene in the state welfare programs.[39] Proponents of firm federal action thought there was plenty of room to intervene. They pointed out, first, that differentiating between children by denying aid to one because his home is unsuitable and granting aid to another in a suitable home has no relation to the respective needs of the children; second, that a state so differentiating is not conforming with federal statutory requirements, perhaps even with constitutional guarantees of equal protection.[40] Others "urged the Department to look behind the statute. If it is satisfied that it was in fact adopted to threaten Louisiana's Negro citizens' pursuit of equal treatment, it would be unnecessary to examine further into the subtleties of Louisiana's ADC program."[41]

Passage of the suitable home legislation redeemed a campaign pledge of Governor Jimmie Davis — who took office in May, 1960 — to

[39]*New York Times*, September 23, 1960, p. 30.
[40]"Source Materials — Editorial Note," *Social Service Review*, XXXV (June, 1961), 205.
[41]*Ibid.*, p. 206.

halt the flow of tax dollars to unwed mothers who continued to bear illegitimate children. It left the Republican national administration in an awkward position. In the battle for southern support in the 1960 national election, a Washington ruling that Louisiana was out of conformity would not have been helpful to the Republican cause in that state. On the other hand, sustaining the state's action would have provided John Kennedy with the opportunity to accuse the Republican administration of disregarding Negro rights. The department apparently suffered from election paralysis: it was September before it first communicated with Louisiana, although the children were removed from the rolls in July. Then, to the probable relief of all parties, the hearing scheduled for late October was postponed until a week after the election. Some modifications of the original plan were agreed to in the course of hearings in November and December, modifications that were, however, largely procedural, involving written notices of the right to appeal and to a hearing, and referrals to juvenile court for children whose homes were deemed unsuitable.[42] Representative Otto Passman of Louisiana, usually known for his role in slashing foreign aid appropriations, testified at the first hearing on the intention of the writers of the Social Security Act to rule out federal interference in states' affairs.[43]

To rule Louisiana out of conformity on the basis of a denial of equal protection would have invited a judicial test of the ruling; to withhold funds on statutory grounds would have provoked a prompt effort to authorize a suitable home test in the Congress convening in January, 1961. Whether the suitable home law could have survived even the temporary cutting-off of federal ADC funds to the state is doubtful, but it would have been a ruling that could easily enough have been justified. Social Security Commissioner Mitchell and Secretary Flemming chose to go the other way. The Commissioner, taking note of the proposed procedural changes in the state plan and of the state's assurances with respect to its administration, found himself "constrained" to conclude that there was not sufficient basis for a finding of nonconformity "in the absence of any requirement prohibiting states to use 'suitable home' as an eligibility factor."[44]

In order to correct this situation, Mitchell asked for, and Flemming agreed to, a revised administrative policy providing that a state ADC plan may not deny assistance on a suitable home test unless and

[42]*Ibid.*, p. 205.

[43]*New York Times*, November 16, 1960, p. 25.

[44]"Decision of the Commissioner of Social Security: Opinion." Quoted in *Social Service Review*, XXXV (June, 1961), 208.

until appropriate provisions have been made otherwise to meet the needs of the child. In short, Louisiana was not to be penalized for outfoxing the federal people, but the hole was to be plugged and the state would then have to conform. The Flemming administrative ruling was established with a July 1, 1961, effective date. Legislation establishing an ADC program for children of the unemployed, passed in 1961 as a first order of New Frontier business, delayed implementation of the Flemming rule until September 1, 1962. The Public Welfare Amendments of 1962 then wrote into law that a state with a suitable home statute would not lose federal funds if provision were otherwise made by state statute for the adequate care of and assistance to the children involved. The effect is that suitable home statutes do not debar a state from federal funds. Children born out of wedlock may not be cut off from public assistance, but they may be treated differently from dependent children born of married mothers.

Protected from federal withholding for two years, Governor Davis did not do badly. In the end, even his law survived. When Secretary Flemming opened the exchange on the Louisiana law with the comment that there was very little room to intervene in the state welfare programs, the tone of federal action was established. To make a spirited attack on the Louisiana act, which was superficially aimed at discouraging illegitimacy, would have put the federal agency in the awkward position of opposing positive action to counter this social evil. At a time when the growth of the ADC program was a major fiscal problem, its defense was going to have to be made on some more generally acceptable grounds. On the basis of the outcome of the suitable home issue, neither Louisiana nor any other state had reason to feel that the federal leash was shortening.

Defining "Unemployment" in ADC-U

Any assumption based on the Louisiana outcome that a state could discriminate between classes of needy children was dispelled by the Department of Health, Education, and Welfare's firm stand against a 1963 Michigan ADC-U proposal. That proposal defined "unemployed" as persons who were eligible for unemployment compensation (which in Michigan is restricted to persons employed by employers of four or more employees) or who had drawn unemployment compensation after January 1, 1958.

Several features of the Michigan situation made it different from that in Louisiana. First, the Flemming decision in the suitable home case made the federal people look weak. A reassertion of federal authority was in order. Second, no one in authority at the national level had any reason to court the state leadership. George Romney, the new Governor (the first Republican elected to the office in 16 years), was considered a potential national political candidate and was actively espousing a states' rights position. Although formal responsibility was with Anthony Celebrezze, Secretary of Health, Education, and Welfare, Romney's real protagonist on the federal level was Wilbur Cohen. Cohen, who came to the job of assistant Secretary from a professorship at the University of Michigan, could claim a knowledge of the state, had been associated with the original professional drafters of the Social Security Act, and was in a secure position in the administration. He could not be cheerful about his own state adopting something less than what he regarded as an adequate plan. Third, the department had a kind of high level, unofficial representative in Michigan in the person of Fedele Fauri, Dean of the University of Michigan School of Social Work, former Legislative Reference Service specialist in the welfare field, and Cohen's old friend and colleague. Most important, however, Health, Education, and Welfare controlled the money. It was not obliged to provide the state a hearing. This was not so much a matter of cutting off support that had once been provided, with all the trauma and dislocations involved in such action, as a matter of just maintaining the *status quo* until the state decided whether it would capitulate or continue to go it alone.

On May 1, 1961, the Social Security Act was temporarily amended to permit the federal government to match state aid to dependent children if they have been "deprived of parental support or care by reason of the unemployment (as defined by the state) of a parent. . . ." The 1962 amendments made this provision a feature of the categorical assistance program until 1967. Michigan had not submitted a plan to the federal government to take advantage of the 1961 temporary provisions; however, Democratic Governor John B. Swainson had recommended two bills which the Republican-controlled legislature had refused to pass. In 1963, Romney proposed to a Republican legislature a state ADC-U plan that had been drawn by Willard Maxey, long-time Director of the State Department of Welfare. Maxey died only days before the state-federal controversy began. His successor, Lynn B. Kellogg, later suggested that the major reason Maxey recommended the moderate plan was the history of legislative disinclination to adopt a more liberal plan.[45] The strategy seemed effective when the Romney-endorsed Maxey plan passed the Michigan

[45]*Detroit News,* March 27, 1963.

House 89-14 and appeared to have clear sailing in the Senate. A month earlier, Maxey had taken the proper precautions by inviting an opinion from the Chicago Regional Office of the Department of Health, Education, and Welfare. The plan was approved in Chicago, a factor that is of considerable importance in later developments.

One of the first formal voices of protest to the ADC-U plan was from a Democratic state senator, one Philip A. Rahoi of Iron Mountain in the Michigan Upper Peninsula. On the very eve of expected Senate passage of the Romney bill, Rahoi telephoned Wilbur Cohen to raise the question of whether the bill met federal standards. But Fedele Fauri had already alerted the department so that after two calls from Cohen's office to Rahoi's secretary, the federal agency was ready to rule. A telegram from the Acting Director of the Bureau of Family Services, John J. Hurley, stated that the Michigan proposal which disqualified people "solely on the grounds of employment not covered under unemployment insurance is [an] unreasonable classification and not approvable under the social security act."[46] Denying that the measure was defective, Romney announced that he intended to sign the bill into law if the Senate passed it. The next day nine Democrats joined the Republicans to bring the vote for passage to 27-6. Romney, again promising approval, asserted that federal law gives the state – not the federal government – power to determine eligibility, and that he saw the matter as a question of states' rights versus federal dictation. In a speech before the Detroit Economic Club, the Governor took his stand on the preeminence of congressional rather than administrative policy-making and on his unwillingness to allow the federal government to "bring a state to heel for a federal handout."[47]

Celebrezze and Cohen based their argument on the department's right to judge the adequacy or inadequacy of standards rather than on the substantive adequacy of the proposal itself. In other words, unlike its position in the Louisiana case, Health, Education, and Welfare now adopted the position that its right to approve or disapprove, on the basis of its own interpretation of the law, was legally unassailable. The issue was thus moved from a question of whether or not the Michigan act was or was not "adequate" by some objective standard to a question of the federal administrative agency's legal right to make the decision. Romney, permitting Celebrezze to turn the question to one of authority, made it part of the national political debate by saying of the possibility of a victory for the department, "it would be something to keep eternally in mind when weighing the advantages of federal aid for

[46]*Detroit News,* March 19, 1963.
[47]*Chicago Tribune,* March 26, 1963.

medical care, for education, and in all other areas of social welfare."[48]

In his nationally syndicated column, William S. White put in a strong plea for the state position, arguing that not all wisdom resided in Washington. Perhaps more significantly, White found the dispute to be the "first truly gut clash" between the Kennedy administration and one of the powerful "new Republicans." Noting Romney's position as a possible Republican presidential candidate, White suggested that the national Democratic administration regretted the loss of party power in Michigan and was anxious to cut Romney down to size.[49]

One of the tactics employed by Romney, now in Washington to argue his case, was to attempt to obtain bipartisan congressional support for the contention that the federal government was flouting the "intent" of Congress. The Governor conferred with Celebrezze, but talked first with Michigan's Republican member of the House Ways and Means Committee, Victor A. Knox. Knox confirmed Romney's view that the federal government was invading state prerogatives as they had been established by Congress. Moreover, Knox stated that this opinion was supported by Ways and Means Chairman Wilbur Mills, a Democrat, and by the Democratic majority's legal counsel, John Martin.[50] Michigan's United States Senators Phillip A. Hart and Patrick McNamara, both Democrats, issued a guarded statement deploring the Michigan legislature's arbitrary restriction but remaining silent on the question of whether the plan could properly be rejected.

The alignment of groups within the state pitted the Republican Senate majority, Governor Romney, and the Director of the State Department of Social Welfare against the Democratic state senators, led on this issue by Rahoi who was later joined by Democratic Attorney-General Frank J. Kelley. The state Democratic organization kept its distance after the initial skirmish. For example, its chairman claimed that the Democrats had nothing to do with Rahoi's action, that if it meant "losing the bill, I'm going to regret it very much."[51] Former Governor Swainson made no comment on the issue, was never mentioned in the press. To be sure, once the issue became federalized, the state Democrats no longer needed to commit themselves to a policy position. If the plan was ultimately disapproved, they could point a blaming finger at the Republicans for the $9 million annual loss to the state and local units; if the plan was approved, they could show that it was less liberal than the one originally advocated by Democrats in the previous legislative session. Silence was the optimum strategy.

[48]*Ibid.*
[49]*Detroit News,* April 9, 1963.
[50]*Detroit News,* March 23, 1963.
[51]*Detroit News,* March 19, 1963.

This strategy was spoiled with the entrance of Attorney-General Kelley into the controversy. Kelley, criticizing Governor Romney for not submitting to him the legal opinion of Health, Education, and Welfare's counsel, Alanson Willcox, announced that he would go to Washington to obtain his own version of the issues. Romney goaded Kelley with a letter daring him to submit an opinion — an opinion that Romney certainly could guess would be hostile to the state's position.[52] On April 11, Kelley, who claimed "I am concerned only with the law," sent his opinion to the Governor and to Rahoi saying that the state ADC-U plan was unconstitutional because it was a denial of the "equal protection clause" of the Fourteenth Amendment and of the state constitution. He added that Romney was trying to take "food and clothing away from 20,000 children and make it look like a noble accomplishment." Kelley warned that he would support any suit that was brought on grounds of denial of equal protection of the laws — thus stripping the state of its legal counsel.[53]

The relative ease with which the objectors to the Romney plan were able to shift their legal ground is impressive. Regional Office approval of the proposal was explained away by Cohen as "unfortunate."[54] He said the officials there apparently looked at the bill according to the 1961 federal ADC-U act rather than the 1962 amendments, thus suggesting that the latter did something to change the allowable limits of state freedom to define unemployment. The original wire to Rahoi had also observed that "With the extension of the federal act, we now conclude that . . . [the Michigan plan] is unreasonable classification and not approvable."[55] But the 1962 amendments had made no change in the pertinent part — section 407(a) — of the Social Security Act. Introduction of the change in federal law to justify Health, Education, and Welfare's reversal of the opinion of its Regional Office seems to be one of those magnificent smokescreens which was so effective that the opposition was too blind to read the record. The subsequently released opinion of the General Counsel of the Department did not allude to the new law as contrasted with the old, while Kelley's legal position depended on the "equal protection" clause of the Constitution rather than on any language of the Social Security Act. The department might candidly have confessed error in judgment in the Chicago Office; instead, it suggested that its own people were operating under old rules.

Doing battle with the Romney plan caused Health, Education, and Welfare some additional embarrassment when it was pointed out that

[52]*Detroit News,* April 9, 1963

[53]*Detroit News,* April 12, 1963.

[54]*Detroit News,* March 20, 1963.

[55]*Chicago Tribune,* March 20, 1963.

approved plans operative in Oklahoma and in North Carolina utilized the unemployment definition proposed in the Michigan act. High-level officials in Washington simply had not been aware of the Oklahoma and North Carolina precedents up to that time. "But because we had not known," said one of them to an interviewer, "was no reason to ignore it when we found out." Both North Carolina and Oklahoma were then told that their plans were no longer acceptable and would have to be changed. Oklahoma, with only a handful of cases, agreed to make necessary changes; North Carolina was not prepared to be so coopera-tive, but the department could not back down. The North Carolina law was scheduled to expire June 30, 1963. Setting the date for compliance to coincide with the state's own expiration date was a convenient solution. Federal payment stopped at that time, either because the statute expired or because of the state's failure to meet the new requirements — depending on which explanation best suited the particu-lar spokesman.

In the fullness of time, Romney signed the Michigan act, the State Department of Social Welfare submitted the state plan, Celebrezze formally rejected the plan, and the state found itself in the frustrating position of being outmaneuvered by superior political strategy. Within Michigan, Romney's position evoked support from editorialists and his own party people. Many Michigan Republicans were privately convinced — on the basis of the North Carolina and Oklahoma prece-dents and the earlier approval by the Chicago Regional Office — that Michigan's real problem was Wilbur Cohen's seeking to advance a comprehensive welfare program he had supported since the days of the old Committee on Economic Security. If Swainson had still been governor, the argument goes, the 1963 plan would have been easily approved in Washington because the political desirability of opposing Romney would not have been an element to lend strength to Cohen's intellectual distaste for the plan. Moderate Republican legislative leaders considered the ADC-U dispute a made-to-order case for nonsegregationists to argue the cause of states' rights. No question of race discrimination was involved here; no evidence of any hidden motive was produced.

But the money was federal money. It became increasingly clear that Romney could solace himself only with the pleasures of standing on principle. Solace of this kind was expensive — the more so because the Michigan plan had not been developed to accomplish some special purpose dear to the heart of the governor or his associates. The plan had been developed, as has been noted, by an experienced professional welfare administrator who viewed it as administratively workable and politically feasible in the Michigan environment. As it became more and more apparent that the state administrative and political environment could not be viewed apart from the federal-state relationship, Romney was forced to rethink his position. The plan that he had supported because it seemed expedient turned out to be inexpedient. Since expediency had been the major criterion for selection, it was possible after a while to abandon the original plan in favor of a new try at an expedient plan that took the reality of the need for federal approval into the calculations.

Unlike the Louisiana case where the suitable home issue had racial overtones which seemed to underlie the state's interest in the policy, Michigan's proposed ADC-U policy was not designed to achieve a goal that could not be openly stated. It was designed to be adopted. Since it could not be adopted for an initially unanticipated reason, there was no rational alternative to trying to get another plan through both the Michigan legislature and the federal agency. Romney announced in November, eight months after the dispute, that he would follow such a course, this time choosing to start with what he knew the federal people would approve rather than with what he thought he could pass in Michigan. This was a tacit admission that the power balance cannot shift to a state's side until it is safely on the approved list for the federal grant. Deviants are likely to be pampered; holdouts are not tolerated. No one can play against the house unless the banker first admits him to the game.

CHAPTER V

The Politics of Eligibility

PUBLIC POLICY DOES not make hunger a sole criterion for relief. Federal law restricts categorical assistance to "needy" persons; it requires states to provide an opportunity for a fair hearing to any individual whose claim for aid is denied or is not acted upon with reasonable promptness; it nowhere provides that all "needy" persons must be deemed eligible for assistance. Long-time residence in the area, adherence to established standards of moral conduct, and a willingness to trade in certain personal liberties are among the common formal and informal noneconomic factors that go to make up eligibility in many jurisdictions. There is an implicit assumption in these requirements that a really needy person will not be a newcomer, will not sin, will have nothing to hide and therefore will submit to whatever searches of his physical premises are asked of him, and will accept intrusion into his emotional privacy by the welfare agency that dispenses services along with money.

Formal standards of eligibility for categorical assistance are spelled out negatively in the national act. No state plan can deny aid to a citizen of the United States, no OAA plan can fix an age requirement higher than 65, no residence requirement may be imposed that is longer than five of the previous nine years in the adult categories or longer than one year in ADC. The states are privileged to go beyond the areas of citizenship, age, and residence. In limiting formal economic eligibility, most states have enacted lien laws, relative responsibility provisions, and income and property limitations.[1] Noneconomic eligibility is a more subtle question.

---

[1] For a convenient compilation, see U.S. Department of Health, Education, and Welfare, Bureau of Family Services, *Characteristics of State Public Assistance Plans Under the Social Security Act* (Public Assistance Report No. 50; Washington, 1962).

I. NEED IS NOT ENOUGH

Eligibility in public assistance really turns on how much sacrifice a recipient is prepared to make. Initial and continued relief will depend on whether the sacrifice is deemed to be adequate to justify the granting of money without work. The decision is based on a complex of factors — some of which are reasonably objective and some of which are highly subjective — because, in addition to an economic sacrifice, the sacrifice required of a public assistance client may be physical, emotional, moral, or civil libertarian. These can be illustrated, respectively, by the very existence of the aid to the blind category, by insistence that public assistance recipients accept casework services as a condition of continued aid, by denial of further support to an ADC mother who does not maintain a "suitable home," and by unannounced searches of recipients' homes for evidence of circumstances of fraud.

There is disagreement both within the welfare groups and among politicians as to the merits of any particular one or another of these kinds of sacrifices. For example, most welfare people do not consider the need to accept casework services to be a sacrifice at all, but rather a bonus for the recipient. Others suggest that economic and psychological dependency may be separable, that either one may be the cause of the other, "but they may be found each without the other, and the existence of one does not automatically bespeak the existence of the other."[2] Conditioning relief on morality by imposing a "suitable home" test on the mother of a second illegitimate child has been proposed in more state legislatures than have ever adopted it as policy. But a requirement that, as a condition of eligibility, the ADC applicant who has been deserted by the father involved give aid to the law in tracking him down is part of the national act. The unannounced search is defended as a protection for the properly qualified recipient; it is also attacked as an intrusion of personal liberty in violation of the guarantee of the Fourth Amendment to the United States Constitution. A self-supporting person is free to move at will from a state with a lower minimum wage law to a state with a higher minimum; a public assistance recipient who moves to another state jeopardizes his continued assistance because of state residence requirements designed to discourage boundary jumping in a program that permits wide variations in benefits between states. If the precise forms of the sacrifice or sacrifices demanded of the recipient of public assistance may vary, it is clear that uncomplicated economic need will not bring uncomplicated economic relief.

[2]Helen Harris Perlman, "Are We Creating Dependency?" *Social Service Review,* XXXIV (September, 1960), pp. 323-33.

The Newburgh Crisis

When viewed in the framework of noneconomic sacrifice as a real if not explicitly stated condition of relief, events like the great Newburgh, New York, welfare crisis of 1961 become understandable, albeit not palatable. Joseph Mitchell, the Newburgh City Manager, promulgated a 13-point code of welfare regulations that dismayed the New York State Board of Social Welfare, the American Public Welfare Association, the International City Managers' Association, and most liberal and most middle-of-the-road groups concerned with social issues. The Newburgh code stands as an extreme expression of the position of those who demand noneconomic sacrifice as a condition of relief eligibility.

One important difference between the Mitchell directive and the position taken in other jurisdictions where there has been no national outcry is that Mitchell attempted to add to need 13 further eligibility conditions; other politicians have moved on only one or two fronts at a time. Another difference is that the tone of the Newburgh order was crass and punitive rather than legalistic. For example, while Item 8 of the 1961 Mitchell directive, providing that "all applicants for relief who are new to the city must show evidence that their plans in coming to the city involved a concrete offer of employment," was attacked along with the rest of the package, New York State that same year amended its social welfare law to require an investigation of newly resident applicants suspected of entering the state in order to receive public assistance and a denial of assistance where the suspicion is confirmed. Item 5 in the Newburgh package denied relief to all applicants who left a job voluntarily, "who have not been fired or laid off." This is not so different from the plight of ADC mothers in some California counties who have been in comparable jeopardy for declining employment. The Oregon ADC-U law denied relief to applicants who without good cause had quit a job. Good cause involved unusual hazards or substandard wages. The difference between Oregon and Newburgh on this issue is the difference between careful and sloppy draftsmanship.

Again, Item 7 of the Newburgh code stipulated that all files of all ADC cases were to be brought to the office of the corporation counsel for review every month; all new cases of any kind were to be referred to the corporation counsel before certification of payment. The City's Commissioner of Welfare was asked, during the State Welfare Board investigation, what appropriate state or federal statute he had cited to the City Manager in an effort to countermand Item 7. Objecting to the reply that there was nothing to cite, the board's Counsel suggested the existence of both state and federal statutory requirements for agency notice to a law enforcement officer in ADC desertion cases.[3] In other words, a basis for objection to Item 7 was a preexisting comparable federal requirement of notice. This is quite a different thing from objecting to the item because it imposed an undue or improper requirement on the recipients.

In the exchange regarding Item 2 which mandated work relief for "all able-bodied males on relief," Board Counsel Felix Infausto took pains to point out that the New York State law itself mandated work relief for employables in cases not covered by federal assistance. Federal objections, however, limited the extension of that policy to employable fathers in the ADC-U program. To seal the point, Counsel asked rhetorically, "And haven't you heard that the State Department of Social Welfare has indicated to Federal authorities that it doesn't agree with that policy?"[4] We are as much for work relief as is Mitchell, Infausto appeared to be saying; however, the imposition of work relief as a state eligibility condition comparable to the Newburgh condition was precluded by federal law.

The very first point on Mitchell's list would have overturned the practice of cash payment in relief and substituted voucher payments. Infausto's formal interrogation of Newburgh's Welfare Commissioner O'Donnell on this point was limited to a review of the applicable cash payment provisions of the state law and of similar provisions in the various titles of the Social Security Act. The conclusion was that the directive could not legally be implemented. But the Board Chairman, Myles Amend, later reverted to the voucher payment issue to go beyond the strict legalisms involved. Amend attempted to show that an allowable exception to the cash payment provision of state law—an exception surely designed to permit protective voucher payments where it is in the interests of the recipient himself—already made it possible to deviate from cash payments in exceptional cases. Moreover, he took the witness back to the depression period to establish that the system of voucher payments then used in New York resulted in "fairly widespread" abuses, so that the conclusion would be that "the change from cash to voucher doesn't necessarily mean the elimination of abuses where they occur."[5] In this line of inquiry, Amend was making no frontal attack on voucher payments as a technique that sets welfare recipients apart from the rest of the population. The merits of

[3]New York State Board of Social Welfare, Hearing, *In the Matter of Investigation of Public Welfare in the City of Newburgh* (Albany, N. Y., July 7, 1961), p. 81.
[4]*Ibid.*, p. 67.
[5]*Ibid.*, p. 78.

voucher payments were not being considered beyond the questions of (1) legality under preexisting statutes, and (2) efficiency in reducing costs and eliminating abuses.

It is quite possible that the New York State Social Welfare Board had concluded that the Newburgh program was intolerable as a matter of ethics, but most vulnerable as a matter of law. Its subsequent statement ordering the Newburgh officials to refrain from implementing the Mitchell directive had an angry tone; the criticism used such language as "inhuman and indecent" and "intimidate the needy and helpless."[6] But it was really an easy case. Mitchell, acting from instinct and without information, was vulnerable to an information-oriented response. Newburgh did not have the kind of relief load that Mitchell claimed it had, its expenses for welfare were not what he said they were, the welfare program in Newburgh was not attracting "the dregs of humanity into this city . . . [in a] never ending pilgrimage from North Carolina," and the city was not subsidizing "the migration of unemployable people."[7] If Mitchell had been more careful of his facts and his statistics, if he had consulted a lawyer and hedged rather than hollered, if he had been pushing a more limited program restricted perhaps to three or four points rather than a grandiose, sloppily developed list of 13, he would have created less attention and might have been able to implement his program. The Newburgh directive really asked the recipient to make a maximum number of noneconomic sacrifices all at once. In other jurisdictions, only one or two of them are asked for at a time, and this is less likely to create a *cause célèbre*.

II. CONSTRAINTS ON CLIENT BEHAVIOR

The overriding policy conflict in public assistance is between those who would impose constraints on the behavior of relief recipients and those who focus on need as the sole issue. Clients whose claims are based on physical sacrifice are the least harassed. There are few continuing fundamental battles regarding the aid to the blind program or the aid to the disabled program, largely because the physical impediment is understood to be an act of God entirely beyond the control of the individual to have prevented it. This special status that is bestowed on aid for the blind was illustrated in a proposal to amend the Illinois Constitution, offered in February, 1963, by five state legisla-

[6]New York State Board of Social Welfare, Press Release, July 18, 1961.
[7]Meg Greenfield, "The 'Welfare Chiselers' of Newburgh, N. Y.," *The Reporter,* XXV (August 17, 1961), 37. Mitchell subsequently left the manager field and in the summer of 1964 became a field director of the Citizens Councils of America, a segregationist group.

tors. The amendment would have added to age, citizenship, and residence qualifications for the right to vote, a further qualification that the voter not have received poor relief or other public assistance for eight months prior to the election. Recipients of aid to the needy blind, however, were specifically excepted.

OAA is a less clear-cut case because, although aging is obviously involuntary, there remains the suspicion that irresponsibility is involved in the failure to have provided for one's later years during a working lifetime. There are complicating factors in the old age problem, however, and if a failing in character is noted the politician is likely to attribute the failing to children who neglect responsibility for aged parents rather than to the recipient himself. (Even Newburgh exempted the aged, blind, and disabled from a three-months limitation on relief payments.) In any event, the situation is beyond repair by the time that OAA is required. Little can be done beyond urging recipients to cooperate in seeking help from responsible relatives. The aged cannot as a matter of free will control their age, nor can the blind control their lack of vision, nor the disabled control their disabilities. No *quid pro quo* for relief payments can be demanded of these groups. Just becoming a victim of blindness, disability, or old age represents the recipients' part of the barter. It may not be a fair trade, but it is entered into in good faith by both sides.

Because fewer and fewer ADC cases involve comparable involuntary physical sacrifice, that program is caught in sharper political conflict than the others, and in sharper political conflict than it was in earlier years. Within the ADC group, there is a striking decline in death of the father as a cause of dependency, a sharp increase in deserted and unmarried mothers. Many politicians view this as a shift from a program to meet involuntary dependency to a program that meets voluntary dependency. At the core is the nagging and compelling argument advanced by the politicians that conception is a voluntary act, that conception outside of marriage is frowned upon by society, that illegitimacy is antisocial even when the child does not become a public charge, that the unwed mother who conceives again when she is already dependent on public assistance does not come with clean hands and thereby forfeits any claim to unrestricted freedom of action. As the adult ADC recipient group has changed, noneconomic eligibility conditions have been developed to fit the dominant new group.

The dependent children program was largely ignored for the first dozen years of its existence because it fit the original public assistance model: the exchange of involuntary helplessness for public support. Death of a father was in the same class as blindness or disability;

imprisonment was beyond the control of the felon's family. The test was whether or not the recipients could control their own fate; clearly, widows could not. When 88 per cent of state supported children's aid cases involved death of the father[8] (which was the case in the period immediately preceding passage of the Social Security Act), politicians found no problems associated with voting public funds to support the program. The figure declines to 37.2 per cent in 1942 and to 21 per cent in 1951, downward shifts that are in part attributable to the survivorship insurance program adopted in 1939. The present turmoil in ADC may be best understood when it is noted that by 1962 barely 7 per cent of ADC cases involved death of the father, a drop of 30 per cent in two decades, and a revolutionary change from the circumstances that brought about the original program.[9]

The Noleo Amendment

A half-way point in the voluntary-involuntary dependency continuum exists in the case of desertion. Here, the crisis leading to ADC status is not an act that requires compliance of the mother as is the case in illegitimacy. On the other hand, it is consistent with a theory of self-determination to argue that the deserted mother is able to take steps that may lead to finding the father and compelling him to support his family. The deserted mother is not helpless in the same fashion as the widow or the prisoner's wife. Predictably enough, desertion became the first area in which there was an important move to impose a new noneconomic eligibility condition.

In the late 1940's, ADC desertion cases were a more significant problem than illegitimacy, and they were catching up on death cases.[10] The political response was an effort to make aid dependent on the willingness of the deserted mother to cooperate in attempts to reestablish the socially accepted pattern of responsibility of the father for his family. The mechanism was a legal requirement that law enforcement officials be notified of desertions in order that efforts could be made to locate the father. Congress wrote the requirement — popularly referred to as Noleo (for "Notice to Law Enforcement Officials") — into the

[8]Committee on Economic Security, *Social Security in America* (Washington: Social Security Board, 1937), p. 242.

[9]U.S. Department of Health, Education, and Welfare, Bureau of Family Services, *Trend Report, Public Assistance and Related Data, 1962* (Washington, May, 1963), p. 21.

[10]U.S. Congress, House, Committee on Ways and Means, Subcommittee on Social Security, Hearings, "Analysis of the Social Security System," 83d Cong., 1st Sess., 1953, part 3, pp. 301, 304; and *Proceedings of the Governors' Conference, 1951* (Chicago: author), p. 90.

Social Security Act in 1950 while welfare groups were still trying to decide whether or not to support anything other than need as a condition of eligibility.

Noleo was an attempt at compromise in the conflict between a belief that support of dependent children is a socially desirable act and a belief that society should not countenance the delinquency of a father who fails to assume his obligation to support his children. The effect of the amendment is to require state public assistance agencies to develop plans for prompt notice to law enforcement officials in all cases in which aid is furnished to a deserted or abandoned child. For notice to be furnished, it is obviously necessary that the applicant for aid furnish the agency with the name of the deserting father. This feature imposed a qualification for aid that is unrelated to need and unrelated to the other traditional qualifications of residence and citizenship. "To the established functions of the public welfare agency," Maurine McKeany wrote in her study of Noleo, "the Noleo amendment adds a new function which makes the welfare agency a vehicle of social compulsion."[11]

Devised as a constructive means of aiding support to families without imposing difficult conditions on the recipient, the amendment was directly stimulated by the decision of a House Judiciary subcommittee to hold hearings on the question of making abandonment of dependents a federal crime.[12] The Department of Justice opposed putting problems of domestic relations in the federal courts. Spokesmen for the Children's Bureau and for the Federal Security Agency took a similar position. A pending bill offered by Representative Tom Steed of Oklahoma, however, was obviously getting some support, and a compromise arrangement was worked out by Fedele Fauri, then a specialist with the Library of Congress Legislative Reference Service. The Steed measure, providing for federal prosecution of deserting parents who cross state lines, also made it mandatory for welfare workers to advise prosecuting attorneys when a child of a deserting parent received public aid. Fauri's compromise served to eliminate the federal criminal aspect of Steed's bill. This removed the sting of requiring a deserted mother to take the first steps in a path that could lead to federal prosecution of the father of her children, leaving the option of pursuing or not pursuing the father to local prosecuting

[11]Maurine McKeany, *The Absent Father and Public Policy in the Program of Aid to Dependent Children* (University of California Publications in Social Welfare, Vol. 1; Berkeley and Los Angeles: University of California Press, 1960), p. 67.

[12]U.S. Congress, House, Committee on the Judiciary, Subcommittee Number Two, Hearings, "Making Abandonment of Dependents a Federal Crime," 81st Cong., 1st and 2d Sess., 1949, 1950, pp. 25-26.

attorneys who frequently lack the facilities and the inclination to chase deserting fathers. In 1955, Social Security Commissioner Charles Schottland explained that for a local prosecutor to go after a father "is a long and expensive process. To get a father and get support or to prosecute him is a longer process and costs more money than to handle a major crime in the local courts where you can get the persons in that county."[13] Viewed purely from the standpoint of economy, it would likely be more efficient to use federal facilities for the prosecution, but the objection to federalizing domestic relations law is a substantial one.

Welfare people found it difficult to make up their minds about Noleo. The lobbyist for the American Public Welfare Association explained that the association had not made a formal study of the legislation; in her opinion, however, "a law of this kind would in part keep people from being needy."[14] With this kind of in-part approval there went opposition to including support legislation of any kind in the Social Security Act and an expressed preference for separation of support legislation from welfare legislation.

Noleo was a hesitant, tentative step. It required only notice, included no sanction to compel notified officials to proceed to action. What Noleo did do was to transfer the element of discretion from welfare to law enforcement officials. "Congress, in initiating and adopting the amendment," explained Wilbur Cohen, "was responding to public opinion and at the same time attempting to work out something constructive without infringing on states' rights or broadening the area of Federal control over family matters or changing the basic principles of the ADC program."[15]

The transfer of discretionary authority on the horizontal level from welfare to legal agencies of local or state governments is more significant than the maintenance of the nice balance between federal and state power in the domestic relations arena. This transfer of discretion, removing from the welfare professional the opportunity to make subjective judgments about his cases, flies in the face of the professionals' efforts to provide economic, emotional, and social services as an integrated whole. Sometimes those services will be more effective, the argument goes, if the recipient is not compelled against her will to become an instrument of the law. In some circumstances, a recipient will deprive her child of the benefits of a public program created to aid

[13]U.S. Congress, House, Subcommittee of the Committee on Appropriations, Hearings, "Departments of Labor and Health, Education, and Welfare Appropriations for 1956," 84th Cong., 1st Sess., 1955, p. 1235.

[14]McKeany, pp. 43-44.

[15]Wilbur J. Cohen, "Factors Influencing the Content of Federal Public Welfare Legislation," *The Social Welfare Forum, 1954* (New York: Columbia University Press, 1954), p. 209.

the child rather than participate in legal harassment of the child's father. The social worker feels that she alone should be in a position to make decisions about these kinds of problems.

At the time that Noleo was being worked out, positions of the two sides were not as firm as they were to become the following year when the same basic conflict in philosophy emerged in the Jenner amendment over the issue of confidentiality versus open access to the names of public assistance recipients. Later, the questions of suitability of the home as a test for ADC eligibility and of so-called midnight searches involved some of the same underlying differences. The continuing dispute over the provision of birth control services to relief recipients is another reflection of the same problem although it has some more complicated twists. The Noleo amendment of 1950 was a sign that legislative good will toward public assistance had passed its peak, that "Congress lacked confidence in the exercise of discretion by welfare agencies and feared that they were indifferent to whether the absent father fulfilled his family obligations or not, so long as the children's needs were being met."[16] The particular type of noneconomic eligibility condition prescribed by Noleo was a mild one, but it made clear that special behavior not applicable to nonwelfare recipients – in this case mandatory reporting of desertion – would be expected of recipients.

One hard-core problem that stands between public assistance professionals and political professionals is that politicians assume that any public agency should be available for use as an instrument to help compel compliance with any social policy that has achieved the status of statute law. They assume further that the beneficiary of a public program must provide any information pertinent to his application for aid, certainly including information that could conceivably lead to a change in status. Professional welfare people, on the other hand, believe that agency goals – in this case, the fulfillment of need – are not only primary but exclusive considerations. They would meet need without restraints, restrictions, limits, or any other factor that will act to distinguish recipients of assistance from nonrecipients. The ADC mother who chooses not to divulge the name of her deserted child's father is no less needy than the mother who does provide the information, and it is the function of the public welfare program and the public welfare agency to meet need. It is a legitimate enough governmental function, says this argument, to try to punish desertion and to secure support, but it is a legal agency's function. To involve welfare through a hard and fast requirement for notice may impair the value of casework services.

[16]McKeany, p. 120.

Politicians are less client-oriented and more constituent-oriented than social workers. Casework services in a public assistance agency, say the politicians, are provided by tax dollars. Where a mother declines to provide the name of a deserting father, a legitimate opportunity to conserve some of the taxpayers' money is lost. The politician thus notes that where the function of the welfare agency may be to satisfy need, the function of the politician is to provide funds to satisfy that need but also to provide funds for other public purposes. If, in order to conserve public money for other purposes, the welfare agency must be made in McKeany's terms, "a vehicle of social compulsion," so be it. And if it is a vehicle of social compulsion to enforce constitutionally valid social policy for which there is widespread approval, neither regrets nor apologies are necessary.

The Welfare Search

The problem is quite a different one when the noneconomic eligibility condition imposed cannot survive a civil liberties test. Free citizens in a free society are accustomed to controlling their own time and to restricting access to their homes to invited guests, but public assistance recipients are expected to accept intrusions on the privacy of their homes by unannounced investigators whose time of arrival is designed to be inconvenient for the recipient. Except in the limited number of states that since 1961 have adopted programs accepting unemployment as an eligibility factor, ADC mothers are supposed to run "manless" households. The unannounced search of the home of a recipient of assistance is part of the effort to insure manlessness, presumably part of the effort to eliminate fraud in the program. In the manner of the big-city police department that sends its prowl cars to pick some classes of citizens off the streets late at night for interrogation, some communities play no less recklessly with the civil liberty of their welfare clients. Rationalizations made by the police that a crime has been committed and that there is reasonable ground to suspect the particular person picked up cannot usually be made applicable to the unannounced midnight welfare search. The latter is carried out without the probable-cause element. The welfare search is one thing when carried out with a warrant at the home of a particular client who has given probable cause to suspect fraud; it is another thing when it is established as a general check or as a policy to harass recipients as a class.

Although an occasional unannounced search for hidden treasure is part of the OAA antifraud machinery, ADC cases bear the brunt of the search problem. The disposition to be tolerant of hidden resources that might affect OAA or aid to the blind eligibility is greater than the disposition to be tolerant of a man in the house whose presence would be a barrier to ADC eligibility. The ADC recipient who hides a man in the house has, after all, made no physical sacrifice comparable to that made by the OAA client or the blind client to earn his grant. By sustaining a paramour, the ADC mother rejects the alternate sacrifice — chastity — that is demanded. In accepting ADC, the client has made the public welfare agency guardian of her morals, has contracted away any right to live in sin. Because some clients cheat on the contract, the public that dispenses charity has added the requirement of a sacrifice of civil liberty — the welfare search.

Is there any basis in American constitutional law for a defense of the welfare search? Charles A. Reich, writing in the *Yale Law Journal,* notes that if such searches are not to be in violation of the Fourth and Fourteenth Amendments to the United States Constitution, they would have to be justified by one of the following arguments: that the searches are conducted with the expressed or implied consent of the recipients; that the object of the searches is not to secure evidence for criminal prosecution or forefeiture; that the searches, under all the circumstances, are reasonable. But Reich concludes after an analysis of the appropriate case law that there is no theory under which it can be said that public assistance recipients consent, expressedly or by implication, to searches of their homes; that the object of welfare searches generally is to put the recipient in jeopardy of criminal prosecution or to subject him to deprivation of benefits which might well be considered the modern equivalent of a forefeiture; and that inspecting the homes of public assistance recipients without warrants is, regardless of variations in circumstances, unreasonable. "In sum," Reich says, "midnight welfare searches, as commonly practiced, are a flagrant violation of the fourth and fourteenth amendments."[17]

Public assistance clients are not in a position to argue that the niceties of constitutional law preclude the admission of an unannounced welfare investigator. Even in the unlikely case of a client who is aware of these niceties, the choice is either to waive the constitutional protection and continue to receive economic assistance, or to waive continued economic assistance and draw sustenance from the bill of rights.

One of the comments made by the Comptroller-General of the

[17]Charles A. Reich, "Midnight Welfare Searches and the Social Security Act," *Yale Law Journal,* LXXII (June, 1963), 1348, 1355; See also Reich, "Individual Rights and Social Welfare: The Emerging Legal Issues," *Yale Law Journal,* LXXIV (June, 1965).

United States in his critical appraisal of the adequacy of the nationwide review of eligibility in the ADC program—a review stimulated by the Byrd inquiry into fraud and ineligibility in the District of Columbia program—had to do with the techniques for home visits in the review process. Noting that Health, Education, and Welfare instructions to the review teams were silent as to the extent that the premises of the recipients should be inspected, and that the instructions did not comment on the time that home visits should be made other than to suggest "evening or weekend visits to some families if deemed necessary" in order to see all members of the ADC assistance group and other members of the immediate household, the Comptroller-General reported to the Senate Appropriations Committee his own views as to where to inspect:

1. Inspection of the sleeping arrangements may disclose the presence of people not included in the assistance group or that the father has returned to the home. . . .
2. Personal property of measurable value may be observed in any room. . . .
3. The observation of uniforms, badges, or other articles in bedrooms or closets may be indicative of employment and income affecting either eligibility or the amount of the assistance payment.

As for the timing of visits, the Comptroller-General comments that "there are fact-finding advantages in making initial visits to homes of AFDC recipients at other than normal weekday hours. It would appear that visits made at other times would more likely disclose the actual persons in the regular household unit."[18]

In the abstract, the idea of an investigations officer checking on eligibility of a client through a field visit appears both reasonable and sensible. But abstractions are not realities, and welfare searches are not field visits. The public agency would not be properly discharging its responsibility to its taxpayer clientele if it did not look behind the formal application. It is the description of "the normal procedure" followed in the making of a night call that makes it evident that there is a substantial difference between what is blandly called an unannounced field visit and the actual midnight welfare search. Consultants to the California Welfare Study Commission visited twelve California counties in 1962 to study relationships between welfare departments and law enforcement agencies. Sixty-nine per cent of the ADC case load of the state was found within the twelve counties involved. Night calls were

[18]U.S. Comptroller General, "Observations on the Adequacy of the Nationwide Review of Eligibility in the Aid to Families with Dependent Children Program," *Report to the Committee on Appropriations, United States Senate* (Washington, 1963), pp. 20-21, 22.

made in seven of the twelve counties visited. The consultant describes the calls:

Under the normal procedure one investigator goes to the front door, another to the back door (to make certain that the man does not escape that way), the door bell is rung, the investigators identify themselves, and ask if they may come in. They may say they want to look for a man, or they may say they are "making a routine check and want to see the conditions of the home and how the children are being cared for." The investigators then go through the house looking in closets, drawers, attics, medicine chests, children's bedrooms, and under the bed. They look not only for the man but for evidence of clothing, toilet articles, and personal effects that would indicate a man is living there. The search is usually made between 10 p.m. and 4 a.m. Most investigators prefer to wait until the house is dark as they say this increases the possibilities of catching a man in bed and makes for a stronger fraud case.[19]

There is only limited concern about the constitutional rights of welfare recipients — and particularly is there little interest in the constitutional rights of ADC mothers. Although Reich calls the midnight welfare search a "common practice" in many states, none of the several recent national administrators have raised the question of the propriety of continuing federal aid to a state that administers its state plan in apparent violation of the Fourth and Fourteenth Amendments. The September, 1961, Ad Hoc Committee Report did not deal with this question nor did the report submitted to the Secretary of Health, Education, and Welfare a month earlier by his special consultant, George Wyman.[20]

A recent interest in the problem of protecting the legal rights of the indigent has extended to the issue of bail for the accused indigent person. In the now celebrated Gideon case, the issue of providing counsel for the poor was resolved. Protecting the assistance recipient from improper searches, however, presents some special problems. There is no easy way to force this issue in the courts. Clarence Gideon did not choose between having a public defender and not having a public defender.[21] Denied a public defender and subsequently imprisoned, he had everything to gain by challenging the system. But the welfare recipient would have to put principle over relief. It is simply

[19]California State Department of Social Welfare, Welfare Study Commission, *Consultants' Reports* (Sacramento, Calif., January, 1963), pp. 299-300.
[20]Sanford Solender, Chairman of the Ad Hoc Committee, did attack midnight raids as a violation of civil liberty in his 1963 presidential address to the National Conference on Social Welfare; see *New York Times,* May 20, 1963. The National Association of Social Workers also issued a statement on the right of public assistance recipients to privacy; see National Association of Social Workers, *Midnight Raids* (New York: author, 1964).
[21]See Anthony Lewis, *Gideon's Trumpet* (New York: Random House, 1964).

too much to expect that an alert and high-principled client will refuse entry to an investigator, be dropped from the rolls, and with the help of a civil liberties group seek judicial relief. The stakes are too high for the client to play that game.

Legislative prohibition of the practice or a finding by the federal agency that unannounced night welfare searches constitute grounds for disapproval of a state plan may be more practical approaches, but there is considerable doubt that they are any more realistic. Few congressmen give evidence of knowing or caring much about the details of public assistance policy or administration. Where the announced goal is to uncover suspected fraud, Congress on the basis of the Noleo and confidentiality precedents would be likely to support an antifraud drive. The prospect of the federal administrative agency taking the initiative in this area is not bright. Leaders in the agency will push hard on behalf of equal protection for children in the program. This is the consideration that was dominant in the issuance of the Flemming ruling in January, 1961, forbidding imposition of a suitable home qualification unless adequate provision is made for the support of the children affected by the consequent denial of aid. Again, the department's explanation of its firm stand in the Michigan ADC-U controversy is that the principle of equal protection of children was the point at issue. But the welfare search cannot be said to discriminate between classes of needy children. Although the emotional upset to a child whose home is being searched may be considerable, it is the privacy of the mother that is being invaded. Clearly, the political position of the department would not be strong if it moved to deny aid to a state that was using methods recommended by the Comptroller-General to keep assistance rolls clean of fraud.

The conclusion is apparent. No practical mechanism appears to exist for the protection of the constitutional rights of public assistance recipients in the matter of improper searches other than the self-restraint of the state investigating agency or the willingness of the client to trade economic assistance for the return of his civil liberty. In the latter event, of course, the client has ceased to be a recipient of public aid and the issue no longer exists. The likelihood of self-restraint being exercised by the appropriate state agencies is an imponderable, although there is evidence that some responsible officials may be willing to switch from search to surveillance. But the welfare search persists because the sacrifice of the constitutional protection is virtually the only noneconomic sacrifice that can be enforced against some ADC mothers, when public policy still seems to demand that the assistance recipient be disadvantaged in some way in addition to just being poor.

Birth Control

Birth control has been an important issue in ADC since 1950 because of the large reduction in that part of the ADC dependency rate caused by death. Incapacity, family conflict, and unmarried motherhood which now account for 79 per cent of ADC cases all carry the possibility of further procreation and consequent additions to the public assistance rolls. Family conflict, which includes separation and desertion, as well as divorce, and unmarried motherhood both present special social problems because of the likelihood of impulsive cohabitation as part of a temporary reunion or as part of a trial relationship that breaks up quickly. Temporary or casual sexual relationships is one of the luxuries most relief clients are expected to sacrifice.

Both the unmarried mother and the married ADC mother would benefit from avoiding pregnancy. Indeed, it is expected that this will be the case; deviants are punished in some cases by removal of the child from the home, in others by the need to work budget miracles. Although abstinence is not demanded of the married welfare recipient in the ADC-U program, the typical budget standards discourage additional births. A personal allowance of $19.85 per month for a child under 6 (in a liberal state) could hardly encourage any rational recipient to plan on additional children. A child of dependency brings only a meager economic reward to the parent. Paradoxically, although public policy expects the relief client to avoid conception it usually denies the client information on and materials for birth control. The ideal client is simply expected to be more chaste than the rest of society.

Illegitimacy is the great political problem area in the dispute over birth control for ADC cases. Recent evidence stemming from a bitter fight in Illinois in 1963 over efforts to provide birth control materials to public assistance clients at public expense suggests that even in a state with a heavy Catholic population a prompt compromise arrangement is feasible, at least allowing state payment for contraceptive materials furnished to a married welfare recipient living with her husband. But such a restricted policy, reaching only a small percentage of ADC cases, is inadequate as a way of controlling the birth rate in the dependent group. The ADC manless household is far more procreative than is the ADC married couple.

Those groups that would make birth control information and devices available to welfare recipients at public expense and without restriction are led by the Planned Parenthood Association which has an interest in birth control that transcends the public assistance aspect. The vocal opposition is led by spokesmen for the Catholic Church which has an antipathy to artificial birth control that similarly transcends the public assistance aspect. Where public funds are not involved, the birth control battle is waged publicly in moral, ethical, and spiritual terms; in the last analysis it is a personal decision that can be and is made in secrecy and privacy. Where public funds are paying the costs involved, however, the decision for or against birth control is taken out of the secret classification; it becomes especially important to each of the protagonists to be on the winning side. In 1960, Norman St. John-Stevas' convincing report on *Birth Control and Public Policy,* recognizing the intensity of the dispute over public funds for birth control, concluded that conflicts of principle between Protestants and Catholics as to whether birth control advice should be given in tax-supported hospitals are irreconcilable, that only a working compromise is possible. Significantly, St. John-Stevas also concluded that Anglicans and Protestants would limit the role of law, in relation to contraceptives, to preserving public order and decency, and might favor a ban on sales to unmarried persons under a certain age.[22] In other words, although non-Catholics might favor giving birth control advice in tax-supported hospitals, they acknowledge that public order and decency may require some legal restraints on the availability of birth control devices. If this is so, it seems most unlikely that there will be widespread support for a public subsidy for contraceptives for unmarried welfare clients whose use of the materials would presumably violate commonly expressed standards of public decency.

There are some unmistakable signs of a breakthrough on the birth control front. Michigan's Social Welfare Board has authorized the provision of information and services without regard to marital status. New York State's board announced its intention to do the same. An Illinois legislative commission recommended extension of publicly supported birth control services to mothers, married or unmarried, who are welfare clients; the legislature complied. Everywhere, however, there has been strong opposition, and it is not certain that these new policies will survive legal or legislative attacks. A few years ago, the weight of objections quietly smothered a comparable Pennsylvania effort after board action was taken but before it could ever be implemented.

Political decisions in this sensitive field are never easy. They are made especially difficult now because of the stakes involved. If widespread distribution of contraceptive information and material among public assistance clients could make a sizable dent in the ADC unmar-

[22]Norman St. John-Stevas, *Birth Control and Public Policy* (A Report to the Center for the Study of Democratic Institutions; Santa Barbara, Calif.: The Center, 1960), pp. 76ff.

ried mother class alone—without regard to the unknown totals of dependent legitimate children born out of a highly temporary reunion of basically incompatible parents—the consequences could be dramatic in both economic and social terms. Illegitimacy accounts for two-thirds of a million persons now on ADC at a probable annual cost of at least $300 million. Yet, while the reduction of illegitimacy in general is not argued in the political arena, the reduction of illegitimacy in ADC is. Because ADC illegitimacy is a political issue, the politician who pushes birth control as a remedy invites Catholic opposition. The politician who shies away from public support for birth control in this situation may be castigated by Protestants and Jews for failing to support a program to reduce costs and misery. While trying to resolve that problem, he is not likely to be comforted by official Health, Education, and Welfare assurances that the great majority of illegitimate children do not receive public assistance: "Only about ½ of 1 per cent of the total child population are illegitimate and receiving aid to dependent children, even though about 4½ per cent of the Nation's child population are illegitimate."[23] That ½ of 1 per cent still translates into a little under 700,000 mothers and children on relief.

Most of the problem would go away if women without resident husbands and without resources would stay away from men. Then, of course, the issue of tax funds for birth control would become moot and both proponents and opponents could be satisfied as the dependency totals leveled off. The fact that this is the optimum arrangement, plus the fact that, unlike suddenly acquiring a high school education or a marketable skill, it is possible of fulfillment by the recipients, accounts for the midnight welfare search, for the continuing and hardening political efforts to demand that suitable home tests be applied in ADC cases, and for the proposals that a second illegitimate child be considered evidence of unsuitability of the home. In Louisiana, Governor Davis sloughed off the children with the parents in 1960, an action, it will be recalled, that resulted in a ruling by Arthur Flemming to the effect that no state may deny ADC on account of an unsuitable home unless arrangements are made for the care of the child. Failure to overcome the birth control barrier coupled with the imposition of the Flemming rule—now written into law—may ultimately result in a massive, foster care program which will simultaneously make it possible to deny relief eligibility to "immoral" mothers and provide for the

[23]U.S. Department of Health, Education, and Welfare, *Public Assistance 1961,* reprinted from the *Annual Report 1961* (Washington), p. 31; see also U.S. Department of Health, Education, and Welfare, *Illegitimacy and Dependency,* reprinted from *Health, Education, and Welfare Indicators* (Washington, September, 1963), pp. xxiii-xxiv.

offspring they are not taught to prevent. Until birth control materials are as readily available to the welfare client as to other citizens, the former is deprived of "equal protection" in not one sense, but two.

The Incentive Dilemma

One of the most evident policy lags in public assistance involves what may be termed the incentive dilemma: whether or not to permit clients to retain some earned income as an incentive to achieve self-support. Public assistance was written into the Social Security Act on a categorical basis with the categories restricted to actual or presumed unemployables – the very old, the very young, the blind, and later the disabled. Inclusion in 1961 of unemployed parents as a cause for ADC eligibility was the first basic shift in the policy of presumed unemployability. Until 1961, therefore, the question of the earning capacity of public assistance recipients could be treated as a largely unrealistic problem, hence, one that required no effort at solution. If the categories to be aided were supposed to consist of people who could not work, there was good reason to ignore the question of whether or not they could keep all or a part of their earnings. The logic was reasonably sound during the depression years when 65 did represent a practical chronological limit on self-support among marginal economic groups at least, and during the period when ADC cases were largely made up of orphans and of widows who were expected and encouraged to stay home and care for the orphans. With the labor shortage and the full employment of the war period some of this changed. In the period of postwar plenty, there have been some part-time employment opportunities for the aged, the working mother has become commonplace, and the importance of the mother in the home has been downgraded. Most important, the formal injection of self-help, self-care, and rehabilitation into the language of the public assistance law suggests a public interest in preparing clients to get off the rolls rather than a public willingness to maintain the recipient indefinitely.

Although self-help, self-care, and rehabilitation would all seem to carry with them the idea of self-improvement, the latter has not been encouraged in most of the programs. Except for a 1950 change affecting the blind, more recent and much less liberal changes affecting the aged, and some very new (July, 1965) provisions dealing with children under 18, a public assistance client could not help himself by working unless he could earn more than his budgeted grant and thus go off the rolls completely. The basic requirement that any income of the client be considered in determining the size of his grant is a critical constraint on self-improvement entirely out of keeping with the presumed new look in public assistance. It remains part of the law because a frontal attack on it would be a frontal attack on the idea that welfare clients may not behave in the same manner as persons who are not welfare clients. The man who "moonlights," who holds two jobs in order to improve his family's standard of living, is admired as an example of the American way; the welfare client who holds one job is prohibited from improving his family's standard of living beyond what it would be if he held no job. This peculiar approach to self-help is only slightly modified by the 1962 Public Welfare Amendments, or by the 1964 antipoverty legislation. Public assistance recipients must be prepared to sacrifice the possibility of marginal improvements in their economic status, to adjust to the budgeted grant as an income ceiling, work or no, unless they can perform the miracle of total self-support. This need to sacrifice any chance for small, seemingly attainable improvements over the legal minimum standards or the less than minimum standards of the relief ceilings of many states is a more demanding sacrifice than many of the others expected of public assistance clients. To say to a client that as a condition of support he may not sin, or even to say that he will not be secure against unreasonable searches, seems less self-defeating than to say that he may not earn to improve himself.

Initial recognition of the earning capacity of aid recipients came in the aid to the blind program partly because only the blind, of all categories of aid cases, maintain an effective, highly respectable, and thoughtful lobby operation. Maintaining such an organization is possible since the legislative needs and interests of the blind and the common cause involved go beyond public assistance. If all of the nation's blind were magically provided a substantial annual income, the National Federation of the Blind would continue to have a reason to exist; there is doubt that the same could be said about the senior citizens' pension groups that have put in appearances through the years. The ADC group is entirely unorganized; even if it were organized, it is hard to see what could hold it together beyond legislative goals.

Since its founding in 1940, the National Federation of the Blind has tried to make programs of aid to the needy blind a force for rehabilitation, thus antedating by some years the official interest in the rehabilitation of public assistance clients. The federation encourages incentive and initiative, insisting that, given help and opportunity, recipients of aid to the blind could take their place as contributors to the community. "Our purpose has been the encouragement of incentive and initiative, not the smothering of it," says John F. Nagle, chief of the federation's Washington office.[24]

Because of the persistence of the federation and its on-the-spot lobbying opportunities, and because their obvious physical sacrifice makes the blind a most favored aid group, the 1960 amendments to the federal law required states to disregard a portion of the earned income of a blind recipient in computing income and resources that would otherwise become part of the individual budget calculations. Since July 1, 1962, the amount to be disregarded has been $85 per month plus one-half of earned income in excess of $85. In addition, the 1962 amendments require a state to disregard all the earned income of a blind recipient for a period up to 12 months if he has a state-approved plan for achieving self-support.

In 1962, too, an initial breakthrough was achieved in permitting OAA recipients to have earned income without penalty. Having been previously persuaded of the desirability of such a provision, Senator Robert Kerr permitted Paul Douglas to put through a floor amendment authorizing (but not requiring) states to disregard up to $50 per month of the earned income of an OAA client. The provision was watered down in conference to permit a state to ignore the first $10 completely, plus one-half of the remainder to $50. The foot in the door was achieved this time after years of stubbed toes; it should be noted, however, that it was the OAA door. In the ADC category, the only changes were to require that a state, in determining need, take into account any expenses that may reasonably be attributable to the earning of income, and to permit states to disregard income set aside for a child's future identifiable needs. Before this, an aid recipient whose budget included earned income had no assurance that even his expenses would be taken into account in figuring the budget.

The antipoverty program, enacted in 1964 as the Economic Opportunity Act, recognized the incentive problem without doing very much about it. Title VII of the act did mandate a monthly exemption of all of the first $85 plus half of the payments over $85 from the determination of income and resources in all federally aided categories. It is an exemption, however, limited to payments under the Youth Programs and Community Action Programs of this act; it is not a general exemption covering income earned in private enterprise. A grace period that extended to July 1, 1965, makes it impossible to evaluate the usefulness of the exemption yet, but it is worth noting that

[24]U.S. Congress, House, Committee on Ways and Means, Hearings, "Public Welfare Amendments of 1962," 87th Cong., 2d Sess., 1962, p. 474.

although New York City expects "several thousand New Yorkers will find places in the Job Corps during the course of the program,"[25] not all of them will be public assistance cases. Probably useful enough for attracting participants to the Job Corps and to the work-training programs, the exemption inexplicably fell short of covering the much more extensive problem of ADC mothers and adolescents and unemployed fathers who might secure occasional part-time private employment if there were an appropriate incentive.

This was finally remedied, in part, by the public assistance amendments accompanying the Medicare act of 1965: states were permitted, in computing benefits under the ADC program, to exempt up to $150 a month earned by dependent children under age 18 in the same home, with a $50 limit per child. OAA and APTD permissible earnings exemptions were raised to $20 per month, plus half of the next $60. Ironically, at a time when there is increasing concern about the need to shore up the role of the father in the Negro family, public policy now makes it possible for dependent children to improve the family's situation but does not encourage an unemployed father to accept casual work.

Taking stock, then, the situation is that the blind have been provided an important incentive to develop self-support programs; the aged have been provided a token incentive. For ADC cases, adult earned income is debited against the budgeted grant. In the case of an ADC mother with a capacity for limited earnings, in a reasonably generous state there can be no economic incentive to work even if she is capable of working. Lacking specific amendments like those dealing with the blind and the aged, the basic federal act requires that states consider "any other income and resources of the individual" in establishing need. Like some other features of the law, the provision is an anachronism. It was adopted in 1939, with confidentiality and the merit system requirement, as an administrative reform to meet some special needs of the times. The income and resources provision was enacted in order to overcome (1) public and administrative confusion between pensions and public assistance; (2) favored treatment by several states to their needy aged, due in large measure to Townsend group activities; (3) judicial decisions which ordered assistance payments to aged individuals in spite of the fact that they were living with their adult children and being adequately supported; and (4) administrative malpractices in the states which discriminated against other needy groups.[26] Personnel in the Bureau of Public Assistance first proposed the

[25]*New York Times*, March 17, 1965.
[26]Jack R. Parsons, "The Origins of the Income and Resources Amendment to the Social Security Act," *Social Service Review*, XXXVI (March, 1962), 51-61.

income and resources addition to the Social Security Board. Although the board did not formally recommend it to the Congress, Arthur Altmeyer did personally suggest its approval to the appropriate congressional committees in executive sessions. Designed to protect the needy public assistance client against political favoritism and administrative incompetence, the mandate to consider any other income and resources has lost its original justification. It now serves as an impediment to encouraging recipients to go to work, a possibility that simply did not exist realistically in 1939.

Since proposals for an exemption of small amounts of earned income for OAA cases were lost in Congress at least twice before ultimate token adoption in 1962, it is obvious that the limitation does not hold on just because it has been overlooked. Admittedly, its amendment or repeal has not been a major goal of the American Public Welfare Association. The Wyman Report to Secretary Ribicoff, however, did recommend both administrative and legislative action in this area, and the Ad Hoc Committee on Public Welfare recommended what was ultimately adopted in 1965: partial exemption of earnings of youths in ADC families to provide incentive for work and the development of responsibility. But the administration's 1962 draft bill, which went so far as to reduce maximum permissible residence requirements to one year, shied away from the question of the retention of earned income, dealing only with the exemption of expenses attributable to a job.

Common sense suggests that it would take a person of extraordinary moral standards to report income that would be deducted from a welfare grant already figured on a minimum or below-minimum subsistence standard. For many a client who can work, the difference between retaining his wages and reporting them is sufficiently important to take a chance on being detected and cut off for fraud. Nor is there a middle ground for adults in the ADC program as there now is in OAA and in aid to the blind where some earned income may be retained. In ADC — aside from payments made under the poverty act — it is all or nothing at all, so that the most expensive and the most socially troublesome program is the one that does not provide an adequate incentive for adult recipients to try working if they can.

Taking advantage of a 1962 provision that allows any part of a state plan to be suspended for demonstration or experimental purposes, New York City Welfare Commissioner James Dumpson and the Ford Foundation joined to provide low-skilled jobs for ADC mothers, permitting them to retain their earnings with the expectation that the experience and the presumed increased sense of self-respect would encourage the participants to try to make their own way in the labor market. Failing that, the program will at least improve the status of some families for a time, in itself a socially desirable goal. Whether the jobs created for this purpose would actually be available in a free economy is problematic—an uncertainty that exists with the jobs established by the poverty program too—so that the results of the experiment will lack some of the conclusiveness that might be expected from an authorization for adult ADC recipients to retain up to a fixed amount of earned income from any job. The Ford Foundation is not likely to be able to fabricate job opportunities for great numbers of ADC cases for an unlimited period of time.

Retention of earned income as an incentive represents more of a political problem than its proponents acknowledge. Even in the insurance side of social security, where the claimant is encouraged to believe that he has a vested right to benefits related to contributions, a charge against benefits is made after a stipulated amount of earned income is reached. Only after age 72 may social security recipients have unlimited earnings without loss of benefits. As long as some social insurance benefits are forfeited by earned income, it is fanciful to suppose that politicians will allow public assistance benefits to go on without regard to income. The current exception of a significant amount of earned income in the case of the blind program is traceable to the overt, extreme, physical *quid pro quo* for relief that blindness offers. The recent, small, breakthrough in OAA is a rough measure of how the physical sacrifice of old age is ranked in this market. Once again, if ADC were a program serving widowed mothers, it would probably be easy enough to enact an earned income exemption for them. It is not so easy where illegitimacy and family conflict together represent the cause of so high a percentage of the cases because it would require the politician to tell his constituents that he is supporting a public policy which seems to equate promiscuity and lack of family responsibility with old age and blindness as reasonable grounds for assistance beyond the bare subsistence level. The compromise arrangement of the Economic Opportunity Act will probably affect job corps enrollees rather than ADC mothers; in any event, it is not an exemption of earnings, but, as the statute says, "of payments" made by government. If Ford Foundation money can show that the incentive value of an earned income exemption can make a serious dent in the number of ADC cases, such a public policy may become palatable as an investment. In the meanwhile, it is only foundation policy, and foundation policy demands no behavioral sacrifices from its grantees; public policy does.

III. RESIDENCE AS AN ELIGIBILITY FACTOR

The barter arrangements that are implicit in the public assistance program do not operate in a totally free market. Some rules are imposed on the exchange of economic assistance for personal sacrifices. There is a point at which decision-makers in a superior hierarchical position intrude on the terms proposed by their subordinates because those terms, while perhaps acceptable to the unorganized recipients, are offensive to other organized groups whose peripheral interest in the problem is touched by certain extreme proposals. Organized labor, for example, would not abide a local policy that would put ADC-U fathers to work as strike-breakers, and state or national legislative or administrative intervention would be demanded. Another limit on local freedom becomes operative when conditions are established or proposed which recipients themselves are not likely to be able or willing to meet even at the risk of jeopardizing the relief grant. The consequences of shutting off relief to persons who are apparently without other means of support are neither readily predictable nor pleasant to contemplate. Consequently, when recipient willingness or ability to comply with the sacrifices demanded is exceeded, the demand is likely to be softened or rescinded by order of higher authority. This limit was reached in Newburgh. It was reached again in Louisiana in the suitable home controversy of 1960; it is being approached in the practice of unannounced searches.

On the other side, there are some sacrifices that appear to be considered almost as fundamental as economic need in the eyes of the politicians, some sacrifices about which they are adamant. High on this list is state residency as a condition of eligibility. Wholesale efforts to eliminate this requirement have been just as unsuccessful as wholesale efforts at the other extreme to impose a new flock of restraints. Residence requirements have been a prime target at both federal and state levels of welfare groups who claim that such requirements are arbitrarily imposed barriers to meeting human needs and that they consume time which the welfare workers might better use to provide therapy than to investigate duration of residence. Ideally, for most welfare spokesmen, the federal act should be amended to prohibit the imposition of residence requirements as a condition for continued approval of a state plan. Second best would be a reduction in the allowable adult maximum of five years to coincide with the ADC one-year maximum, although it is certainly not clear how such a change would be significant in conserving the workers' time. Once it becomes necessary to check proof of residence at all, the period to be checked—

within half a decade anyway—is not likely to be a major determinant of staff time investment in dealing with the aged.

During its period on the offensive, the Social Security Board never missed an opportunity to urge federal and state liberalization of residence standards. In the first years of the federal program, virtually every state had adopted the maximum allowable requirements, but the board urged adoption of the ADC stipulation as a model for the adult categories. Typical was the statement in the annual report for 1942: "The residence requirements of State plans for old-age assistance and aid to the blind should be liberalized to accord with provisions under approved plans for aid to dependent children."[27] As some of the states eased their restrictions somewhat between the beginning and the end of the war period, the board pressed the advantage and urged congressional action to abolish residence requirements entirely. By 1944, it was suggesting that free movement would result in automatic adjustments on the theory that "in-and-out migration of persons who were receiving or might apply for assistance would cancel out in many States, with little change and possibly reduction in State costs."[28] This bit of undocumented speculation did not move Congress; thereafter, the board, for the period that it continued to make legislative recommendations, settled into regularly characterizing residence requirements as "an anachronism in modern society."[29]

Progress in the states has not been swift. New York, Hawaii, Rhode Island, and Connecticut are the only states ever to make presence and intention of residence the sole residence qualification for all categories, although states as different as New Jersey and Georgia both abandoned the ADC residence provision. In New York, it has been a continuing battle. After vetoing one bill that would have reimposed an eligibility requirement, Nelson Rockefeller subsequently signed legislation to debar persons who are shown to have come into the state solely for the purpose of collecting assistance. After three decades, the "no residence" states are more than counter-balanced by California, Florida, Michigan, Texas, Arizona, and New Hampshire, among many others, which continue to require the maximum residence permitted by the federal act. Just under half the states have settled on a one-year eligibility provision in the adult categories and retained the similar requirement in ADC.

No feature of the public assistance program has been more con-

[27]U.S. Social Security Board, *Annual Report 1942* (Washington), p. 21.

[28]U.S. Social Security Board, *Annual Report 1944*, p. 43.

[29]U.S. Social Security Board, *Annual Report 1947*, p. 114; see also *Annual Report 1949*, p. 134.

sistently under political attack than the residence feature. At hearing after hearing, proposals have been put forth to eliminate residence requirements. *Ad hoc* councils and advisory committees reporting to the Congress and to the administration have attacked residence and urged reduction or elimination by federal action. Liberalization or elimination are entirely possible by state action, however, and Congress shows no interest in mandating a change that would upset the assertion it accepted in 1935 that "A few standards are prescribed which the States must meet to entitle them to Federal aid but these impose only reasonable conditions and leave the States free of arbitrary interference from Washington."[30]

One line of attack has been that citizens of the United States should not be deprived of the benefits of a program supported largely by federal money because they move from one state to another. The argument would probably carry more weight if a legal right to free movement could be shown. As a matter of law, a majority of the Supreme Court has never concluded that there is, as an incident of national citizenship, a right to move freely from state to state. The Court has held invalid a state statute making it a misdemeanor for anyone knowingly to bring or assist in bringing into the state a nonresident "indigent person"; the majority decision, however, was based on the exclusive right of Congress to regulate interstate commerce.[31] Even if his brethren were to agree with Justice Douglas' concurring view that the question of freedom of interstate movement of human beings should not rest on the commerce clause, but is protected against state interference by the privileges and immunities clause of the Fourteenth Amendment, it is still a long way between establishing a constitutional right to free movement and a constitutional right to public assistance without regard to previous residence.

In a classic demonstration of what Morton Grodzins has characterized as the "multiple crack" aspect of American politics, the opponents of residence requirements, having failed in Congress and with the state legislatures, directed their attention to the state governors in 1958-1959. At a 1958 meeting, the Governors' Conference provided for a special committee to study the problem. According to Glenn Brooks, biographer of the Conference, "the states had previously been criticized severely for their failure to make adequate provision for these stateless persons."[32] A year later, the report was received, discussed,

---

[30]*House Report 615*, 74th Cong., 1st Sess., 1935, p. 4.

[31]*Edwards* v. *California*, 314 U.S. 160 (1941).

[32]Glenn Brooks, *When Governors Convene* (Baltimore: Johns Hopkins University Press, 1961), p. 70.

and approved. It included a recommendation to Congress that the Social Security Act be amended to impose a uniform one-year ceiling on all four categories and a recommendation to the states that an interstate compact be developed to cover the problem of nonresident applicants for general assistance. Health, Education, and Welfare Secretary Flemming participated in the discussion of the report. Unlike a Democratic predecessor, Oscar Ewing, who once told the Governors' Conference that "another thing that might be done to improve matters would be for the states to lengthen the residency requirements for eligibility,"[33] Flemming gave his support to reductions in residency requirements. Views on public assistance policy cannot be stereotyped according to political party affiliation.

But if American federalism permits a multiple crack, it also permits a multiple pose. The governors not only adopted their committee's report; they also adopted a companion resolution stipulating that "The individual Governors be requested to support the findings and recommendations of the Committee's report in their messages to the legislatures."[34] The prospect of championing easier public assistance eligibility was more appealing to the governors in San Juan, however, than when they were facing their respective legislatures at home. Rhode Island's Governor Del Sesto did urge on his legislature adoption of interstate compacts waiving residence requirements, an appropriate enough stand in a state where there had been no requirements for more than a decade. Among the others, apparently only John Reed of Maine heeded the conference resolution by recommending repeal of existing residence laws to his legislature. (To be sure, when the New York legislature enacted a one-year residence bill in 1960, Nelson Rockefeller struck it down.) To Glenn Brooks' characterization of the Governors' Conference action in this area as "studious and comprehensive" may be added the statement that it was "without follow through." Governors are making no serious moves to wipe out the state option in residence allowed by the federal law, or to wipe out the *status quo* in residence requirements at home.

It is consistent with the professionals' general objective of making need the sole criterion for assistance to argue against residence. But need as the sole criterion is not an objective that has ever been adopted by the policy-makers, so they have no difficulty in turning aside the antiresidence argument. In the last analysis, it is an objective that even some professionals find discomforting when they view the possible consequences to their own well-regulated systems. The residence

[33]*Proceedings of the Governors' Conference, 1951* (Chicago: author), p. 93.
[34]*Proceedings of the Governors' Conference, 1959* (Chicago: author), p. 138.

dispute has compelled a separation between the welfare locals and the welfare cosmopolitans. State leaders without the need to meet a frequently hostile legislature take the cosmopolitan approach, acknowledging the artificiality of political boundaries and the reality of individual human need. But American politicians, state-oriented by the nature of the political system, and those welfare specialists who have to protect a state program that has come to include special advantages, are locals who find it quite adequate to show a concern for individual human need within the artificial but practically important boundaries of their own states. In this dispute, as in so many others in this field, welfare ideology never meets political reality. The politicians and the bulk of the professionals do not come to a head-on clash of ideas; rather, they pass each other while running in parallel channels, the one emphasizing human need, the other emphasizing the American political and constitutional system.

Failure to join the issue is illustrated by a dialogue between the late Senator Robert Kerr and Elizabeth Wickenden who often speaks for the National Social Welfare Assembly and a variety of other welfare organizations. Miss Wickenden spoke in 1962 on behalf of the proposal advanced by the administration, but eliminated by the House committee, that maximum residence requirements be limited to one year and that there be a federal reward for compliance. Her prepared statement noted a long professional organizational effort "to bring about a better understanding of the deleterious effect of residence restrictions in public assistance."[35] The statement went on to allege that these restrictions create hardships, place burdens on voluntary agencies, endanger the grant-in-aid principle, are administratively costly, and run counter to the country's basic economic needs. Some of these would be compelling points, if demonstrable. But neither Kerr nor the other members of the Senate Finance Committee were ready to accept the two premises on which the Wickenden testimony was based: first, that because Miss Wickenden and her colleagues asserted a position regarding residence requirements, that the position was therefore empirically valid; and second, that the grounds on which the the position was based are the exclusive grounds on which policy should be based.

Without bothering to address himself directly to the first premise, Kerr made it clear that the second premise could not stand. In the senator's judgment, the important determinant was the nature of the historic contract between federal and state governments as set forth in

[35]U.S. Congress, Senate, Committee on Finance, Hearings, "Public Assistance Act of 1962," 87th Cong., 2d Sess., 1962, p. 188.

the approved state plan. Under the original federal law, five years of residence was a permissible requirement in the adult categories; under that law, the level of payments was fixed and became a pattern in various states. "And many States," said Kerr, "under that pattern have taxed themselves to where they are paying up to $100 a month on a 50-50 basis or paying up to 35 per cent of it, while other States are under $40 and paying only 20 per cent of it."[36] The state which has made its arrangements on the basis of preexisting federal authority to require five years residence should not have its arrangements and its tax system jeopardized by the possibility of an inflow of beneficiaries from other states which follow another pattern. Kerr argued that if the federal government has made a contract whereby it agrees to match the states' money with reference to people who are otherwise eligible and have been in residence for five years, and the federal government then decides to change the terms of the contract to admit people who have not been in residence five years, the change should be paid for at the national level. The proposal being advanced provided for a reward to the states; the small reward, however, would not compensate for the full cost of the change mandated. Kerr carefully distinguished between the requirement with a reward and the incentive without coercion, but no proponent was around to ask whether he would support either an incentive without coercion plan or a requirement with a full cost reward.

Instead, Miss Wickenden began to give assurance of her personal happiness to pay taxes to support public assistance:

Miss Wickenden. I don't want to take too much time on this one point except I would like to make two more points.

I am a taxpayer of New York State. New York State is one of the few States which has no residence requirements and does have a very high standard of assistance. I am happy to pay taxes for that purpose. I think the studies that have been made in New York have showed very little evidence that people move in order to get assistance. They do come to get jobs, and sometimes things happen that make it impossible for them to support themselves. They have to—

Senator Kerr. What time is it in New York now?

Miss Wickenden. What?

Senator Kerr. What time is it in New York now?

Miss Wickenden. Of day?

Senator Kerr. Yes.

Miss Wickenden. The same time as here.

Senator Kerr. What time is that?

[36]*Ibid.,* p. 182.

Miss Wickenden. A quarter of 11.

Senator Kerr. What time is it in Los Angeles?

Miss Wickenden. Well, it is quarter of 8.

Senator Kerr. Now, the fact that the people in New York in their wisdom or that part of the country under the Federal Government are under one time and California is under another, do you think New York ought to have the right to say California ought to adopt our time schedule?

Miss Wickenden. Sir, you are talking about the course of the sun and I am talking about a purely legislative relationship.

Senator Kerr. What you are talking about is the Federal Government taking an action which would be just as arbitrary.

Miss Wickenden. Well, I would like just to add one more word and then go on to something else.[37]

The colloquy again illustrated the separate orientations of the politicians and the welfare spokesmen. The problem with which the antiresidence people must deal on the federal level is that of the alleged federal-state contract and the reluctance of the Congress to abrogate the terms of the contract by fiat. But the contract theory has never been attacked. A later Kerr criticism was that proponents of change in federal residence requirements were seeking to change rules that had been in effect for nearly 30 years. Presumably, longevity of contract is an argument against change—but failure to change further increases the age of the contract and by this test strengthens it. Senator Kerr hinted at one possible resolution: voluntary abandonment of contractual rights by the states based on federal financial incentives. The incentive would have to be great enough to cover costs, however, and no one appears to have studied the question of costs intensively.

Absence of really certain information about costs or consequences of a change in residence requirements is certainly part of the reason for the politicians' consistent rejection of the welfare premise on this question, *i.e.,* that eliminating residence requirements will not result in any significant shift in the dependent population from the low-benefit states to the high-benefit states. Proponents of change do have an especially difficult problem here because the professionals themselves are not united. Despite the fact that both political and professional opposition turn on the inadequacy of data about the probable consequences of change, there do not appear to be any more such data now than there were in 1950 when a recommendation for change was under serious consideration because it got a boost from the Advisory Council on Social Security. (The Council had been created in 1947 by the 80th Congress to take a total look at the country's social security pro-

[37]*Ibid.,* pp. 183-84.

gram and to make recommendations for change. Chaired by Edward R. Stettinius, Jr., its membership covered the fields of business, labor, professional economics, and social welfare.) The report of this cosmopolitan group endorsed reduction of the OAA residence maximum to one year and elimination of all other residence requirements. When the proposal came to be considered by the Senate Finance Committee, the uncertainty of members on both sides of the aisle about possible consequences became apparent; so did the uneasiness of those welfare people who could not afford to take anything but a local view. The latter position was typified by Earl Kouns who successfully administered Colorado's generous program for more than ten years, and who had a liberal program to protect against the chance of dilution:

I know that fundamentally people do not migrate for the sole purpose of getting higher public assistance payments.... But I do know that a good segment of our population are migratory and do move, and I do know that when they do travel from State to State, when they are going to stop some place, it is convenient to stop in the State that pays higher public assistance.[38]

When Loula Dunn, Director of the American Public Welfare Association, spoke on behalf of the residence reduction measure, Colorado's Senator Eugene Millikin asked for statistics on migration from low- to high-payment states. Miss Dunn bucked the question to an associate whose vague answer prompted Millikin to ask for "statistics having any substance to them on that problem."[39] He got none. In 1959, the Governor of California raised substantially the same question with Secretary Flemming who was supporting reduced residency. "We have not made any studies that would produce a cost figure," said Flemming.[40]

The effort to eliminate or liberalize residence requirements has been singularly unsuccessful; policy-makers have not been willing to adopt a policy that would have unpredictable fiscal and social consequences and abandon a policy with known consequences. Many welfare spokesmen invoke everything except empirical data to support their contention that residence requirements do not deter potential public charges from flocking to generous (and sunny) states. For more than twenty years, the proponents of change have argued that because

[38]U.S. Congress, Senate, Committee on Finance, Hearings, "Social Security Revision," 81st Cong., 2d Sess., 1950, p. 325.

[39]*Ibid.,* pp. 172-73.

[40]*Proceedings of the Governors' Conference, 1959* (Chicago: author), p. 85. Statistics from New York City indicate that in both August, 1959, and June, 1962, 8.3 per cent of the public assistance recipient group had less than one year of residence. See Citizens' Committee for Children of New York, Inc., *Public Welfare: Myth vs. Fact* (New York, January, 1963), pp. 10-11.

federal money is involved in the categorical programs, the recipients should be permitted to qualify as residents of the United States rather than as residents of some particular state. Proponents of the *status quo* argue that it is a nation of states, that the states should not have their existing arrangements disturbed by unilateral national action. This whole argument, emphasizing an attachment to government levels, hides the real issue: opponents of residence requirements still hope to make need the sole determinant of assistance eligibility; supporters of residence requirements do not want the needy flitting around in hopes of bettering their income or getting more sunshine. And on this latter point, there is more firmness than on any of the other noneconomic eligibility conditions. Poor people are expected to stay put.

Neither proponents nor opponents, however, really know what the consequences of change would be. Indeed, the stability of policy in public assistance is generally related to the uncertainty about the consequences of change, an uncertainty that is traceable in turn to the absence of a system for gathering and transmitting information.

CHAPTER VI

Influence, Information, and Innovation

AMERICAN PUBLIC ASSISTANCE policy has been stable for 30 years. This stability—or, from another point of view, sterility—is more readily traced to an absence of innovative proposals than to any consensus that the categorical assistance programs spelled out in the Social Security Act of 1935 have continuing validity. Stability is less a matter of widespread satisfaction with the program than it is the absence of an informed, influential group with a better idea.

Policy innovation cannot come without recognition of and positive response to differences in an economic or political or social condition that originally stimulated a specific public policy. Recognition and response are likely to be dependent on information. The greater the flow of information to those authorized to effect change, the greater the likelihood of change; without a flow of information, policy becomes guesswork or the legalization of prejudice or intuition. Of course, information will not always lead to policy change. One obvious reason is that the character of the information may be such as to sustain existing policy. But without information, and with media of communication available to broadcast blunders widely, policy-makers sensibly find the *status quo* to be the only possible policy. Information has the added advantage of providing protection for the sympathetic but hesitant policy-maker. In public assistance, for example, the record of the Louisiana hearing made possible the 1962 provision that requires a state to arrange for the care of a dependent child before cutting off aid to an unsuitable home. Much earlier the Ohio record, coupled with information about political use of the relief rolls in other states furnished to the House Ways and Means and Senate Finance Committees in executive sessions, made possible the 1939 confidentiality provision. The examples are not easily multiplied.

I. TIME FOR A CHANGE

There is now no adequate system for assembling and transmitting public assistance information to policy-makers. Potential information-gathering agencies among the various groups concerned with policy in this field either avoid the role entirely, or operate in a closed circuit wherein selected case information is used to reinforce the preexisting convictions of those who neither need to be persuaded nor have control over public policy.

We have seen the data gap at work in the long history of undocumented assaults on the maximum allowable residence requirements. Costs are still unknown, and actual data on causes of migration of clients have yet to be reported. Opponents of residence requirements assure each other that costs would be nil; it is their impression that people do not move with expectations of obtaining relief. A very good argument may be made for eliminating residence requirements even if the costs would be high and even if assistance benefits are a factor in the movement of poor people, but the case will never be argued on those grounds until some defensible data are at hand. In the interim, policy-makers prefer the *status quo* to unpredictable consequences of change.

There is some recognition within the trade of the inability of many welfare people to substitute information for impressions. Having read the statements made by social welfare professionals to the House Ways and Means Committee in 1961, an otherwise sympathetic faculty member of a school of social work was sufficiently disturbed to write that welfare power "might more strongly be felt if representatives of the profession were better prepared to back up their professional impressions with the kind of 'hard facts' that make sense to hard-headed, practical legislators."[1]

This is a finding similar to the one reached a year earlier by another insider, Joseph Vigilante, now dean of the Adelphi College School of Social Work. Vigilante examined the social policy and social action activity of 17 national social welfare organizations, almost all of which claim at least a peripheral interest in public assistance. "There is," says Vigilante delicately, "some evidence of rather loosely constructed policy statements and action appeals based largely on emotion." His perusal of copies of letters sent to policy-makers by

[1]Alan Wade, "Review of Hearings of House Ways and Means Committee," *Social Service Review*, XXXV (December, 1961), 471-72.

members or affiliates of some organizations revealed inaccuracies, maudlin appeals to emotion, and careless consideration of important legislative proposals. "One can understand criticism from policy makers after examining some of this material," Vigilante concluded.[2]

A few of the professionals do study the scattered research data that are available. In one of his first editorials, Robert Morris, new editor of *Social Work,* the journal of the National Association of Social Workers, was acknowledging that "accepted techniques of just increasing the volume of services for dependent families is not as effective as we would like to believe . . . if economic independence is the measure of success, assistance clients who use current services do only a little better than those who do not."[3] Yet, in precisely the same month, speaking as if from another world, *Social Casework,* journal of the Family Service Association of America, editorialized that "periodic attacks on public programs are based on lack of information about the causes of economic need and about the effectiveness of rehabilitative services."[4] Morris' close examination of California and New Jersey reports led him to a conclusion at least partly out of keeping with the one that had been pushed by most welfare spokesmen for the previous 18 months and that was so uncritically accepted by the editors of *Social Casework*: that is, that noneconomic professional services are especially necessary in public assistance and that they are the way to a reduction in dependency. The conclusion itself was based on a paucity of rigorous data, although there were plenty of official and semiofficial reports being passed around and approved of just as if they were something more than "impressions."

Around 1961 the handful of public assistance policy specialists all at once discovered that it was time for a change. Special projects, consultants' reports to the new Secretary of Health, Education, and Welfare, task force reports to the new President, and *ad hoc* committee reports all concluded that 1961 was not 1935, but that one would never know it from examining public assistance law and administrative arrangements. Policy, it was discovered, had been stable; clients were different. Either no one had been keeping tabs on the program, or those who had were not heard.

The group of specialists numbers not more than a dozen, the inner club only three—one a federal administrator, one the dean of a school

[2]Joseph L. Vigilante, *Study of Social Policy and Social Action Activity of Selected National Social Welfare Organizations* (New York: National Social Welfare Assembly Committee on Social Issues and Policies, 1960), p. 120.
[3]"Editorial," *Social Work,* VII (October, 1962), 2.
[4]"Editorial Notes," *Social Casework,* XLIII (October, 1962), 437.

of social work, and one a "technical consultant on public social policy." (None of these three is a professionally trained social worker. One of them says lightly that they would not be admissible to a school now because "we lack the proper mental attitude.") As persons of intelligence, high motivation, and intense loyalty to the cause that they hold in common, they are concerned about the fact that they are not multiplying, that the old China hands will retire without successors. None of the members is below fifty, and their average age is probably closer to sixty. They talk to each other frequently, although they are scattered geographically and by career attachment. They are all public assistance veterans in the sense that they either participated in the work leading to the basic federal act or joined the field shortly thereafter. They are committed to the principle of social insurance, but having concluded that a social insurance system adequate to meet human needs is not practicable in the present state of American political and social thinking, they now concentrate instead on improvements in the basic scheme of public assistance as a residual feature of social security. Since most members of the larger group, and all of the inner club, can remember the creation of the Social Security Act and its provisions for categorical assistance, the possibility that these latter provisions have already acquired anachronistic features may not be as readily considered as it would be by a second generation. These are the veterans who have served as observers, draftsmen, lobbyists, administrators, consultants, historians, apologists, and teachers. Innovation comes hard to an in-bred group that has once made a major policy contribution.

The member who is the focal point for continuing attention to public assistance policy is Elizabeth Wickenden, once Washington representative for the American Public Welfare Association, now officially Technical Consultant on Public Social Policy for the National Social Welfare Assembly, and unofficially a kind of executive secretary for a nonexistent association for public assistance. Thus, testifying before the Senate Finance Committee in 1962, she was exclusive spokesman for ten organizations from the Salvation Army to the National Association for Service to Unmarried Parents, spoke for six other organizations—from the National Council of the Churches of Christ to the National Association of Social Workers—who testified in their own behalf but nevertheless recorded themselves as in agreement with her statement, and reported the endorsement of fourteen individual welfare leaders from Jane Hoey, former Director of the Bureau of Public Assistance, to Sanford Solender of the National Jewish Welfare Board who had been chairman of Health, Education, and Welfare's Ad

Hoc Committee on Public Welfare. Unlike many self-designated focal points, Miss Wickenden has an excellent understanding of the situation and very good contacts as befits a former Washington lobbyist. Any doubt about her contacts was resolved early in 1964 when a wire service picture of Miss Wickenden affectionately pecking the cheek of President Johnson, "an old friend," was widely printed. She is more easily available to groups with a peripheral interest in public assistance than are government officials. As an independent operator, married to a staff member of the United Nations, she is able to carry on without the distracting responsibility of attachment to a formal government or university or welfare agency. Miss Wickenden, in short, facilitates communication between and advances the views of those with professional or intellectual interests in public assistance. But she is an individual, not an institution, and, consequently, there are limits to her ability to gather information and to analyze it.

An important illustration, both of Miss Wickenden's role as communicator and of the limits of the information she deals with, is seen in a project on public services for families and children established in November, 1960—in anticipation of the change in national administration—under the sponsorship of the New York School of Social Work with Miss Wickenden as Director. The concern of the people involved in the project was with national controversy about public welfare programs, and with "their own awareness of the need for changes in the program."[5] By choice, however, it was restricted to "self-criticism from within the field of social welfare." To develop specifics to flesh out a program, an inquiry went to 349 individuals or agencies—every state welfare commissioner, many local welfare commissioners, every head of a national welfare organization, every dean of a school of social work, and every local community council or state welfare council. Of this group of highly involved professionals, only 52 per cent answered; more than one-third of the replies lacked enough substance to permit analysis. Analysis and review turned out to be something of a problem. "How to handle this veritable treasure trove of thoughtful, expert opinion has constituted a major problem for this project," it was reported. "Altogether these responses reflect a healthy well-spring of vital thought but are difficult to handle in any of the typical patterns of research analysis."[6] One interpretation of this

[5]U.S. Congress, House, Committee on Ways and Means, Hearings, "Public Welfare Amendments of 1962," 87th Cong., 2d Sess., 1962, p. 408.
[6]Elizabeth Wickenden and Winifred Bell, *Public Welfare: Time for a Change* (New York: New York School of Social Work, 1961), p. 7. Reprinted by permission of the Columbia University School of Social Work.

statement is that there were no specific questions and no specific answers. But the 118 "useful" replies from within the profession somehow became the field data available for developing policy proposals.

The conclusion drawn from replies of the professional respondents, separately complemented by a collection of reports from ten state and local public welfare departments, was that more professional social service is required; more professional social service, when tried in demonstration projects in the ten reporting jurisdictions, invariably had "a practical value" which resulted in improved family relationships, better housing, employment, or sometimes self-support. No failures were reported. This idea of social service by a trained staff with small case loads, skilled supervision, and intensive counseling was the critical element in the Wickenden report. It became a critical element in the official Ad Hoc Committee report, and was at the heart of the program accepted by Congress on the basis of the presentation by Ribicoff. "The answer is through professional, skilled services," he said. "We believe that services represent the key to our efforts to help people become self-sufficient so that they no longer need assistance."[7]

The Wickenden methodology had some obvious deficiencies. One was the failure to identify how much self-sufficiency could legitimately be expected from the total number of clients in the nation, the failure to isolate just what groups of relief clients could be brought to the point where they "no longer need assistance." The methodology did not invite reexamination of the legitimate uses of a welfare program. What the investigators and the respondents must have known as men and women but blocked out as welfare professionals is that the particularly sticky issues in public assistance are, first, emergence of ADC as a seemingly insoluble problem related to race discrimination, immorality, undereducation, and underemployment, none of which have been affected by social services; and, second, some public and political doubts that the program's defenders are willing to use public assistance to achieve social change.

Public welfare, asserts Miss Wickenden's report, should not be expected "to compensate for a social deficiency which lies basically beyond its jurisdiction and competence."[8] This is not a new contention, having been asserted at the time of the Noleo fight in connection with desertion cases. But what social deficiencies lie beyond the jurisdiction and competence of public welfare? What else is a system of casework services to economically or psychologically dependent people than compensation for social deficiencies? Of course undereducation is not the fault of public welfare, but why should not welfare

[7]Ways and Means, Hearings, 1962, p. 166.
[8]Wickenden and Bell, p. 37.

assistance be made contingent, wherever practical, on school attendance, an innovation attempted by Raymond Hilliard in Chicago? Failure of the urban centers to find ways of preparing new residents for some of the emotional shocks of big-city life is not the fault of public welfare either. Yet this social deficiency is one that public welfare actively seeks to compensate for by insisting on providing social services along with money. And the Wickenden report itself urges that "public social services should be expanded to cover cases of noneconomic need as rapidly as personnel, finances, and public acceptability permit."[9] It is a particularly neat trick to deal with noneconomic need without compensating for a social deficiency that lies beyond the jurisdiction and competence of public welfare.

The plethora of reports produced in 1961 and 1962 offered no information about the different public and political attitudes toward widows on the one hand, and toward unwed mothers on the other hand, information that might at least lead to an important improvement in the level of support accorded the noncontroversial former group. Some nonprofessionals feel it is time to raise the question of whether Congress would be receptive to providing support at the social insurance levels for the act-of-God ADC cases if they were established as a separate class. For the professionals, wed and unwed mothers on ADC are both people in need, and that obliterates all other differences.

In any event, subsequent legislation did reflect the assertions of the several reports by emphasizing and providing federal funds for services presumed to have a practical value. Policy-makers are receptive to attempts of national organizations to influence welfare policy. The legislation did not mount a frontal attack on the questions of race, undereducation, illegitimacy, and ghettos in ADC, perhaps because the specialists have come to believe that there can be no useful attack, that, to quote one of them, "some problems are insoluble," and that it is useless to exacerbate the issue by inviting it to be raised outside the welfare profession. A year after the amendments passed in response to the time-for-a-change drive, New York City's Welfare Commissioner was announcing that he could see no diminution in the foreseeable future of a client load amounting to 6 per cent of the city's population, that the welfare role had increased despite efforts to expand rehabilitative services.[10] It is not much of a change that leaves a steady 6 per cent of the people tied to a program that its sponsors invented in another era to meet a different collection of problems. Is it not time to ask different questions? Is it not time to be fussy about what constitutes useful information?

[9]*Ibid.*, p. 50.
[10]*New York Times,* December 14, December 31, 1963.

II. IMPEDIMENTS TO CHANGE

It would seem a fair guess that proposals for policy innovation in public assistance would come from the identifiable groups most directly involved in its operation: administrators, both those working at the high policy levels and those working at the caseworker level; congressmen and congressional agencies through which public assistance legislation must move; commissions and committees officially created and invited to advise on the program; and the recipients. For a variety of reasons, however, each of these groups has been less of an instrument of change than one of retaining the particulars of a program with which they all acknowledge dissatisfaction.

The American Public Welfare Association

The dispensing of public assistance is a job shared by semiprofessionals and professional social workers in a ratio of about 96:4. The American Public Welfare Association, the national organization of state and local public welfare departments and of individuals engaged in the business of public relief, understandably attracts more of the semiprofessionals than of the professionals who have their own more exclusive but numerically larger club. Membership in APWA includes federal, state, and local welfare administrators, welfare workers, and board members from every jurisdiction. By the circumstances of its creation, however, APWA is at least as much an organization to service its members as it is an organization to improve the condition of its members' clients.

At the time that the depression was beginning to expose the paucity of public organization to meet relief problems, a New York foundation—the Spelman Fund—under the direction of the man who was later to invent income tax withholding, Beardsley Ruml, was pushing the possibility of improving the quality of state and local administration generally.[11] Goals were modest: associations of officials able to provide their members year-round service, to keep in touch with members, and to make current replies to inquiries. Ruml sent his emissary, Louis Brownlow, to the 1930 National Conference on Social Work meeting in Boston with authorization "to intimate to public welfare officials assembled there that it would be favorably disposed to make a grant if a new organization of public welfare officials was

[11]My discussion of the organization of the American Public Welfare Association within the Public Administration Clearing House depends on Louis Brownlow, *A Passion for Anonymity* (Chicago: University of Chicago Press, 1958), ch. 22.

established.''[12] From this intimation, there was promptly founded the American Association of Public Welfare Officials. Six months later, the Public Administration Clearing House set up its shop in Chicago with Spelman Fund money and Brownlow direction. One of the organizations constituting the Clearing House cluster was the new American Public Welfare Association. Like its older colleagues in the group including the American Municipal Association, the International City Managers' Association, the Municipal Finance Officers' Association, and the American Legislators' Association, APWA was bound to adhere to Brownlow's belief in the difference between administration and politics. This was a belief in the difference between providing a clearance of information, of ideas about techniques, and providing support for a cause.

For Brownlow and for the leaders of the Clearing House, the optimum arrangement in public affairs was two organizations in each field, one composed of citizens interested in the promotion of reform and political improvement at the polls and before legislative bodies, and the other composed of administrators interested in techniques, methodology, and training. For the International City Managers' Association (ICMA), the arrangement has been most successful because the National Municipal League took up the reform and lobbying goals shucked off by ICMA. The latter concentrated on running an employment exchange for its members and on producing training manuals in administration and an annual *Municipal Year Book* which is at once a directory and an important source of statistical data. With the Municipal League dealing with politics, ICMA went into business and grew rich on the sale of training manuals.

But since APWA has had no complementary political organization to meet Brownlow's model, it has tried to be both kinds of organizations without making that fact very explicit. There is no conspiracy to hide policy activity, only an automatic filling of a vacuum which has grown larger as the welfare policy problem has grown larger. The result is an association with a split personality, one part of it providing service to members and the other interested in policy improvement. Neither part is thoroughly dominant, and the APWA is neither rich nor powerful.

In mid-1963, APWA claimed some 7,700 members—a small, annoying decline from 1961 when an all-time high of 8,000 members had been reached—approximately 1,700 of whom were agency members. The 6,000 individual members represent only one-eighth of the estimated potential, and only 40 per cent of the modest membership

[12]*Ibid.,* p. 226.

149

goal of one-third of the potential, adopted by the APWA national membership committee.[13] Neither an information center nor a members' service agency in a class with the City Managers' Association, APWA also lacks ICMA's ability to command membership from virtually all practitioners in the field. Perhaps even more significant than numbers in evaluating APWA as an innovative agency in welfare legislation is distribution of membership. Its strength is more in the nonurban areas than in the urban centers, more in the south than in the north or west. Thus it is not an organization dominated by welfare workers from the big-city departments who are most likely to be regularly confronted with some of the new problems of public assistance: race discrimination, illegitimacy and desertion, automation, and slums. With as many individual members in Tennessee alone as in Massachusetts and Connecticut together, and with as many in Mississippi as in Oregon, the work and the goals of the organization can hardly parallel those of the Urban League.

APWA's executive leadership has performed an important function in a skillful manner by holding together in a single organization the disparate collection of state and local administrators and workers who, left on their own, would be likely to present to the public and to Congress a whole variety of interpretations of public welfare. The uneven character of the membership, however, serves to limit the scope and depth of APWA activity. The highly skilled New York and California welfare commissioners have programmatic commitments far deeper than the Caseworker I in Wichita, Kansas, who is likely to be passing through en route to marriage, or children, or a more tranquil job. The public welfare group is not composed largely of members with an educational investment and a permanent professional interest in the program. Members have not grown accustomed to being serviced by the association, unlike the city managers who expect their association to be a combination employment exchange, sponsor of short courses, information center, and nonpolitical exponent of the virtues of local government in general and of professional, city-manager, local government in particular. APWA is in the position of having to support public welfare programs at all governmental levels which makes it a closer relative of the Public Personnel Association (PPA) or of the American Society of Planning Officials (ASPO) than of the city managers' association. But unlike PPA and ASPO, the APWA cannot focus on professionalism as a common denominator in its membership cause, because APWA membership goes much beyond the professionally educated welfare worker.

[13]American Public Welfare Association, "Membership Statistical Report as of April 30, 1963" (Chicago, process duplicated).

Within the limiting framework described here, APWA has found it possible to fill a highly useful role as a gathering place for the varieties of people who work in the public welfare field or who have an intellectual, religious, or social interest in public welfare problems. It has been able to speak in Washington as a unified association because it supports increased federal funds and primary state responsibility for policy development within nationally established goals and guides, a package that all elements of the association can support.

In recent years, the association put a good deal of energy into a project with the ambitious goal of enlarging public understanding of public welfare. The project fuses the members' service job and the policy reform job. That it is an effort to enlarge welfare administrators' understanding of public welfare is evidenced by the membership of the project's two "shirtsleeve sessions," weekends of "no prepared papers for formal talks, only informal but very intensive discussion on a free-for-all basis." The friendly group at the first such session included nine state and two metropolitan welfare administrators, a public welfare board member, the executive director of United Community Funds and Councils, and the Commissioner of Social Security. To round out the seminar and to allow APWA to function as reform advocate, there were two newspaper editors and Charles Percy, then Chairman of the Board of Bell and Howell Company, and who had been 1960 national Republican Platform Committee Chairman. Leader of the session was Virgil Martin, President of Carson Pirie Scott and Co., the Chicago department store.

Both the project director and the then executive director of APWA pronounced the session an unqualified success, using excerpts from participants' letters of appreciation as supporting evidence. Just how success was to be measured—or whether there was any chance of failure—is not so clear. The official memorandum report to the Board of Directors of the association claimed that the "real value in sessions such as these lies not so much in the ideas that come out but in the process that takes place—the individual thinking and reacting that each participant goes through, and the ideas this generates in himself."[14] But Martin himself had already done his best to enlarge public understanding of public welfare by resigning as Chairman of the Illinois Public Aid Commission in protest against a plan by Governor Otto Kerner to cut public assistance budgets. Like the eleven welfare administrators present, he had been trying to enlarge public understanding of the problem for some years. Percy, who appeared to be the least committed member

[14]Memorandum from C. Virgil Martin, Chairman, Project Advisory Committee, to Board of Directors, American Public Welfare Association (Chicago, November 15, 1962), p. 1.

of the group, apparently did not have his understanding enlarged as much as the sponsors would have liked. Running against Kerner for Governor of Illinois in 1964, Percy announced himself in favor of ceilings on public aid payments.

Representation at the second "shirtsleeve session" was planned to be, and was, essentially the same, but with a different set of participants. The "uncommitted" participant on this occasion was Miss Barbara Johnson, President of the Association of Junior Leagues of America. There is no evidence of whether Miss Johnson has enlarged Junior League understanding of public welfare. Another phase of the project for the enlargement of public understanding involved sponsorship of a Public Affairs Pamphlet on public welfare by Emma Harrison of the *New York Times*.[15]

Earlier foundation grants had permitted APWA to sponsor sessions comparable to the "shirtsleeve" meetings, albeit more prosaically titled. A Project on Aging, supported by a Ford grant, produced three 1961 "institutes" on aspects of public welfare services for the aging. Between 1958 and 1961, the Rockefeller Brothers Fund supported seven institutes on subjects ranging from the objectives of public welfare administration to medical care in public welfare. Two highly academic studies of the ADC program have been sponsored by APWA, a decade apart.[16] On both occasions, a special grant from the Field Foundation made the work possible; it was farmed out each time to the Institute for Research in Social Science at the University of North Carolina; both reports were for specialized readers. For the nonacademics, APWA publishes short, inexpensive pamphlets on various aspects of public welfare problems.

In the words of one of its leading spokesmen, the American Public Welfare Association "is a democratic organization in the sense that it permits participation by all of its members in the development of its policies and the development of its programs." The strength of this kind of organization—working at many governmental levels, drawing from varied levels of professional skill and commitment, yet "democratic"—is maximized if it concentrates on external enemies and discourages internal sniping. The association's statement of basic principles reflects this wisdom by focusing on the obligation of a democracy to assure equitable opportunity for family life, healthful

[15]Public Affairs Pamphlet No. 343 (New York: Public Affairs Committee, April, 1963).
[16]Gordon Blackwell and Raymond Gould, *Future Citizens All* (Chicago: American Public Welfare Association, 1952); and M. Elaine Burgess and Daniel O. Price, *An American Dependency Challenge* (Chicago: American Public Welfare Association, 1963).

living, and maximum utilization of potentialities; the desirability of contributory social insurance; a preference for family-centered public welfare programs which would make financial, protective, preventive, and rehabilitative services available to all who need them; the need to make the benefits of modern medical science available to all, if necessary through governmental or other social measures. It is not a statement of conviction that will unnerve any member in any job in any public welfare agency.

To sum up, APWA's major thrust has probably been in pushing for increased federal funds in the public assistance grant program. As an association, it must still be concerned with increasing membership in a group that derives minimum benefits from membership. Only a limited number of members have an important stake in the association because it does not serve the economic protection function of a labor union or provide the psychological satisfactions of an exclusive professional guild. It agrees on "objectives" but it can make few "findings" because many of its members are really not experts. Its strong southern membership—there are more members from the southeastern states than from the central states, and twice as many from the southwest as from the west coast—may enhance its influence with congressional committees led by southerners. An informed, determined group of public assistance specialists could make APWA a vehicle for innovation in the program by explicitly abandoning the Public Administration Clearing House tradition, making the organization instead an association for the advancement of public welfare policy. It could then gather data on such issues as the constitutional rights of relief recipients rather than on how to behave as a member of a welfare board. Elizabeth Wickenden has already found, however, that there is really no market for an association for the advancement of public welfare policy. APWA is likely, therefore, to try to make the best of its split personality and avoid deeper involvement in either national policy or membership service.

The Recipients

Probably no beneficiaries of a public subsidy have less real influence on the terms and conditions of that subsidy than do the recipients of public assistance. The various agricultural lobbies, spokesmen for one or another segment of the farm population, are expected to speak for the farmer in the formulation of price subsidy legislation. By the same token, the views of the publishing industry are solicited through its specialized associations in the course of fixing the mail subsidy provided that group. Even in the case of economic and military subsidies provided foreign countries, while the representatives of the nations involved are kept out of the spotlight, it is perfectly clear that many of them have been involved in the tentative allocation that precedes the formal legislation. Only in public assistance does it seem to be taken for granted that the interests of the group most directly and particularly affected, the recipients, will be indirectly protected in the course of the public policy struggle by some caretaker.

One group of assistance recipients speaks through its own leaders rather than through Elizabeth Wickenden or anyone else. While the National Federation of the Blind covers public aid only as part of its broader interests in problems of the blind, assistance recipients are part of its membership. The federation is understood, therefore, to be representative of rather than just sympathetic to the aid to the blind group. It is regularly accorded a respectful hearing on issues dealing with aid to the blind.

There is no comparable mechanism for ferreting out the views of deserted or widowed mothers as to the adequacy of the ADC program, its impact on the beneficiary, and grass roots suggestions for change in that category. While numerous other factors contribute to the end result, it is still worth noting that the most highly organized beneficiary group—the blind—has been the most favorably treated category; the beneficiary group with a smattering of organization—the aged—is runner-up; the totally unorganized beneficiaries—those in the ADC group—whose political interests are handled by several trustees have been least favored.

The leading formal organization of public assistance beneficiaries is that led, until his death in July, 1965, by George McLain, centered in California as the California Institute of Social Welfare, with ties outside the state through the McLain-created National Institute of Social Welfare and his National League of Senior Citizens. In McLain's words, he had "for the past 22 years been engaged daily for the elderly in the field of administration of the public assistance section of the Social Security Act." During one period, the scope of his activities was broadened to include the blind as well as the elderly, a marriage that fell apart when leaders of the blind group threw their strength against legislation geared to need rather than rehabilitation. McLain never attempted to bring ADC recipients within his orbit.

McLain's primary goal was the organization and mobilization of an unstable constituency. Thus, much of the institute's work has been directed inward but there has been no lack of pressure group activity as an important element in successful organization. The struggle for increased benefits has aided in the recruitment of new members and reinforced the commitment of old members. By helping to justify the institute's existence, attempts to better members' situations have served as a rationale for internal fund-raising and for the maintenance of the organization's solvency.

Because the operation has been sustained by OAA recipients who are tempted by the possibility of marginal improvements in benefits available under a program they know and understand, no reconsideration of the basic structure of the program is possible. The anxiety and insecurity of the old age group make it necessary to provide assurance that the *status quo* will be safeguarded as a minimum goal. Accordingly, as Frank Pinner and his colleagues have put it:

> The entire program of the California Institute of Social Welfare has been developed by McLain as a response to the Old Age Assistance law and its administration. The measures proposed by McLain and endorsed by his members refer to specific sections of the law and specific kinds of administrative behavior; they do not call for radical changes in laws and institutions or for revolutionary innovation.[17]

Concentrating his efforts in California between 1941 and 1955, McLain demonstrated that an organization with pension goals less comprehensive than those of the Townsend Plan or of Upton Sinclair's End Poverty In California effort could have an important measure of success. OAA maximum grants were increased during that period from $40 to $85, an improvement which McLain credited to his own efforts although his opponents are skeptical. Pinner suggests that the truth is somewhere between the extremes. McLain's use of the initiative and referendum techniques were important elements in whatever success he had. In the 13 years between 1941 and 1954, the California institute sponsored four initiative measures for statewide vote. In addition to furnishing a path around the legislature, the initiative method helped to keep the organization together by giving the members an opportunity to collect signatures and so enjoy a sense of participation in a direct effort to improve their status. One measure, on the ballot in 1948, was successful. It increased the maximum OAA grant from $60 to $75; reduced the eligibility age from 65 to 63; abolished relative responsibility; centralized control of the program in the state Department of Social Welfare; and elected Myrtle Williams, Secretary-Treasurer of the California Social Welfare Institute, as Director of the Department. A year later, the measure was repealed by popular vote after the

---

[17]Frank Pinner, Paul Jacobs, and Philip Selznick, *Old Age and Political Behavior* (Berkeley and Los Angeles: University of California Press, 1959), p. 21.

California Chamber of Commerce, the County Supervisors' Association, the Taxpayers' Association, and the California Council for the Blind allied in favor of repeal, spending a million dollars in the effort. It was after that campaign that McLain avoided the mistake of combining programs for the aged with those for the blind.

Gradually shifting attention to the national scene, McLain formed the National Institute of Social Welfare in 1956 as a national federation of state pension organizations and, since that time, kept a regular lobbyist in Washington when Congress was in session. McLain personally tried for the Democratic nomination for the House of Representatives in 1952 against the late Clyde Doyle, but ran badly. In 1964, when he entered the Senate primary against Pierre Salinger and Alan Cranston, McLain won only 7 per cent of the vote.

The activity of McLain's organization of public assistance recipients is important because of the contrast it affords with the practices of groups able to apply some sanctions to enforce their claim on the public fisc, or the public conscience, or both. Organized labor's use of the strike weapon, the farmer's abandonment of the land or his withholding of produce, the schoolteacher's refusal to supervise extra-curricular activity have all resulted in public policy designed to improve the economic condition of the groups involved. But public response in these cases had an element of self-protection — strikes, agricultural shortages, and inadequate schools are highly inconvenient. Marginal or submarginal relief budgets can be ignored. There is no ready sanction available to the client. He has nothing to withhold.

Developments in civil rights have some useful points of comparison with those in public assistance. The hope that education, persuasion, and voluntarism would in time overcome discrimination against the Negro may be compared to the hope that social insurance would wipe out the public assistance problem. Both hopes failed. New treatments were proclaimed. Failure of nonlegal methods to cope with race discrimination was acknowledged with the school desegregation decision of 1954 and with the Civil Rights Act of 1964. Failure of social insurance to drive out public assistance was recognized with the service emphasis proclaimed in 1956 and reaffirmed in 1962. While neither the school desegregation ruling nor the services amendments themselves effected much change very quickly, the former did trigger organization for change. The Negro has been organized and trained in the use of sanctions — the sit-in, the wade-in, economic boycott, extensive use of the judicial process to seek protection of constitutional guarantees. Now the payoff is not measured in marginal improvements in the economic and social condition of the Negro; it is measured in revolutionary innovation that scorns token gains and actually provides special advantages for Negroes in some areas of American life even while the desegregation battle continues in a bloody phase.

Is the public assistance client so much more insecure, so much more depressed than the Negro that a comparable pattern of organization and a comparable nonviolent drive for revolutionary change is precluded? Coupling the impact of Francis Townsend and Huey Long on the development and enactment of the old age titles of the Social Security Act with the success of the current organized Negro movement for equality now suggests that an organization of participants with an articulate leader may be more effective in working for improvements in the status of public assistance clients than are the numerous welfare associations now purporting—with the best of intentions—to represent the interests of the recipients in the political arena. The idea of self-help by direct action of depressed or dependent groups has been pushed—and shown to be effective—by Saul Alinsky, a Chicago sociologist who is a specialist in organizing such groups. Alinsky furnishes blueprints and guidance for action programs by depressed groups in particular locales; he does not deal in public policy leadership. The latter kind of leadership is hard to find among the very poor. To the present date, such leadership has been virtually nonexistent within either the OAA or ADC recipient groups. But it is certainly not impossible that the groups themselves can be organized and led by a compassionate clergyman or other outsider. George McLain was no Martin Luther King. When the Martin Luther King of public assistance does appear, client-sponsored proposals for innovation will be worth watching. In the meantime, innovation will have to come from another source.

Congressional Committees

Operating over a limited jurisdiction—District of Columbia appropriations—Senator Robert Byrd has given a chilling demonstration of how effective an inquiring legislator with a specialized subcommittee and a little staff help from the Comptroller-General can be in changing some of the premises on which public assistance policy has been based. Byrd pushed the inquiry beyond Miss Wickenden's letters to friendly administrators and schools of social work deans, and beyond the American Public Welfare Association's effort to enlarge public understanding. He pushed for information that finally made it necessary for someone to make a summary comparison of myth and reality in the District of Columbia's welfare program. Byrd invited the Chief of the

Public Assistance Division of the District Welfare Department to do it himself:

Sen. Byrd. Now, Mr. Scholz, I think that you are in the best position to indicate to us what should be done to put this department on its proper course, weed out the ineligibles, provide for the needy, cut out the red tape and the paperwork, and thus permit the Department to go forward with a well-charted program which will earn for it the respect and high regard, not only of those people who are being served by it, but also of the people who help support it with their tax dollars.

Now could you in a somewhat brief fashion let us have your advice and counsel on this matter before we recess?

Mr. Scholz. All right.

I believe that we have learned from the painful experience of the past few months that our social service staff is not equipped to do the job it is expected to do with today's caseload. We are operating with social workers, and when we hire case workers all our specifications are written that way, all our instructions are written that way, we expect them to do the old type of social work which is a helping relationship. We tried to create a public image that the social worker is not a snoop who looks under the bed and in the closet, but is as one well known training film put it, a friend at the door. And as a result a relationship has been built up which is not realistic, where the social workers, as the Social Security Administration puts it, uses the clients, the applicant, as the primary source of information. And we find this information is not reliable.

This may all have been true at the time when the program started, when we had the so-called "nice" people on relief, the widows and orphans who have been siphoned off since then by the survivors benefits program, and when we had the families that were unbroken, where the man was disabled and except for the financial assistance they would not have been able to manage. They have been siphoned off by the disability insurance program. And what we are having now is the bottom of the barrel, without wanting to cast any aspersions on the worthwhile people we have on assistance. Most of them, as our investigation now has shown, are problem cases. They are, as Mr. Lang pointed out, people with problems of alcoholism, drug addiction, with criminal records, and are not the type of people whom social workers are trained to deal with.[18]

The Byrd activity in the public assistance field assembled some data on ineligibles and fraudulent cases, compelled an airing of the characteristics of some of the case load, and touched off a national audit of the ADC rolls based on a presumption of high levels of ineligibility. Byrd focused less on the inadequacy of policy and more on the inadequacies of petty administrators. Unfortunately, there is not a

[18]U.S. Congress, Senate, Subcommittee of the Committee on Appropriations, Hearings, "District of Columbia Appropriations for 1963," 87th Cong., 2d Sess, 1962 part 2, pp. 1638-39.

congressional agency equipped to devote comparable energy, hard work, and imagination to reexamining the basis of relief policy, to considering its applicability to its present clientele. The latter would be a more rewarding inquiry than was the search for fraud which has never been shown to be widespread.

Congress has shown relatively little interest in the whole question of public assistance policy, least of all in anything unconnected with the federal percentage of the grant-in-aid. Even the much heralded 1962 amendments provoked a minimum of legislative attention as measured by attendance and questioning at committee hearings, by floor debate and discussion, or by important changes made in the bill sent down by the administration. Until the addition of the Kerr-Mills program of aid to the medically indigent aged in 1960, and the more recent political activity connected with efforts to substitute a medical care program tied to social insurance, there was occasional congressional confusion between old age assistance and old age insurance. Much of the legislators' seeming indifference can be traced to the diminishing importance of public relief in the postwar period when international affairs, atomic energy, space, health, and civil rights developed as the glamor issues. Any intelligent young member of Congress who decided to turn his attention to public assistance, hoping to achieve recognition as a specialist on the subject, gambled against the chance that, before he could complete his "cram course," public assistance would further decline in public interest and congressional interest to the point where the investment would yield no political benefits. Neither atomic energy nor space held similar uncertainties.

In addition, there is a built-in deterrent to congressional specialization in public assistance and to the consequent likelihood of congressional pressure for reexamination of policy. The deterrent stems indirectly from the original decision of the constitutional lawyers to make the taxing power the key to constitutional safety for social security. As a tax matter, for purposes of legislative committee jurisdiction, all social security bills — including public assistance — come to the House Committee on Ways and Means and to the Senate Finance Committee. The structuring of these two committees, their staffing features, the significance of the legislation competing for committee attention, and even the Constitution of the United States combine to make it difficult for a member of either committee to narrow in on public assistance.

Scheduling is one discouraging element. The time of a Ways and Means or Finance Committee member is cut to periods of varying length but almost uniform high intensity while the committee concentrates on legislation dealing with revenue rates, tax reform, the bonded debt, customs, trade agreements, or social security, each to the exclusion of all the other subjects. The constitutional requirement that revenue measures originate in the House is used as justification by leadership in the Senate Finance Committee not to schedule Senate hearings until bills have gone through Ways and Means hearings and executive session, have been reported to the floor, and are passed by the House. This unwillingness to conduct even preliminary hearings on important bills delays bringing the policy issues involved to the members of Senate Finance until a relatively late date. In 1963, for example, while Ways and Means was arguing tax reduction for nine months, Finance was marking time with trivial legislation. The House Committee then proceeded to a brief consideration of a necessary increase in the debt limit, but the year ran out before subsequent hearings on medicare could be completed.

In every instance, Ways and Means functions in full committee and follows public hearings with extended executive sessions at which expert witnesses are in attendance. Ways and Means moves slowly, deliberately, and cautiously. Because the prospect of having tax or tariff legislation written on the House floor is too frightful to contemplate, Ways and Means legislation will ordinarily come to the floor from the Rules Committee with a rule prohibiting amendments. Therefore, once the Ways and Means Committee finishes off a bill, its members can be confident that they can go on to the next subject. It is a little like the student who faces half a dozen final examinations in a week. He becomes a specialist on a single subject on a particular day, but cannot afford to give that subject any of his attention on any other day.

Committee staffing is nonexistent in public assistance. Staffing of the Ways and Means Committee bypasses the whole social security field, thereby further lessening the chance for information-gathering and for innovative proposals. "To me," said Representative Thomas Curtis, an active member of the committee, "one of the great tragedies . . . is that this great Committee on Ways and Means, which has jurisdiction over these important matters, does not have a permanent professional staff in the field of social security . . . it is almost impossible really, in my judgment, for this Committee to conduct an adequate and meaningful study into this very important area."[19] The Senate Finance Committee, "the most centralized committee in Congress," with one of the lowest budgets, is also without social security staff help.[20] The Finance Committee has a staff of six, only one of whom is a professional, a tariff expert.

[19]Ways and Means, Hearings, 1962, p. 175.
[20]George Goodwin, Jr., "Subcommittees: The Miniature Legislatures of Congress," *American Political Science Review,* LVI (September, 1962), 603.

In his now famous blast at the Senate Establishment, Senator Joseph Clark—not a member of the committee—pinpointed three reasons for what he called "untoward delay" in the reporting of important measures to the floor from the Finance Committee. The first was the committee's traditional insistence on waiting for House action before opening hearings. Clark found the staff problem equally troublesome: "it has not an adequate staff in terms of the numbers of qualified men and women able to sift and analyze and report to the members of the committee . . . besides advising other Members of the Senate who may feel impelled by reason of an interest in the subject matter to seek the advice of members of the staff of the Finance Committee."[21]

A third Clark complaint about the Finance Committee—the absence of a subcommittee pattern despite a jurisdiction as extensive and as complicated as that of any Senate committee—would be equally applicable to the Ways and Means Committee. The practice of meeting in full committee eliminates, in each case, the possibility of simultaneous hearings on different matters and the more prompt consideration of legislative proposals on a variety of subjects. A subcommittee pattern in Finance would have the additional advantage, in the view of some liberals, of opening the way to staff expansion. It would have the disadvantage, in the view of those happy with the *status quo,* of cutting up the power of the committee chairman. Division of the Ways and Means and Finance Committees into subcommittees is probably the most likely way to encourage specialization by members. While every member is formally involved in every subject, there has been no sign that public assistance can challenge reciprocal trade or excise taxes as a matter of specialized interest.

Specialization should not be equated with influence. It is important not to overstate the likely impact of congressional specialists. Respect, deference, and power may be earned through specialization, but it is not an unfailing route. Influence does not flow automatically to the knowledgeable member, a conclusion illustrated by Senator Paul Douglas' role on the Finance Committee. As an academic specialist on the economics of social security, Douglas can speak on the question with authority. Nevertheless, his impact on Finance Committee action in this field is certainly not great; indeed it is characterized by one close administration observer whose job it is to know these things as "virtually zero." The advantage Douglas has as a specialist is overcome by the disadvantage associated with his "out" status in the ruling elite of the Senate. Douglas' success in securing an earned income exemption for OAA recipients in 1962, by floor amendment, his third try in six

[21]*Congressional Record,* February 20, 1963, pp. 2524-25.

years, is attributable less to his expertise than to the fact that Senator Robert Kerr had been independently persuaded to support the proposal.

It is not as much of a problem for the influential senator to get specialized help as for the specialist to acquire influence. Not only can a member bring experts to the hearings, he can bring them to the floor with him as did Kerr in the 1961 debate on increasing the federal share of public assistance benefits. The experts were not even Kerr's own staff members or congressional committee personnel. Two members of the staff of the Library of Congress and an Assistant Secretary of Health, Education, and Welfare were brought to the Senate Chamber "in order that their advice and information may be available." Actually, it is the judgment of those who follow public assistance legislation as lobbyists or administrators that Kerr himself combined influence with a capacity for work, with intelligence, and with an understanding of public assistance. But Kerr is dead.

Innovation by Congress is more likely when the legislative sponsor has both influence and a specialized knowledge of the subject matter, and less likely when one or another is lacking. Specialized knowledge alone is not likely to produce any action. Influence alone may bring the short-run result desired by the sponsoring groups; it will not maximize congressional understanding and participation. Senator Scott Lucas threw his influence behind the ADC caretaker grant provision in 1950 because he was told that it had the support of the American Legion. Although the caretaker grant was adopted, Lucas never cared especially about public assistance policy. Men of influence — particularly southerners — have been active through the years in supporting an unrestricted increase in federal public assistance grant funds: Ernest McFarland, Russell Long, Robert Kerr, Wilbur Mills all pushed successfully for changes in the grant-in-aid formula to benefit the states and the recipients if the states chose to pass on the increases. But the institutional arrangements — lack of staff in Senate Finance, lack of social security staff in Ways and Means, absence of a subcommittee pattern in both Finance and Ways and Means, the extensive jurisdiction of both committees, with public assistance low in relative importance — discourage the combining of influence and specialized knowledge that might produce congressional innovation on the policy side.

Federal and State Administrators

In the first years of public assistance, top federal administrators represented an important source of innovative proposals. Arthur Altmeyer, one of the major architects of the Social Security Act, became a member of the Social Security Board during its period as an independent board (1935-1939), retained this attachment when the board was made part of the domain of the Federal Security Administrator (1939-1950), and became the Commissioner for Social Security in the Federal Security Agency when the board was replaced by a single administrator (1950-1953). When the Republican reorganization of 1953 wiped out the job of Commissioner for Social Security, replacing it with a Commissioner of Social Security in the new Department of Health, Education, and Welfare, Altmeyer's tenure ended. (The change from Commissioner "for" to Commissioner "of" was innovative in that its purpose was to eliminate Altmeyer and permit a new image to be developed that would emphasize the role of the states and downgrade the federal role.) From 1936 until November, 1953, Jane Hoey served as Director of the Bureau of Public Assistance. Altmeyer, Miss Hoey, and one or two others monopolized high-level bureaucratic knowledge of the origins, details, philosophy, and expectations of the public assistance program. It was Altmeyer who proposed the important 1939 amendments dealing with inclusion of all income and resources, confidentiality of assistance records, and the merit system requirement for state personnel.

Altmeyer looked on the role of the federal administrator as that of a policeman alert to misdeeds by state welfare agencies believed to be subject to state political control. Using audit exceptions, and withholding federal funds when he thought it necessary, Altmeyer built up the image of a tough administrator, insensitive to political needs, bent on national control. But by 1940, the program was stabilized; federal administrative activity became routine; the states had come to understand that public assistance had to be more professional than political. Federal administrators in public assistance coasted easily in the 1940's. They had experience, specialized information, and influence. There was no evidence that the program was not "right"; Presidents Roosevelt and Truman were sympathetic; money was adequate; waiting lists were outlawed, an ADC caretaker grant adopted, a new disability category established, and medical vendor payments approved; the big remaining goal of federal administrators was to cut back on the maximum permissible residence requirement.

This picture faded with the 1952 election when a Republican administration came to power for the first time in the life history of the Social Security Act. Experience and stability in federal administrative leadership declined. Altmeyer went out quietly after his job was abolished, declining an opportunity to remain on the payroll in a special capacity for the few months necessary to improve his pension situation. Miss Hoey went out noisily, formally discharged, having declined to resign after her job was reclassified from civil-service-protected to a new "policy-determining," civil-service-exempt classification. Between 1953 and 1961, when it was increasingly apparent that things were not right with the public assistance program, there was a parade of Social Security Commissioners; from 1954 to 1959, the "policy-determining" position of Director of the Bureau of Public Assistance was filled by Jay Roney who jumped from child welfare representative of the Children's Bureau in the Kansas City Regional Office of that bureau. Roney clearly could not match Jane Hoey in prestige or in experience. Professional positions in the Bureau of Public Assistance dropped to 136 in fiscal 1954, the lowest number since 1940 when there had been 130 positions for only two-thirds as many state programs. The number dropped further to 125 in 1955, and then started a slow climb back to 140 in 1960. Loose bodies in Washington or in the regional offices were not encouraged during this period of emphasis on state responsibility.

Now there are signs of a renewal of the old days. Ellen Winston, long-time Commissioner of Welfare in North Carolina, is Commissioner of the new Welfare Administration. Wilbur Cohen, who worked with Edwin Witte and with Altmeyer in the development of the Social Security Act thirty years ago, served first as Assistant Secretary of Health, Education, and Welfare for legislation, and has more recently become Under Secretary of the Department. Fred Steininger, former director of the Lake County, Indiana, Welfare Department, past president of APWA, and a member of the fraternity, is Director of the Bureau of Family Services. The federal war on poverty is reminiscent, of course, of the New Deal days. But there is an important difference. While federal public assistance bureaucrats are again in a strong position, important innovation may now demand an overhaul of policies and principles they themselves helped develop rather than a starting from scratch. Abandoning old policies is one thing when they are someone else's policies. It is quite another thing, and appreciably more difficult, to reconsider one's own work. Yet it is not easy to uncover fresh new administrative talent.

Finding federal-level administrators in public assistance was a problem in 1953 when Jane Hoey went, and it was still a problem in 1963 when a new job had to be filled, that of Welfare Commissioner. Until 1963, public assistance did not have a life of its own in the federal chain of command, since it had always been tied to the social security apparatus. Belated administrative recognition of the separability of public assistance and social security (and tacit recognition of the permanence of public assistance) came in 1963 with the creation, as a legacy from Secretary Ribicoff, of a separate Welfare Administration within the Department of Health, Education, and Welfare. When the Kennedy administration turned to filling the job of welfare administrator, it found that the pickings were just as thin as had been the case when the Eisenhower people were seeking a successor for Jane Hoey. In both cases, it was easier to decide who would not do than who would do. "I don't think there were five people in the United States from whom a choice could be made for Commissioner of Welfare," complained one official who was involved in the 1963 selection.

One reason for the difficulty in finding a properly qualified person for Welfare Commissioner is the relative weakness of the state administrators who would normally be expected to constitute a pool of available talent in accordance with the training ground theory of American federalism. State welfare administrators do not fit the model. As a group, they come up through the political lines rather than through professional career lines and, therefore, are heterogeneous in backgrounds and values. Pressures from welfare and reform groups for the appointment of a professional conflict with the appointing authority's desire to find someone who will be sensitive to local problems. The resulting compromise candidate rarely represents the best of either the welfare or political worlds. Frequently preoccupied with trying to make a respectable showing with limited funds, and having more in common with their own states' political leaders than with each other, many state administrators have attachments and loyalties to the political leadership and to the dominant values in the state rather than to the more distant programmatic goals of the American Public Welfare Association.

A dramatic case in point is that of Mrs. Mary Evelyn Parker, Commissioner of the Louisiana Department of Public Welfare who, in a letter to the editor of the APWA journal, *Public Welfare,* in January, 1959, acknowledged that public welfare programs did not meet needs, and asserted the importance of welfare administrators in educating politicians to these needs. "If public welfare programs are to come nearer to meeting the needs of people," Mrs. Parker wrote, "elected officials must understand, in general terms, the present program and the needs that are not being met. We must take advantage of every opportunity for interpretation."[22] Less than two years later, Mrs. Parker was administering the Louisiana suitable home law which *ex post facto* struck more than 20,000 children — principally Negro — from the ADC rolls because they were living with mothers who had borne an illegitimate child or children after receiving public assistance. In the

[22]"Letter to Editor," *Public Welfare,* XVII (January, 1959), 39.

course of the ensuing dialogue with federal officials on the conformity of the state act to the federal law, Mrs. Parker denied that racial discrimination was involved, noted that none of the national welfare groups had protested while the law was pending, and complained that the federal agency "sat by and saw these children removed in July and did not send any word to Louisiana until September."[23] Prior to the formal hearing, she announced rejection of two federal demands: to a demand that the department advise the affected mothers of their right to reapply for assistance, Mrs. Parker replied that "the Welfare Department is not in the business of soliciting applications for assistance"; to the proposal that all ineligible cases be referred to the courts for possible removal of children from unsuitable homes, she answered that "to refer all ineligible cases to the courts would place an impossible burden on the courts and the department."[24] The Mrs. Parker who, in January, 1959, had felt that "we must take advantage of every opportunity for interpretation" apparently yielded to the Mrs. Parker who read the Louisiana election returns in January, 1960.

There are many differences among laws of the states governing selection, retention, and responsibilities of public welfare administrators. In 1961, only three states — Colorado, Maryland, and Michigan — provided merit system selection and protection, thereby allowing the welfare administrator the security that might be conducive to generating innovative proposals. When Judge Thomas J. S. Waxter who had served as Baltimore's Welfare Director from 1935 to 1953, and as Maryland Public Welfare Director under merit system protection since 1953, died in November, 1961, the *Baltimore Sun* reported of Waxter that "He was a tireless proponent of new approaches to welfare problems." It is not a description readily applicable to many state administrators, a goodly number of whom, whether appointed by the governor or by a quasi-independent welfare board, have neither tenure nor an escape route to a comparable job elsewhere. Some of them safely choose to become familiar with the old approaches rather than to propose new ones. This is not to deny the independence, competence, and originality of many state and municipal welfare administrators. To take one example at the municipal level, Raymond Hilliard in Cook County, Illinois, pushed literacy training programs and vocational training for employable recipients long before it became the fashionable thing to do, urged the resumption of a Civilian Conservation Corps program before it became part of the war on poverty, and has spoken out sharply against moves by both Democrats and Republicans to cut

[23]*New York Times,* September 18, 1960, p. 70.
[24]*New York Times,* November 3, 1960, p. 49.

back levels of public assistance support. Again, with pardonable pride in his program, James Dumpson, New York City's Welfare Commissioner, told an interviewer that "there is nothing new for us [in New York] in the 1962 Public Welfare Amendments." Dumpson left his job in 1965. The opportunities for continuous high-level service in public assistance administration are too limited to stimulate development of a class of innovative state and municipal welfare administrators.

An illuminating commentary on the federal administrator's view of the role of state administrators is Secretary Ribicoff's statement to the House Ways and Means Committee to which he was presenting the "new direction" amendments of 1962: the "State administrators of public welfare programs conferred with us here in Washington on our administrative changes and legislative prospects. They expressed their wholehearted approval of the goals we have set . . . unanimously backed up what we are trying to do in our efforts in this field."[25] State administrators are people to whom a policy program in public assistance is unveiled; they approve of goals set by others.

Among the factors that discourage reexamination of the fundamentals of relief policy is the delicacy in reporting that characterizes both state and federal public assistance administrators. The early Ohio, Illinois, and Oklahoma scandals were treated circumspectly in the annual reports of the Social Security Board, so much so that the story of the unhappiness in Oklahoma was passed over entirely. Results of statewide reviews of eligibility carried out in the 1950's were not reported, although they might have provoked more intensive concern with eligibility-determination techniques and procedures. Typically, the 1954 Annual Report of the Department of Health, Education, and Welfare noted that "In 11 States statistically selected statewide samples of case records were reviewed to determine the eligibility of persons receiving assistance and the accuracy of payments made to them," but it did not have anything to say about findings.[26] Three years later, "administrative reviews were conducted in 23 States, covering 920 local agencies. . . .Findings from these reviews were used in strengthening program operations both in the States and in the Bureau."[27] Whatever the findings were, they did not make their way to the report.

[25]Ways and Means, Hearings, 1962, p. 297.
[26]U.S. Department of Health, Education, and Welfare, *Annual Report 1954* (Washington), p. 56.
[27]U.S. Department of Health, Education, and Welfare, *Annual Report 1957* (Washington), p. 51.

More recently, the federal reports somewhat reluctantly acknowledge the troublesome questions of illegitimacy and of race, and hasten to explain, in a general way, how to account for them. In 1962, the department said the following:

In recent years, public concern about welfare expenditures and dependency of welfare recipients has been reflected in widespread publicity about individual instances of fraud, unmarried parenthood, desertion, and other social problems. But there has also been an increasing recognition that the economic need of some groups is a consequence of a healthy, growing industrial society in which technological change and automation have produced economic and social problems with which some individuals, families, and even communities, can no longer cope.[28]

But this is not the real point. The fact that unmarried parenthood and desertion are often consequences of an inability to cope with economic and social problems does not make them any less real matters of concern. The critical issue must be whether social and economic problems are sufficiently different now from the problems of 1935 to raise a question about whether the public assistance categories themselves are still appropriate. Are the cases attributable to social problems extensive enough to merit formal separation? Are the widows and orphans on the ADC rolls, persons whose dependency stems from an act of God rather than from an act of society, being victimized by the perpetuation of a single classification when there are really major differences within the class? If there were no public assistance legislation and we were now drafting a program *de novo,* would the existing patterns be maintained? Should the problem of Negro dependency be acknowledged by the creation of a formal unit in the Welfare Administration? Does OAA still belong in a federal-state program at all? Should eligibility stipulations be rewritten to provide a direct federal grant to the needy aged, thereby freeing limited staff to work with new categories and eliminating OAA from state welfare budgets?

These are questions not dealt with in the federal reports or reexaminations. They are not likely to be dealt with until some mechanism develops for an uncommitted influential group to gather information and transmit it without fear of jeopardizing welfare progress in the process. Although this is theoretically the job assigned to several advisory committees, it has not been done because federal administrators responsible for selecting members have consistently played safe and named a preponderance of members who have an attachment to the *status quo.*

[28]U.S. Department of Health, Education, and Welfare, *Annual Report 1962* (Washington), p. 55.

Advisory Councils

Tripartite advisory bodies representative of employers, employees, and the public have been a favored official technique for the development of new policies in social security. The first such group, the Advisory Council on Economic Security, was created to advise the small Committee on Economic Security appointed by Franklin Roosevelt to produce a social security program. That Advisory Council was less than a great success because it actually was a kind of competitor of the committee it served, itself a *de facto* advisory body to the President and to the appropriate committees of Congress. Thereafter, the technique has been successful in establishing a focal point for policy proposals, partly because the advisory bodies subsequently created have had no competition from any official agency. Social security advisory bodies have taken on both the specialized subcommittee and the social security staffing jobs that the congressional committees have not developed. In addition, because they are advisory bodies of private citizens, and because their original conception involved a balanced representation of the interest groups concerned, advisory bodies are presumed to be uncommitted.

Before 1958, public assistance and social security were fused for advisory council purposes in accordance with the still prevailing myth that assistance was a residual aspect of social insurance. Tripartite councils on social security worked in 1937-1938 and in 1947-1948 with the understanding that both problems were within their scope. Enactment of two important public assistance improvements — the caretaker grant in ADC and separate medical vendor payments — "was immeasurably aided," according to Wilbur Cohen, by the support given these proposals by "a distinguished advisory council. . . . The contribution of the advisory council [of 1947-1948] was of great significance."[29] Ten years later, public assistance and child welfare were split off from social security and made the subject of separate advisory council inquiry. President Eisenhower hoped that one result of the work of the public assistance advisory council created in 1958 would be a recommendation for increased state and local financial responsibility in the categorical assistance program, that the council would put a brake on the prevalent congressional disposition to add to the federal grant over administration opposition.

Creation of a separate public assistance advisory council posed a unique kind of problem in the selection of members. The earlier advisory councils concerned with social security could, by their tripar-

[29]Wilbur J. Cohen, "Factors Influencing the Content of Federal Public Welfare Legislation," *The Social Welfare Forum, 1954* (New York: Columbia University Press, 1954), p. 212.

tite character, represent the principal beneficiaries, the principal bene-factors, and the general public. Social insurance, after all, involved special tax levies against employees and employers and the creation of a trust fund for the benefit of contributors whose views would under-standably be solicited in the governance of the program. Tripartitism allowed for participation of the major groups directly involved — employ-ers and employees — while protecting the interests of groups only peripherally involved by including public members. Resulting activity can range from free collective bargaining to mediation to arbitration, depending on whether public members sit silent, work for an agreement satisfactory to both the employer and employee groups, or impose an agreement by siding with one of the groups against the other. To achieve this tripartite character, the earlier social security councils were drawn from organized labor and from the organized business community with most public members holding government or uni-versity attachments.

An advisory council on public assistance alone required either a new theory of tripartitism or a complete substitute for tripartitism to govern the designation of members. Public assistance is not a contribu-tory program; it is supported by general revenue. No special trust fund is established; the program competes with all other public causes for public funds. No organized group can be said to be even remotely representative of the beneficiaries; no employer organization can be said to have a particular stake in the program directly comparable to that established by the social security tax on employers. An advisory council in the established tradition would be a case of using an old model for a new purpose.

The statute creating the council in 1958, however, was part of the sweetening used to produce presidential approval for a bill increasing public assistance benefits after the President had specifically requested a reduction in the federal share. There was neither time nor disposition to theorize about the niceties of the applicability or inapplicability of tripartite councils in view of the new, separate emphasis on public assistance. On signing the bill, Eisenhower warned that "increases in the proportion of the public assistance programs which are financed by the Federal Government can lead only to a weakening of the responsi-bility of the states and communities."[30] Charged with worrying over the presumably frightful consequences of spending more federal money on public assistance was a council of 12 "who shall, to the extent pos-sible, represent employers and employees in equal numbers, per-

[30]*Congressional Quarterly Almanac*, XIV (1958), 159.

sons concerned with the administration or financing of the State and Federal programs, other persons with special knowledge, experience, or qualifications with respect to the program, and the public." That the job of the council was to worry about the distribution of costs between governments was made clear in its assignment: to review the status of the public assistance program in relation to OASDI (where there is no state money), in relation to "the fiscal capacities of the States and the Federal Government, and [to review] any other factors bearing on the amount and proportion of the Federal and State shares in the public assistance program."[31]

Whether by chance or design, the Health, Education, and Welfare advisory council appointed under the 1958 act lacked a single obvious spokesman for the Eisenhower position, but included a minimum of eight persons either already on record or otherwise certain to support increased federal funds, however they might divide on the issue of federal control. The eight included four state or local officials who could certainly not be against unrestricted federal funds (among them a state welfare commissioner, a state legislator who was also a professional social worker, a liberal southern governor, and the manager of a county supervisors' association), two welfare "professionals" whose views were well known (Wilbur Cohen, then of the University of Michigan Social Welfare faculty, and Loula Dunn, then finishing her tenth year as Director of the American Public Welfare Association), the Assistant Director of the AFL-CIO Department of Social Security, and the Executive Director of the Division of Christian Life and Work of the National Council of Churches of Christ in the United States. Previous public positions of the National Council and of the AFL-CIO left little doubt about the stand of their spokesmen. Nor were all of the four doubtful cases really very doubtful. They were the Secretary of the New York State Catholic Welfare Commission, a Hunter College sociologist who had written on the relationship of juvenile delinquency to various sociological variables, a Cornell University Vice-President for Business who had, however, served as New York State Budget Director for seven years, and the Chairman of the Board of General Mills.

The council made short shrift of Eisenhower's expressed concern about increased federal funds weakening state and community responsibility. "We have considered the concern expressed in some quarters," said its report, euphemistically passing over the opportunity directly to challenge the President of the United States, "that the present degree

---

[31]Title VII, Sec. 704 (B), Public Law 840, 85th Cong., 1958.

of Federal responsibility assumed for public assistance endangers the authority or responsibility of State-local governments. We have found no convincing evidence to support this viewpoint."[32] The 19 other points made by the council all went to liberalization of the program; they included federal grants for general assistance; extension of ADC benefits to a second parent, thereby covering unemployment; elimination of state residence requirements by federal legislative action; equalization of ADC grants with those of the adult categories; federal support for training of public assistance workers and federal grants to schools of social work for training of potential workers; development of more comprehensive medical care programs; and appropriations for research and demonstration grants in the strengthening of family life. After the council's report was filed in January, 1960, no more talk was heard in the remaining year of the Eisenhower administration about increasing state and local responsibility.

Another opportunity to get advisory assistance came in preparing for the 1962 Public Welfare Amendments. An Ad Hoc Committee on Public Welfare was named by Secretary Ribicoff in 1961 and charged to "undertake a careful and thorough review of the Federal welfare laws" in accord with President Kennedy's assertion that in the quarter century since passage of the Social Security Act, "The times, the conditions, the problems have changed — and the nature and objectives of our public assistance and child welfare programs must be changed, also, if they are to meet our human needs."[33] Recognition of the importance of change evaporated when it came to naming members of the Ad Hoc Committee. Members of the closed society were invited to reassemble and again to assure each other that all the old truths had lost none of their validity, that patience and statesmanship would finally overcome partisan political, selfish interests, and that noneconomic services were needed. Committee members were not drawn from a broad spectrum as had been the case in 1937 and in 1947 in choosing social security advisory groups. Instead, like the composition of the 1958 council, that of 1961 could have doubled as the Board of Directors of the American Public Welfare Association. There was overlapping between the 1958 group, the group assembled by Elizabeth Wickenden in 1960, and the 1961 group — and there was to be further overlapping in 1963 when an ADC Audit Advisory Committee was named to help guide the national audit of the ADC program demanded by Senate Appropriations. But there was little diversity within any of the groups. What this meant was that the Ad Hoc

[32]*Senate Document 93,* 86th Cong., 2d Sess., 1960.
[33]Ways and Means, Hearings, 1962, p. 64.

Committee could take on faith as matters of agreement the very kinds of questions that most require reexamination and inquiry. The people whose professional lives were dedicated to services as a necessary element of welfare could neither fail to stress services nor be expected to think it necessary to wipe the slate clean and build a new empirical theory of public assistance.

As it developed, the committee report was no more informative than the charge to it had been. After acknowledging differences between conditions of 1935 and those of 1961, but not mentioning technological change, race tensions, urban slum ghettos, and changed patterns of sex behavior other than by the simple assertions that "there have been sweeping social and cultural changes" and "large numbers of people have changed geographic location, often moving to a totally new kind of community (rural to urban, urban to suburban)," the Ad Hoc Committee went on—without documentation—to assert the importance, as its primary recommendation, of increasing federal grants for rehabilitative and preventive services and for the training of social work personnel. Relying on its own members' experience, the committee had no public hearings, reported only conclusions. For information on which to base its conclusions, the committee substituted platitudinous summary statements. The report included no data, an omission that apparently did not disturb Ribicoff, but provoked one congressman to ask, "How about some of the raw material? ... I am interested in conclusions, but I am interested in finding out the reasons and what data they have."[34]

The report did not, for example, include an analysis of the ADC case load by way of separating out the percentage of cases that might realistically be involved in a rehabilitation program. Rehabilitation became the keystone of the program of services proposed by the committee; the rehabilitation recommendation, however, was not based on the identification of a new situation in public assistance. If most of the client group did not lend itself to rehabilitation, there would not be much innovation. It didn't; and there hasn't been.

Many of the other particulars of the Ad Hoc Committee report have been noted earlier. For the present argument, it is important that, like the members of the earlier advisory council, the Ad Hoc Committee members were not really free to consider the problem of public assistance *de novo*. By virtue of professional attachments, they were to a man committed to liberalization of existing policy which is a different animal—and may actually be less liberal—from creation of a policy

[34]*Ibid.,* p. 175.

adequate to the current problem. No one would know from the 1961 Ad Hoc Committee report any more than from the 1960 advisory council report that 67 per cent of ADC cases are families with an absent parent; that the costs of public assistance are deeply resented by numerous northern governors and state legislators who allege that migrants from the south are an improper burden on their states; that if provision of minimum standards for the needy is the goal of public assistance, variation in benefits between jurisdictions over a protracted period raises some doubt about the validity of the federal-state cooperative arrangement; that race, illegitimacy, and birth control are critical public assistance problems now, while they scarcely existed as issues in 1935. Most important, if release from economic dependency is the test of success, there is little evidence that services to lead to rehabilitation are a solution to the ADC problem. The specific remedy for the ailment is not at hand in present policy.

Advisory councils in public assistance are now built into the system since provision was made in the 1962 amendments for a council to report in 1966 and for subsequent councils to be named by the Secretary of Health, Education, and Welfare. The first such council was appointed by Secretary Celebrezze in July, 1964. It is unlikely that any fair-minded person would question the competence of the 12 appointees, but surely there is a certain futility involved in Wilbur Cohen formally and officially soliciting public assistance advice from Fedele Fauri, who is chairman of the council, and from Elizabeth Wickenden — friends, colleagues, coarchitects of current policy. The council chosen in 1964 is composed of the same kinds of excellent people whose impressions have dominated national policy in the field for three decades; this very circumstance makes it unlikely that they can undertake the kind of "independent review" that the Ways and Means Committee regarded as important.

There can be no drive for innovation as long as an elaborate facade exists which obscures the need for innovation. A critical part of that facade is the advisory or *ad hoc* committee which, to be useful, should be representative of widely divergent groups, uncommitted to any existing way of meeting the problem, committed to assembling information. The recent councils and committees are not broadly representative; neither are they uncommitted, nor have they substituted inquiry for impressions. It is not certain, of course, that there is a better way to meet the problem of public assistance; it is certain that before the question of a better way will even be asked about, it will be necessary to broaden subsequent advisory groups to include a goodly number of those who neither created nor administered the existing policy, nor are bonded to it by faith in professional colleagues. There are critics of present public assistance policy who are neither in favor of antediluvian standards nor ill-informed; none of them has been attracted to one of the advisory groups. Before the philosophers of innovation in public assistance can appear in the advisory groups, the company union must first be dissolved.

CHAPTER VII

The Social Work Syndrome

EVERYTHING IN PUBLIC assistance ultimately turns on the social worker who has unlimited discretionary authority to inquire into a client's fiscal, physical, and emotional affairs in the course of providing service. Because the alternative was thought to be political favoritism, the United States established a system in which social workers handle intake, service, and appeals in public assistance under the Social Security Act. While a small number of locally supported relief cases are disposed of by a town officer, no categorical assistance case involving federal money is disposed of without the participation of a person called a social worker. Opening and closing of cases, budgeting, and supervising are all functions of the social worker, not of administrative analysts, home economists, or lawyers.

Interest in cutting back the costs of public assistance and interest in improving the life adjustment of public assistance recipients each lead to a sympathetic consideration of the role of the social worker. The desirability of a crash program to provide trained social workers for public assistance is widely asserted. Even Senator Robert Byrd, the program's principal congressional critic, still supports increasing the number of social workers in public assistance. More workers and smaller case loads per worker have been continuing goals of welfare-oriented groups. No matter how intense the criticism of the operations of any particular assistance program, the need for social workers in public assistance is rarely challenged. Occasionally, an out-of-patience congressman will suggest that social workers are seeking to perpetuate themselves by keeping the program alive, but this kind of extreme statement is uncommon. While social workers themselves sometimes show insecurity about public acceptance of their role, at least one opinion research report concluded that the public considers the social worker's role as generally worthwhile, and characterized the shortage of trained social workers in public welfare as "a national scandal."[1]

As Hardy Wickwar has written, however, "There is need for a lot of thinking by some other people besides social workers on the proper role of the social worker in the social services."[2] It has been taken for granted in the past, as it seems to be taken for granted now, that social workers have a special claim to the public assistance field, that they are as specifically trained for work in this area as doctors are for coping with physical illness and engineers are for the building of highways. Some people besides doctors, however, have done considerable thinking recently about the costs of medical services. The result is a public policy adopted over the opposition of the professional medical group rather than a policy growing out of that group's own recognition of the obsolescence of the *status quo* in financing medical care of the aged. The highway engineers are finding, too, that their professional judgments about freeway locations can be turned aside when some people besides engineers think about alternative ways of attacking the traffic problem. Professional social workers do not occupy the same exclusive role in the new antipoverty program as they have occupied in the old public assistance program. Officials of the Office of Economic Opportunity are quoted as hailing steps in "deprofessionalizing" welfare and social work.[3] Have social workers, like doctors in medical finance, been too slow to recognize the need for change?

Acceptance of the inevitability of the social worker in public assistance may be too uncritical. Social work education and social work practice have undergone marked change in the last several decades and so have social workers' interests, all without concurrent consideration of their continuing relevance to the problems of public welfare. Some of these changes stem from an anxiety many social workers seem to feel about being accepted as professionals. In this respect, of course, social workers are not different from practitioners in other new fields like regional planning and city management who also agonize over their place among white collar groups that are increasingly certificated, licensed, or otherwise accorded recognition and

---

[1]*New York Times,* May 23, 1963. The survey report was that of the Opinion Research Corporation, Princeton, N.J.
[2]W. Hardy Wickwar, "Social Welfare and Political Science," *American Political Science Review,* XL (June, 1946), 567.
[3]*New York Times,* May 28, 1965, p. 20.

status. Neither the managers nor the planners, however, have agonized over the problem of professionalism as deeply and as constantly as have the social workers. In any event, if social work achieves universal recognition as a profession, legal or traditional conditions for admission to practice could be expected to be operative as they are operative in law, in medicine, and in teaching. The condition most frequently urged involves formal graduate training in social work, a qualification that only microscopic numbers of the present public assistance workers could now meet. It is appropriate, then, to turn to a series of inquiries about the relationship between social work practice, social work training, and public assistance: What is the nature of present-day professional social work? Do professional social workers have an interest in public assistance? Does social work education train for public assistance? What are the implications for public assistance of the social workers' drive for professional status? Does the professional association of social workers represent public assistance workers?

From Charity to Modern Social Work

The old-fashioned social worker of 50 years ago, sometimes known as a "friendly visitor," dealt with a reasonably wide range of problems. The friendly visitor of those days of the charity organization movement was well born, well bred, compassionate. Principal qualifications for the work were efficiency, tact, and humanitarianism. Her job was to improve the condition of the poor by recommending small grants, to counsel those needing advice, and to procure work for those capable of being wholly or partly self-supporting. Her trademarks were good will and good cheer.

Thirty-five years ago, she was known only as a social worker, the "friendly visitor" designation having been cast aside as unprofessional, while the range of problems with which she dealt had widened. The social worker in the urban center then was probably employed by a private philanthropic group with a sectarian interest or bias even if it was not an official agency of one of the established religions. Affairs of the agency were guided by a lay board of directors whose personal contributions of time and money to the cause were usually substantial. The cause might be an orphan asylum, a child care association, a charity aid society for needy families, a home for consumptives who lacked funds for private care, a summer camp for underprivileged children. Potential clients learned of the availability of the services by word of mouth, often from ministers, rabbis, and priests. Sometimes schoolteachers or doctors would suggest a visit to a social service agency. If agency contacts were good, a public utility might ask it to investigate a case before cutting off service for nonpayment of bills.

During the depression period of the early 1930's, it was possible to find private agencies often assigning in excess of 100 families to a single worker. Her job was complex. Some of her responsibilities might be to cope with budget problems, supervise the spending of the allowance made by the agency, recognize and refer mental health problems to competent specialists, arrange for an exterminator, negotiate with local merchants and professionals to provide goods and services at less than established rates, alert employables to job opportunities, personally fight eviction notices with landlords, when unsuccessful find new shelter for the client and his family, cultivate community leaders in order to assure emergency dispensations of drugs or clothing or heating fuel, and through it all keep a thorough agency record of these activities.

Public assistance and prosperity enabled the private charities to take advantage of the drive for professional education in social service, and to shuck off old-fashioned social work and old-fashioned social workers. Boards of directors casting about for a new function for their charitable aid societies happily acquired new administrative leaders who "had been through the school of social work" and who worked for the transformation of the agency from one dispensing charity to one that offered therapy. Almost anyone could be quickly taught to dispense charity; to practice casework required an elaborate education. Some retraining and reassignment of veteran field workers was undertaken, but the big push was on to make social service a professional calling. The worker who had not been to a school of social work had no real future in a private agency that was providing psychosocial help instead of giving away money or services equivalent to money. Case loads went down and prestige went up almost in direct proportion to the number of professionally trained workers on an organization's staff.

Association with those who had been washed in the graduate baths of the New York, Chicago, Pennsylvania, or Western Reserve Schools of Social Work was enough to make even the untrained workers sensitive to the conclusion that only a limited role could be played by concerned middle-class matrons who delivered baskets of food to the poor. The worker who did not herself realize the importance of her professional status was reminded of it in one of the interminable case conferences in which the supervisor and caseworker "shared" their

179

views on the progress of a case. One worker with a case load of underprivileged children in a prewar district on the Lower East Side of New York reports that she found essential her ability to cook thick barley soup. "Whenever a mother wasn't at home, I took over. I cooked and washed and did whatever had to be done. I became part of the family," she recalls. Her supervisor warned her to stop cooking and washing for families, calling it "unprofessional." "I told him that you don't lose your status by washing clothes or making some soup."[4] Presumably, the incident became part of the supervisor's written evaluation of the worker where it was probably acknowledged as a positive factor in establishing a "relationship" with the family but as a negative factor in "professional growth."

(The really ideal workers of today, of course, would suggest that the family make itself known to an agency that provides visiting homemaker service, would provide information to the client about such agencies, and would follow up to be sure that some service had been provided the client. The workers in the respective agencies would thus have an opportunity to "share" their case histories informally or to work independently, but in either event each could dutifully probe for "strengths" in a family that needed someone to cook its barley soup. If the family contacted the homemaker agency, it would count as a positive strength in assessing individual personality within the family group.)

The new social work did not come into its own until the last quarter century.[5] As early as World War I, however, there were some practitioners concerned about ways of using social work to help people lead more satisfactory lives. With the publication of Mary Richmond's *Social Diagnosis* in 1917, that group of practitioners asserted the value of the casework process, a family-centered service involving thorough investigation, accurate diagnosis, cooperation with all possible sources of assistance, and treatment. In each case, the service or process is unique, because there will be no two identical family problems. Although Mary Richmond herself did not stress its significance, her followers emphasized the importance of the relationship between the social worker and the client as the key to the casework process. Individ-

[4]*New York Times,* November 10, 1963, sect. I, p. 128.

[5]For the discussion in the next several paragraphs, I am dependent on Alan Keith-Lucas, "The Political Theory Implicit in Social Casework Theory," *American Political Science Review,* XLVII (December, 1953), 1076-91; Floyd W. Matson, "Social Welfare and Personal Liberty: The Problem of Casework," *Social Research,* XXII (October, 1955), 253-74; and Kathleen Woodroofe, *From Charity to Social Work* (London: Routledge and Kegan Paul, 1962). See also Roy Lubove, *The Professional Altruist: The Emergence of Social Work as a Career, 1880-1930* (Cambridge: Harvard University Press, 1965).

ualization of activity became the distinguishing characteristic of the casework concept.

If initially it was not especially Freudian, American social work in the post-Richmond period quickly took on more and more Freudian overtones. Soon the process became overwhelmed by what social historian Kathleen Woodroofe has called "the psychiatric deluge," and the "era of frenzied Freudianism." Mary Richmond had underplayed "treatment" in her work, thereby inviting a subsequent merger of Richmond and Freud. Emphasizing the need to help individuals adjust to society as it exists, social work joined the Richmond preoccupation with investigation to the Freudian concept of self-adjustment through sublimation or repression. "Whereas in the period from 1900 to the First World War, the caseworker, faced with the problem of man's adjustment to his social environment, had been concerned primarily with the environment and the possible ways in which social action could repair individual failure, now in the post-war years," explained Woodroofe, "it was assumed that if adjustment was not achieved the individual was to blame."[6]

Individual therapy if applied correctly would bring adjustment. In the dispensing of therapy, the social worker may be obliged to explore the subconscious—Freud's sex and death instincts (the Id)—which is not accessible to reason and to contrast it with the life instinct (the Ego) which is subject to conscious control. Because the worker will then come to have a better understanding of the causes of the client's maladjustment than the client himself can be expected to have until it is unveiled for him, the worker must lead the way. "Over the years," Floyd Matson has written, "more and more categories of welfare clients have been adjudged incompetent to lead their own lives. Prospective clients who choose to reject services or otherwise prove uncooperative may find themselves labeled as 'unstable defectives.'"[7]

Until the great depression, social work showed little interest in organized social protest, in movements for social reform, or for governmental action. While the very magnitude of the dependent population during the depression had to give pause to a notion that suppressed childhood poverty wishes could account for those seeking relief,[8] the support given political action by social workers during the depression

[6]Woodroofe, p. 132.

[7]Matson, p. 263.

[8]Gordon Hamilton's *Theory and Practice of Social Case Work* (New York: Columbia University Press, 1940) deplored the fact that some social workers were "unable or unwilling to see poverty except as a purely economic event, without acknowledging the possible existence of childhood dependency wishes which, if they do not actually cause, may certainly prolong dependency." Quoted in Woodroofe, p. 146.

did not become a dominant pattern during the period of war and postwar prosperity. Even today, with group work and community organization available as respectable options, self-adjustment through the therapeutic casework relationship is still the principal interest of social work.

The Freudian basis of social casework was challenged by another current in the psychiatric stream when Otto Rank's theoretical formulations invited a social casework approach that permitted greater emphasis on the likelihood of imperfect environmental factors. Thus the groundwork was laid for a dispute that separated the profession into Freudian and Rankian schools, a dispute that polarized for a time the New York School of Social Work and the University of Pennsylvania School of Social Work as leaders of the large, diagnostic (Freudian) group and of the small, functional (Rankian) group respectively. For the latter, the client was in charge; for the former, the worker ruled. The Rankian position allowed for the treatment of client need on the basis of known facts, and as need was determined and expressed by the client, rather than for treatment of "total need" as revealed to the caseworker through the application of her special skill. For the functional group, the recipient of social aid was to be treated like any other person aside from delivery of the particular aid required. For the diagnosticians, of course, the recipient of aid was *ipso facto* in need of services whether he knew it or not.[9]

No ideological war has been fought with greater fervor. At its height, the Family Service Association of America named an *ad hoc* committee to explore the grounds of difference and look for a way to achieve peace. The committee concluded that the differences between the approaches were irreconcilable.[10] Still, the war has waned, and some social work intellectuals smile softly as if in remembrance of things past and claim that that fight is over now. It is said that although the diagnosticians represented the preponderance of professional opinion — only the Pennsylvania and North Carolina schools and one or two others followed the functional approach — they softened their position to allow for the importance of social action, and that this tacit acknowledgment of possible environmental flaws served to calm the waters. Implicit or explicit efforts at accommodation, such as Helen Harris Perlman's *Social Casework: A Problem-solving Process,* have been warmly welcomed.

[9]Keith-Lucas, p. 1090.
[10]Cora Kasius (ed.), "A Comparison of Diagnostic and Functional Casework Concepts," *Report of the Committee to Study Basic Concepts in Casework Practice* (New York: Family Service Association of America, 1950), p. 13.

Social Workers in Public Assistance

Very little of all this percolated down to the worker in the field, especially to the worker in public welfare who was most unlikely to be professionally trained. It is still unusual for a social worker employed in a direct service position in either private or public welfare to have had graduate education in social work, but it is more unusual in the public assistance field than anywhere else. A 1960 survey of social work manpower showed 89 per cent of public assistance workers in direct service positions had had no graduate study against 69 per cent of workers without graduate training for all social welfare programs excluding recreation.[11] Only 1 per cent of the public assistance group had two or more years of graduate work. Even allowing for the inclusion of supervisors, administrators, and other nondirect service personnel, fewer than 4 per cent of the 35,175 social welfare workers in nationwide public assistance held an advanced degree in the field. In California, there were not 100 trained people out of 3,000 working with clients in the state's public assistance programs.[12] Only a handful of the public assistance caseworkers anywhere have had the time for, interest in, or capacity to understand the great ideological clash. Whatever his educational background, the public assistance worker in the field is usually fully occupied measuring room sizes, computing heating costs, working out food budgets, and otherwise tending to the economic needs of the public assistance client. This is not an activity that a graduate of a school of social work tends to find appealing.

The arithmetic of the situation argues against the possibility of staffing public assistance with real social workers if graduation from a school of social work continues to be the test of legitimacy. In September, 1962, there were 57 accredited schools of social work in the United States, 7 in Canada. They admit students with a bachelor's degree to full-time study leading, in two years, to a master's degree in social work, the mark of a genuine social worker. Enrollment in these schools is approximately 6,000 students, distributed between the two years of the program, with a preponderance of first-year students as might be expected. Fewer than 2,400 are graduated each year. Capacity could be increased to about 8,000 with presumably 3,200 graduating annually. The best current estimates indicate that there are at least 10,000 social work vacancies for which funds are available but

[11]U.S. Department of Labor, Bureau of Labor Statistics, *Salaries and Working Conditions of Social Work Manpower in 1960* (New York: National Social Welfare Assembly, 1961), p. 51.

[12]California Senate Fact Finding Committee on Labor and Welfare, *Aid to Needy Children Program* (Sacramento, Calif., 1961), p. 127.

for which qualified staff cannot be found. According to the Council on Social Work Education, sample studies show that more than 15,000 persons would have to be recruited annually to replace those leaving the field, to staff necessary expansion of existing services, and to man newly developing services.

Assuming a set of circumstances that are entirely unrealistic but which would be the most favorable in terms of bringing social work into public assistance, the goal is still impossible to fulfill. Assume that the 35,000 public assistance workers now in the field all stayed on their jobs and were assigned only to computing basic maintenance grants. Assume even that public assistance rolls dropped off to a total of about seven million persons. Assume further that every graduate of every school of social work in the United States and Canada entered public assistance work in America. With these obviously absurd assumptions, it would be at least 1975 before there was just an equal number of trained and untrained workers in public assistance, and before the ratio of trained workers to recipients was brought as low as 1:200.

The conclusion is inescapable that public assistance, as it has been run up to the present time, has not been a social work program. What the drive for the introduction of services into public assistance really means is that some public assistance leaders want to absorb a greater proportion of the graduates of schools of social work into the public field. So overwhelming a proportion of trained social workers has opted for the private agencies that up to now public assistance has been semiprofessional—or at least not really related very closely to the mainstream of professional social work. Public aid personnel bear something of the same relationship to graduates of the social work schools as the optician bears to the opthamologist. Authority to write a relief check does not make a professional social worker any more than authority to prescribe glasses makes an eye specialist. Non-social workers have been compelled to masquerade as social workers.

What has happened, then, is that the failure of public assistance to wither away made it necessary for public welfare to keep adding to its staff at a time when many private groups were busy glamorizing themselves into the new type of agency. The competition to attract social workers was unequal in that private welfare had the advantages of money, the promise of professional recognition, and the probability of being less nerve-wracking. Trained social workers joined the staffs of the family service associations and bemoaned the terrible condition of social work practice in the public welfare field, where workers were still making budgets and taking anguished calls from clients whose relief checks had not appeared on time. Public assistance was able to recruit neither the old-fashioned social worker nor the new-style caseworker, but its load kept growing, and someone had to figure the budgets. Public agencies recruited the best talent they could find, usually relatively young college graduates who did not stay long. Some of them may have had an undergraduate course with a social work label, but the probability was not high because social work has not encouraged the development of an undergraduate curriculum.

Now we are at the point where professional leaders suggest that public assistance work will be ever thus unless relief is separated from the more significant aspects of the work. "Overburdened again with 'unemployment' cases which should be provided for otherwise under social security," complained Gordon Hamilton, a high priestess of the profession, in 1959, "the worker is prevented from carrying out his appropriate functions. Hampered with routine eligibility determination, snowed under with procedures and papers which could be done by experienced clerks who should not need to earn a master's degree for efficient performance, bedeviled by such antiquities as residence laws and shockingly low levels of assistance, workers stagger along, often delivering a quality of service to clients and community that is all but incredible."[13] Three years later, Miss Hamilton made absolutely explicit her view that relief would have to get out of public assistance before social work could come in. In another editorial in *Social Work,* she said, "Social work to date has never been allowed the tools, even on a minimum level, to make public assistance a helping func-tion. . . . Why not place the basic maintenance grant in a separate unit . . . and staff this unit with well trained civil servants? . . . Why not take the albatross of 'relief' . . . from the neck of social service?"[14]

Private welfare siphons off virtually all of the trained workers, but even private welfare still has a very long way to go before it is close to being staffed exclusively by trained workers. It is not true that private welfare placement possibilities are beginning to dry up so that trained workers are interested in expanding into the public field. We can continue to put our people into the private agencies indefinitely, the Gordon Hamiltons are saying, but we are willing to put them into public assistance if you will make public assistance like private welfare by cutting off the money problem. Then we can treat people.

The challenge offered by the profession seems clear: either public assistance practices must become more like private welfare practices or the trained professionals will continue to shun the public agencies. It is an understandable position because there is no doubt that public

[13]Gordon Hamilton, "Editorial," *Social Work,* IV (April, 1959), 2.
[14]Gordon Hamilton, "Editorial," *Social Work,* VII (January, 1962), 2, 128.

assistance does not allow for the use of graduate training in social work any more than did the job of the old-fashioned worker in the private charitable agency of the depression period. No really clear-cut public policy answer has been given to the challenge because policy-makers can't make up their minds. They recognize the need for bodies, and they can understand that a worker with fewer clients may be able to give more careful attention to each case than can an overburdened worker. Politicians also argue, however, that something is wrong with public assistance now, because if it was working according to theory, it would be less expensive than it is. But to jump to the conclusion that the thing to do is to separate relief from service and encourage the wholesale entrance of professionally trained social workers into the service side is a jump that politicians have been uncertain about making. So Congress refuses to appropriate money for training grants that will allow the Department of Health, Education, and Welfare to subsidize potential public assistance workers in graduate schools of social work; but at the same time Congress authorizes the expenditure of funds for comparable academic training of workers already on the job. The social workers would diagnose such behavior as ambivalence, and provide skilled service.

Does Social Work Train for Public Assistance?

How defensible is the proposition that schools of social work provide special training important and pertinent to public assistance? In making a plea for authorization of funds for social work traineeships in public assistance, one federal administrator explained to the House Ways and Means Committee that the average public assistance worker authorized the expenditure of $100,000 a year, much of it federal money. The year was 1956 and the dollar amount is higher now, but the case for training is made in the same terms now as Charles Schottland made it then. Social work schooling, it was said, would provide a real understanding of the program, and discharge an obligation to the public and the taxpayers, to the people involved, to see that the training of public assistance workers is as adequate as possible. No effort would be made to fashion a special training program geared to public assistance. The only federal requirement envisaged was that traineeship funds, if they were to go to schools, would go only to accredited schools.[15]

The schools of social work affiliated with the accrediting agency in

[15]U.S. Congress, House, Committee on Ways and Means, Hearings, "Public Assistance Titles of the Social Security Act," 84th Cong., 2d Sess., 1956, pp. 225ff.

the field, the Council on Social Work Education, all provide virtually identical two-year graduate programs divided roughly equally between classroom instruction and field work in a cooperating agency. If the school is located in an urban center, the field work is likely to be carried on at the same time as the academic work on a split-week schedule. Schools located in more remote places like Smith College at Northampton, Massachusetts, utilize so-called bloc placements wherein students are in school for several months at a time and then in the field for several months. Bloc placement is less highly regarded than the split-week arrangement because it is believed that the latter is more conducive to mixing theory and practice. Whatever the field work arrangements, academic content of the program will include special social work courses in human growth and behavior, in social welfare policy and services, and in social work values and ethics. These constitute the so-called focusing stage of the social work curriculum. Application of social work knowledge acquired in the focusing stage can take the form of social casework, social group work, social work community organization, social work administration, or social work research. Students, for all practical purposes, may choose only between casework and group work as a specialization and, although they are taught the approved social work methods in both areas, one or the other is emphasized. Casework instruction and casework field training are the important aspects in connection with public assistance.

It is one of the paradoxes of the profession that social workers simultaneously deplore the use of untrained workers and yet turn untrained students loose on clients almost from the minute the students enter a school. Under present arrangements, social work education differs from most programs with internship requirements in that the social work internship starts at the same time as the academic work. In some agencies, student status is not divulged either to the client or anyone else outside the agency. Although licensing has been espoused as a way of protecting the public from unqualified workers, the social work educational system delivers clients to brand new students of unknown talent and unknown stability.

Because public assistance has not conformed to the professional leadership's insistence on small case loads and extensive noneconomic services, students who have had at least a year of graduate training are usually considered too advanced to be assigned to a public assistance agency. The result is that first-year students may be assigned to public assistance, second-year students almost never are, and the great majority of students have no field work whatever in any public agency, although almost two-thirds of all paid social workers are publicly employed; half of those publicly employed are in public assistance. Field work activity in the schools—the heart of social work education—is tailored to what the profession would like social work to be more than to what public assistance actually must deal with.

The fully trained caseworker's training may never bring her any closer to an actual public assistance situation than classroom discussion of a "canned" case provided by the Council on Social Work Education. Nevertheless, since the schools take pride in training students "to practice in any setting," it is assumed that acquisition of the social work degree via exposure to the predetermined curriculum will fit a caseworker to deal with the kind of poverty she has probably never seen in her life. In a typical, highly rated school, all first-year casework field placements will offer a family experience, while the second-year placement involves concentration on a field of practice, *e.g.,* psychiatric casework, medical social casework, child welfare, or corrections. All students in social casework (as distinguished from group work) have the same classes and essentially the same field work learning experiences save for the variety of practice settings possible in the second year. There is no such thing as a social work "major" in public welfare. The student who shows a special interest in public welfare politics or administration will be tolerated and a thesis in that area will be accepted but it is not likely to be encouraged. This is so despite a sharp warning to the profession by Wilbur Cohen to the effect that "[social workers] as a group have not developed sufficient professional knowledge of the process of the Federal level which produces the legislation that has been a major factor in the transformation and increased importance of social work in the last generation."[16] It is a reasonable assumption that an insufficient knowledge of the federal policy-making process certainly means a thin knowledge of state and local policy-making processes as well.

The closer a public agency gets to the hard problems of legislative animosity and limitations on available public funds, the more it is shunned as a fit training ground for social work students. Writing to an inquiring student, the dean of a leading school in a major urban center with a heavy public assistance load explained that "under normal circumstances we regard public assistance agencies as quite suitable for first year field placement. Unfortunately, the financial crisis in [the state] and the uproar that the agency has been in as a result of this has

[16]Wilbur J. Cohen, "Factors Influencing the Content of Federal Public Welfare Legislation," *The Social Welfare Forum, 1954* (New York: Columbia University Press, 1954), p. 200. The point is also made by Charles Schottland, "Social Work Issues in the Political Arena," *The Social Welfare Forum, 1953* (New York: Columbia University Press, 1953), p. 19.

made this agency somewhat less useful as a field placement this year." The New York School replied to a similar inquiry in a positive tone in 1963: "almost 15 per cent of our full time students in casework have a public assistance field experience... a significant increase over the number of placements in previous years." Turned around, the response seems appreciably less positive because it suggests that almost nine out of ten casework students at the New York School — situated in the midst of one of the biggest and most complex public relief situations in modern times — are graduated without direct contact with public assistance work. At Smith College's highly regarded School for Social Work, there are now no training affiliations whatever with public assistance programs. Some years ago such affiliations did exist but they were discontinued by the participating agencies because of their inability to provide adequate supervision or consultation. A school that considers itself strongly oriented in the direction of public assistance — that at the University of Southern California — places about half of all first-year students in public assistance field assignments. At Western Reserve, efforts to improve student attitudes toward public assistance field placement are reported. But such a placement is said to involve an "ego problem" because of the physical surroundings, mass need, policies and practices that reflect only in part the basic philosophy of social work, and newspaper attacks on the program.[17]

Classroom work is not planned to compensate for any possible deficiency in exposure to public relief in students' field placements. Schools of social work have been accused of teaching students more detail about the historical background of welfare legislation in Great Britain than about the evolution of federal welfare legislation in the United States since 1935.[18] Whatever the merits of the complaint, it provoked no reexamination of the adequacy of student training in public welfare. An even more explicit bill of particulars was furnished as long ago as 1951 in the Hollis-Taylor Report made for the national Council on Social Work Education:

> In the areas of public assistance and child welfare, important fields of employment for social workers, there are major problems of policy which call for intensive study and clarification by teams of experts that should include social workers. Among them are such problems as the meaning of the large number and upward trend of assistance recipients in a period of high national income; the astonishing differences between recipient rates in different states, even between states in similar economic circumstances; the determination of the appropriate level of the minimum family or individual budget; the potenti-

---

[17]Rose Meyer and Virginia L. Tannar, "The Use of the Public Assistance Setting for Field Practice," *Social Work,* IV (July, 1959), 35.
[18]Cohen, p. 200.

alities and limits to the role of the institution of public assistance as an instrument for dealing with economic need; and the appropriate relationships between social insurance and public assistance. Most graduate schools of social work do very little to increase the capacity of students to cope with these truly basic social welfare issues.[19]

The kinds of questions spelled out in the Hollis-Taylor work are the kinds of questions about public assistance that legislators ask and to which no answers are forthcoming because social workers are not educated along those lines. In the first place, it is not really necessary to start with specialized knowledge in anything to be admitted to a school of social work. Although some background in social science is preferred, the only indispensable requirements appear to be "an interest in people" and a state of health adequate to meet the rigors of carrying a full-time academic program simultaneously with a half-time field work program. Given the emphasis on the student's interpersonal relations rather than on disciplinary competence, it becomes unnecessary to insist on a distinguished undergraduate record as an admission requirement. Admissions committee members are thus able subjectively to detect aptitude for social work that a university-wide admissions officer cannot detect objectively from a scrutiny of a student's record. The easy availability of places in most schools has also worked to the benefit of the academically weak student who need not compete for an entry permit with an outstanding group as does the medical student, for example. On a more positive note, federal grants in support of some kinds of social work education have increased the application rate in recent years, and a more discriminating admission policy may become possible soon.

In the second place, social work education discourages both independent inquiry and reexamination of the professional myths. Consequently, many products of the schools hardly know how to go about posing and executing a researchable problem.[20] Unlike law or physics or economics or medicine, the professional literature in social work reports not the results of research nor interpretations of basic data but rather vignettes descriptive of daily practice, misgivings about public policy which does not accord with the judgments of social work leaders, or small-scale semiscientific efforts at survey research from

[19]Ernest Hollis and Alice Taylor, *Social Work Education in the United States* (New York: Columbia University Press, 1951), pp. 142-43.

[20]"The plain truth is that social work practitioners are unable to understand the language of social science." From Ernest Greenwood, "Social Science and Social Work: A Theory," *Social Service Review,* XXIX (March, 1955), 29. But for a more optimistic view, see Henry Maas, "Collaboration Between Social Work and the Social Sciences," *Social Work Journal,* XXXI (July, 1950), 104-9.

which large-scale conclusions are drawn. And the case of some "Mrs. P." or a "Henry M." is always available to illustrate the point.

The reports that the student hears and the reports that the student writes are cut from the same pattern which has three pieces: client trouble; social worker help, based on personal or professional experience and professional training; and client rejuvenation or rehabilitation. At a time in 1964 when the civil rights struggle was at an intense point, some social work students were learning a few things from the Annette Rose Case, one of a series of authentic case records distributed for use in graduate schools of social work by the Council on Social Work Education. In this "true record of a working relationship," a Negro child started "treatment interviews" with a school social worker on January 24, 1957, because of recurrent extreme feelings of resentment toward white people, feelings shared by her father but not by her mother. By February 17, five interviews later, "the 'chip' seems to have disappeared entirely," evidence of resentment toward the white schoolteacher and white classmates has dissolved, and the child has written a model essay on the subject of brotherhood. Moreover, after finding on the social worker's desk and bringing home to her father a March of Dimes pamphlet that pictured a Negro girl with a white girl, the child is quoted as saying her father's attitude toward whites is changing too. Before moving to a new neighborhood, Annette and her mother paid a farewell call on the social worker on February 25, exactly one month after the first of the eight treatment interviews. Annette was now said by her mother to be like a different person at home, and the child agreed with the social worker that she felt pretty sure of being able to handle new situations as they arose. There was no evidence of stress or disturbed feelings. Social work, the problem-solving process, had fulfilled itself.

An important function of professional education is to expose the neophyte to the procedures and methods of the trade. Social work education does this job very well. From the beginning, it is made clear that the social work setting involves a hierarchical relationship between worker and supervisor, linked by the case record. Farmed out at once to a field work assignment, the student promptly learns the importance of the process-style case record, the record that recreates a worker-client interview in total detail. In writing a process-style interview, a field work supervisor explained to his charges, one does not say one entered the house, but one says that he knocked on the door or rang the bell as the case may be. The interviews so recorded are made the basis of periodic discussions between worker and supervisor. Process-style reports are not automatically abandoned in nontraining situations, but continue to be required by some professionals who deplore the bureaucratic paper work in public assistance.

Process-style interviews are not developed to make it easier for another agency to learn the case history in the event a client moves or requires a new kind of service. To open case files to outsiders, even fellow social workers, is now considered a violation of confidentiality. In the technical language of the profession, it would provide a worker with guilty knowledge of a client's situation, *i.e.,* knowledge not volunteered by the client himself. Process-style interviews are not read by every new worker assigned to a continuing agency case. For this purpose, each worker writes or dictates periodic summaries of case progress. In fact, in recent years there has been a tendency to shorten such summaries, particularly in medical social work.

Since social workers certainly are too fully occupied to use process records as a kind of busywork for students and junior staff, the rationalization for process-style records must rest on their value in supervision. The supervisor, a kind of mother superior who has always risen from the ranks, is ultimately responsible for the relations between the workers (including students) in her unit and their clients. Supervision is exercised by study and discussion of the case records and through a periodic ritual known as the evaluation. It is the supervisor's job to suggest to the worker where the client's strengths and weaknesses in personality, in social adjustment, and in family ties may have been overlooked. Occasionally, a supervisor will provide information on agency policy that may be necessary. The process-style interview thus provides the supervisor a maximum foundation for case discussion with the less skilled worker. Ultimately, the records, the discussions, and the worker's responses to supervision will be formally evaluated by the supervisor in written form and read to the worker who is offered a chance to write a rebuttal — assuming he wishes to indict himself for "resenting supervision."

Dependence on case analyses in social work schools borrows from legal training, but the case method in social work is not used to train the student in logic or to invite a challenge to the judgment of the court based on a different analysis of the facts or a different line of precedents. The social work training case is part of the process of convincing the student that the trained worker has "special skills and of teaching the student how to use these skills." In a public assistance case record provided by the Council on Social Work Education, for example, the student reads of the activities of a trained worker who, faced with an OAA application from an indigent man apparently alienated from a self-supporting son, brings father and son to a new understanding of each other, culminating in the son's voluntary assumption of financial responsibility for his father. It goes without saying that an untrained worker would never have achieved this result.

For the student who comes with faith, every case is a revelation of social work skills, every bit of speculation by a supervisor is a sign of the insight that will ultimately be acquired by the neophyte. But public assistance usually doesn't provide an opportunity for this kind of thorough inquiry into other people's emotions. There are too many people to be handled, economic needs are so desperate that they must have the highest priority, and there is not time for leisurely supervisor-worker discussions about personal growth.

It is not surprising, then, that public assistance cannot attract trained social workers. During the school training, the cases that the student reads and the cases on which he works are very different from the typical public assistance case. Public assistance workers who take educational leaves of absence abandon the public assistance field at the earliest possible time. Trained workers without public assistance experience shun it. The "ego problem" that the Western Reserve people found to exist in public assistance field placements is really a matter of social workers finding public assistance too depressing. Since the schools do not insist that students come to grips with public assistance, and actually downgrade it in the scale of professional achievement, trained workers select an environment more like the model social work environment pictured in the schools. It is an environment of disturbed people whose money troubles are perhaps bothersome but rarely all engulfing, and who are actively seeking someone who can provide therapy. Public assistance is a different world.

Part of the social work classroom curriculum is designed to stuff useful information into the student. This aspect, dealing with normal patterns of human growth and development, combines basic material in physiology, biology, medicine, psychology, and psychiatry. It has no independent social work content, but it is taught in the school of social work rather than by farming social work students out to other departments in the university. When the school faculty member is over his head—which is frequently and understandably the case—a common practice is to coopt local physicians and psychiatrists to deliver lectures.

Comparable modesty is not as often shown in dealing with curriculum material concerning social welfare policy although this component is also without unique social work content. Social work education does not normally include exposure to the significance of economic trends or personal income statistics. It avoids both politicians and study of the uses of political power. It is more likely to provide a condemnation of inadequate services offered by public agencies than it is to provide an examination of the image of social workers held by politicians. It is more likely to emphasize a professional responsibility to interpret to the public and to the politician than it is to evaluate various lobbying techniques. It is not likely to explore the philosophical problem of the duty of social work to respond to public opinion. For example, noting that society continues to react to public assistance differently from the way professional social workers feel society should react, Dean Alton Linford of the University of Chicago admitted that it was a discouraging situation in view of the profession's "best efforts to convince [society] of the true facts. Yet it is not something to get panicky about. We can only continue our efforts to explain and interpret."[21] Alan Keith-Lucas, one of a handful of social work educators deviating from the party line, examined the principal literature on public welfare administration and was led to the conclusion that the major relationship between the public and the social worker envisaged is an educative one, with the public on the receiving end.[22] Where responsiveness to public sentiment is advocated, this is largely for the purpose of ensuring or protecting current programs.

Some of the problems of training for the public social service might have been exposed in the social work curriculum study sponsored in 1959 by the Council on Social Work Education. The study problem as laid out by its director included consideration of the desirable educational objectives for social work; a special volume was commissioned on education for social workers in the public social services. Unfortunately, however, to reach conclusions on this subject, the inquiry was conducted within the closed social work society. The authors ignored the public, ignored elected public officials, and instead asked social workers in child welfare and public assistance to identify major on-the-job problems handled effectively or ineffectively by various personnel in the professional hierarchy from caseworker through state field director. This critical-incident method was designed to yield data about the kinds of critical problems public agency personnel face in practice and which of those problems tend to be successfully handled. As it developed, the schedule became so complex and so ambiguous that most of the replies could not be used in the analysis. Even if they had been, the subjective character of the effective versus ineffective decision would

[21] Alton Linford, "Which Way Public Assistance Administration?" *Social Work Journal,* XXXIII (July, 1952), 120.
[22] Alan Keith-Lucas, *Decisions about People in Need* (Chapel Hill: University of North Carolina Press, 1957), p. 85.

continue to be troublesome, as would the choice of "behavior categories" within which incidents were reported.

Curriculum implications that are claimed to grow out of this study are understandably "broad": caseworkers should be trained in assessment of human needs, in establishment of the client-worker relationship, and in planning and performing services.[23]

Another volume of the curriculum study touched on the responsibility of social work to the community. It proposed a heavy load for the profession. Not only must social work help people with their problems, but it must help the community itself to respond more effectively to changing human needs, interests, conditions, and ideologies. The role of the profession as an agent of change must be understood universally. Agency and profession, it was said, have a responsibility to bring their relevant experience and knowledge to bear upon community processes of planned change.[24] Precisely what it is that an energetic social worker is to do in order to discharge this responsibility is, like many things in social work, unclear.

The Director of the Council on Social Work Education offered some personal observations on the study including the volume on education for the public social services. He found (1) the use of the critical-incident technique in social work research to be an incidental but important contribution, (2) analysis of the data to prove "conclusively" that social work personnel in public assistance and child welfare "need the best that social work education has to offer," and (3) the full implication of "these rich findings for both in-service and professional education will come only as practitioners and educators decide which of the findings and recommendations they wish to utilize."[25] Practitioners and educators have made their decision. All 13 volumes of the curriculum study now appear to have been quietly laid to rest, including Volume 1 which included a recommendation by the study director that part of the curriculum be moved to the undergraduate level. "Experienced social work educators," wrote one of them, "have registered serious questions about this proposed modification of structure."[26] Somehow, the study failed to comprehend that the trend

---

[23]Irving Weissman and Mary R. Baker, *Education for Social Workers in the Public Social Services* (New York: Council on Social Work Education, 1959), p. 76.

[24]Irving Weissman, *Social Welfare Policy and Services in Social Work Education* (New York: Council on Social Work Education, 1959), p. 75.

[25]Ernest F. Witte, "The Curriculum Study: Some Personal Observations," *Social Work,* IV (July, 1959), 11.

[26]Marietta Stevenson, "Social Work Education," in Gilbert Y. Steiner (ed.), *Public Higher Education in Illinois* (Springfield: Illinois Joint Council on Higher Education, 1961), p. 81.

of professional education is toward graduate work and that social work schools are determined to have the ornaments of professional schools.

Public Assistance and Social Work Professionalism

Within the spectrum of productive human activity, some is considered professional without dissent, some makes no claim to professional status, and some falls in what Harold Wilensky describes as an "in process" category.[27] A principal goal of social work is to make the jump from the "in process" category to the professional category. Acceptance of a claim to professional status will, it is hoped, afford social workers the public deference associated with respect for specialization. Nothing now riles some social workers quite as much as the loose use of the title. A favorite comparison is with medical doctors, another "helping profession," and the likely effect on the prestige of that group if every hospital orderly who carried a bed pan was called Doctor and every aide who delivered a patient's meals called Nurse. The title Social Worker, it is argued, should be guarded no less jealously because practitioners of real social work are also technically trained, are professionals.

Social work's drive for recognition and status has been unceasing. It was manifested in activity that culminated in the formation of the National Association of Social Workers in 1955, as well as in the activity directed toward licensing and certification that both preceded and followed the 1955 organizational changes. Over and over again, however, social work has been caught on the basic question of what independent body of knowledge goes into the trained practitioner that clearly distinguishes her from the untrained. Efforts to delineate social work theory result in some volumes that are either outrageously pretentious or childishly obvious. But an instinct to assert professionalism is omnipresent. Social work may really have its own theory, methods, and other, necessary, professional trappings. Certainly no other calling claims a concept known as reflective consideration of the current person-situation configuration.[28] The trappings do not work to bar people who are not social workers from behaving as if they were, and often doing so with the blessing of a civil service classification as social worker. People who have acquired the dignity of a Ph.D. degree and a job on a college faculty have learned to distinguish themselves

[27]Harold L. Wilensky, "The Professionalization of Everyone?" *American Journal of Sociology,* LXX (September, 1964), 143.
[28]Florence Hollis, *Casework: A Psychosocial Therapy* (New York: Random House, 1964), p. 73.

from ordinary teachers by being termed professor. Social work is still searching for the appropriate equivalent shorthand way of saying that the sweet girl graduate of Pembroke who visits OAA recipients is not a trained social worker.

This suggests that public assistance practice is an impediment to social work's achievement of the status that is desired by its leaders. Unlike practicing medicine or practicing law, or even selling real estate, it is still possible to become a social worker overnight, to be employed by an agency engaged in dispensing money or nonmaterial services to people seeking help without satisfying any standard technical requirements or demonstrating a minimum level of technical skill. The designation is not technician or clerk; it is social worker. One can become a social worker by getting a nonclerical job with an agency engaged in social service, and public assistance agencies make this ridiculously easy to accomplish. Public assistance is really a block to social work professionalization; and social workers have not accepted the block very gracefully, as Gordon Hamilton's reference to the "albatross of relief" suggests. We shall see that, for all practical purposes, public assistance is shut out of social work's professional association.

Another impediment to elevating the status of social work as a profession — but one for which public assistance cannot be blamed — is the inability of its practitioners to demonstrate conclusively that there really is a discrete body of knowledge, the possession of which separates social workers from non-social workers and which lends itself to academic instruction. The Hollis-Taylor Report made this same point:

> Few would deny, social workers least of all, that the public at large has little conception of what casework is or has to offer. More disturbing is the difficulty that caseworkers themselves have in explaining precisely what it is they do, what results they can reasonably expect to achieve, or what criteria they apply in testing professional competence and in distinguishing between the functions of specializations.[29]

Without being very clear about what social work is, social workers' associations have been urging legal restrictions on the right to practice. Restrictions, it is claimed, are necessary both for the protection of the public and for the responsible development of the social work profession. In a report to the 1947 Conference, the National Committee on Registration and Licensing of the American Association of Social Workers (AASW) proposed and had accepted a policy

---

[29]Ernest Hollis and Alice Taylor, pp. 145-46.

statement that asserted as a "major responsibility the development of a long range program of study, education, and action, leading to the adoption of legislation in each state which will restrict the practice of social work to persons designated as qualified practitioners by an appropriate agency of the state."[30] Although the public protection aspect has been a consistent feature of the licensing effort, it has become more and more apparent that the real goal of licensing is official recognition of the professional character of social work.

Restricted entry to practice is the most effective way to multiply any group in accord with standards established by the incumbents. However, if the discriminatory arrangements are to be legally protected, it is necessary to show more than the advantage to the "ins." A democratic system demands evidence of the social evils to be expected from uncontrolled participation of the "outs." For example, architects are licensed partly because the profession can show instances where an untutored designer has jeopardized public safety. But the instances where presumably untutored social workers have been extremely successful are very great. Neither the 1947 report nor any preceding or subsequent effort comes to grips with the question of what happens if social work is not licensed or certificated, of precisely who suffers, and just how the absence of certification has affected social work clients. The case rests entirely on the advantages to the profession.

The Executive Secretary of the AASW, in his review of the activity of the registration and licensing committee and of the policy statement, established professional recognition as the official line. Virtually abandoning the public protection case, the argument now was that licensing efforts would facilitate recruitment and selection of persons with the basic preparation for social work positions, would contribute to the development of progressively higher standards of professional competence, and would help give the profession both status and recognition.[31] Here, for the first time, registration as a technique in the drive for professional status was openly admitted as being an important motivation, while protection of the public was no longer headlined. Understandably, legal licensing of social workers never made much progress.

[30]"AASW Policy Statement on Regulation of Social Work Practice," *The Compass,* XXVII (July, 1947), 17.

[31]"Report of the Executive Secretary," *Social Work Journal,* XXIX (July, 1948), 123. For a discussion of some possible mechanics of licensing and a review of experience with a mild California registration law, see R. E. Arne, "Protection of the Public through Licensing of Social Workers," *Social Work Journal,* XXXIII (October, 1952), 184-90; for a warning to social workers that licensing is not an automatic way to achieve status, see Damon A. Turner, "The Licensing Effort—Seven Years Later," *Social Work Journal,* XXXV (April, 1954), 68-72, 78.

A great push for licensing was not the only postwar social work activity designed to achieve recognition. Indeed, the licensing issue with its uncertainties and ambiguities seems to have been laid aside a year or two after the adoption of the 1947 policy statement in favor of a more direct path to recognition and professional status: reorganization of the existing organizations of social workers from fragmented groups with little influence to a unified association big enough to set restrictive admission standards and still be heard from. At the height of the reorganization activity, public assistance accounted for two-fifths of all social work employees. It was the largest social work program in terms of employment. Involvement of the 30,000 public assistance workers in setting associational goals and standards did not, however, appeal to the professional leadership. When the one big social work association evolved in 1955, the public assistance people weren't even invited as observers.

Origins of the modern movement for organization in social work can be traced back at least 50 years. In 1913, the Intercollegiate Bureau of Occupations of New York City established a special department for social work as a unique field. The National Social Workers Exchange, organized in 1917, took over the work of the bureau. The Exchange became the American Association of Social Workers in 1921, with the counseling and placement functions given a special place in the new organization. In the meantime, there developed organizations of social workers who worked with professionals in other fields but who could not become part of professional groups in those fields. The American Association of Medical Social Workers was organized in 1918, the National Association of School Social Workers in 1919 and, in 1926, the American Association of Psychiatric Social Workers ceased being a branch of the medical social work group and organized separately.[32] Each of the four associations grew, but by 1930 they collectively accounted for less than one-third of the social work labor force as indicated in the census of that year. Nathan E. Cohen, who has been in the business long enough to mix jargon and English, has remarked upon the mixed motivations behind the early striving for professionalization: "For some it represented status; for others a line of demarcation between the volunteer and the paid worker; and for a small group who were conscious of the emergence of a unique metho-

[32]Circumstances leading to the establishment of most of the separate organizations of social workers are detailed in Lubove, pp. 124ff. See also Melvin A. Glasser, "The Story of the Movement for a Single Professional Association," *Social Work Journal*, XXX (July, 1949), 110-17; and John C. Kidneigh, "Social Work as a Profession," *Directory of Professional Social Workers* (New York: National Association of Social Workers, 1960), pp. xv-xvii.

dology it represented the institutionalization of functionally specific technical competence."[33] Presumably for the same mixed motivations, during the 1930's and 1940's, the American Association of Group Workers, the Association for the Study of Community Organization, and the Social Work Research Group appeared on the scene.

After nearly a year of preliminary discussion sparked by problems of certification of curricula in the schools—a primary concern of the American Association of Schools of Social Work—the big American Association of Social Workers succeeded in bringing representatives of four small sister organizations to a January, 1949, ecumenical council. Later, the study groups in community organization and social work research were given accredited status, but the Association of Schools limited itself to the role of observer as did its successor, the Council on Social Work Education. Discussions in the Committee on Inter-Association Structure, which was the legacy of the January council, proceeded swiftly. By July, the entire issue of the *Social Work Journal* could be devoted to its work. The committee suggested then, in effect, that the choice was between continued separation, confederation, federation, and unification. Values of specialized associations were noted and compared with the advantages of unification as a further step in identifying the profession, improving professional publications, and creating an association that would allow social workers to "stand up and be counted."

It took three years for the committee to come to the point of issuing a "Plan for a New Single Organization of Social Workers," and three more years to set up a mail referendum on the issue of unification. The decision was for an entirely new organization, the National Association of Social Workers (NASW), to begin operations on October 1, 1955. The seven old groups went out of business, some of them apparently delighted to avoid folding up for lack of funds. Through the press, NASW announced that it would "strive to utilize more effectively the resources of the social work profession, and to eliminate duplication of organizational efforts." Through the new journal, *Social Work*, sole successor to all the journals and newsletters of the old associations, NASW members were soon assured that the new association was a milestone in the history of social work, and that it was "a professional step."

The referendum leading to formation of the unified association involved a total of 20,585 persons qualified to vote by virtue of membership in one of the seven participating groups. According to the

[33]Nathan E. Cohen, "Professional Social Work Faces the Future," *Social Work Journal*, XXXVI (July, 1955), 82.

Bureau of Labor Statistics, there were 30,110 social welfare workers in public assistance in 1950 with the number growing. Whatever else the new association may have been, it seems clear that it was not representative of the interests of large numbers of public assistance workers. The separation of those in public assistance work from the social work professional association was insured by the decision to make graduate education in social work a prerequisite for membership in NASW. That decision also meant that NASW chose to speak for a closed group of workers meeting each other's standards rather than for the much larger group of workers who meet the legal standards necessary for employment as a social worker.

Critical elements in the unification contract were the provision for the new organization to accept automatically all members of the participating associations, and the restriction of new membership to graduates of an accredited school of social work. The former was characterized as the "one temporary flaw" in the professional nature of the new association. Members of the NASW — including those who had been blanketed-in — were told that graduation from an accredited school was "the new standard toward which we have all worked." Even more restrictive conditions for membership were promptly and enthusiastically envisaged. "Such a [blanketing-in] compromise is not likely again in social work until the doctoral degree is required as the criterion for membership — as it will be someday within the career of the younger of you. It is the next step.... When this temporary compromise is corrected by death and retirement, as it inevitably will be, the Association will be the stronger."[34] Although an expression of this sort in the very first issue of a journal that was distributed to the beneficiaries of the "compromise" might have been characterized as "hostility" if it were observed in a client by a graduate of an accredited school, it was apparently considered understandable professional militancy by fully trained social workers. No one appears to have raised the question of bad manners.

So in 1955, the social workers faced the world with an organization designed "to further a sound unification of objectives and activities, but allowing for flexible diversification in line with the particular interest of members and changing needs of a growing profession."[35] The organization could claim to speak for 20,000 members and to guarantee that all new members would be high-class types, but when it turned its attention to legal licensing or certification there was still the

[34]Louis A. Towley, "NASW — A Professional Step," *Social Work,* I (January, 1956), 111.
[35]Kidneigh, p. xvii.

problem of "interpreting" to the politicians just what it is that fully trained social workers do that reasonably intelligent laymen should be prohibited from learning on the job. As Hollis and Taylor had reminded social workers before the unification, both the essential character of social work practice and standards of competence had yet to be established, and no satisfactory definition of social worker was at hand. NASW leaders apparently concluded, however, that they could not wait indefinitely for state legislators and governors instinctively to grasp the importance of certifying social workers.[36] The association designed a voluntary certification scheme "as an interim step pending the passage of legislation in the several states providing for legal regulation of practice of the licensure form."[37] Preliminary discussions at the 1958 Delegate Assembly followed by chapter reports and committee proposals in 1959 resulted in a recommendation to the 1960 Assembly that NASW create the title of Certified Social Worker. All incumbent NASW members could be blanketed-in again, but new recipients of the title are to be members of the association who have, in addition, two years of paid employment under the supervision of a Certified Social Worker. The thick-barley-soup cooks are clearly not wanted, although in the span of a few years an untrained member of the old Association of School Social Workers might have been swept along into the presumably restricted NASW, and would now be anointed with the CSW designation upon application.

A last-minute legal opinion necessitated an alteration. Delegates were told that by restricting eligibility to members of NASW, the association laid itself open to possible charges of illegal monopoly. If practice ever was legally restricted anywhere to Certified Social Workers, acquisition of the title could not be controlled by a private association. Accordingly, a legal fiction was devised, a separate organization to be known as the Academy of Certified Social Workers run by the NASW board and served by the NASW staff. "That this fiction was specifically designed to circumvent certain legal and ethical requirements drawn up to protect the public evidently held no terrors for sponsors; in any event," reports William Schwartz, "it was not discussed by them." Since nobody wished to certify social workers, he says, they certified each other.[38]

---

[36]"It is a sobering experience to read congressional and state legislative hearings," Eveline Burns wrote in 1962, "and to see not merely how ignorant the legislators are of what social services mean, but even more how unable we who render services seem to be to enlighten legislators in terms they can understand." From "What's Wrong with Public Welfare?" *Social Service Review,* XXXVI (June, 1962), 117.

[37]National Association of Social Workers, *The Social Work Yearbook 1960* (New York: author, 1960), p. 571.

[38]William Schwartz, "On Certifying Each Other," *Social Work,* VII (July, 1962), 23.

A kind of certification has finally been achieved through the academy plan. It is a certification scheme that provides requirements bearing virtually no relation to standards of competence. It offers the public an illusion of protection and an illusion of legal regulation when neither in fact exists, and neither has been shown to be necessary. It avoids meeting the hard questions of precisely what are a social worker's special skills, and what guarantee there is that graduation from an accredited school instills them in a student. But certification obviously had an appeal independent of these questions. It made it possible for the fully trained worker to distinguish himself from the so-called social worker who might once have considered membership in the American Public Welfare Association as satisfactory as NASW membership. Associations are routine in American society, but academies and certified status have prestige. Within six months after introduction of the academy arrangement, 19,000 members joined. More than 4,000 persons joined NASW in order to become eligible for membership in the academy.[39]

With every passing year, NASW comes closer to representing only school-trained professionals. Nevertheless, it does not regard itself as in any way limited in its right to speak out as the voice of welfare. Social workers have no vested professional interests, they say. Nathan E. Cohen explained that "one of the differences between the A.M.A. and the N.A.S.W. is that the doctors lobby for the vested interests of their membership whereas we lobby for the interests of those we serve."[40] Accordingly, although public assistance has not been staffed by more than a handful of the professionally trained social workers admissible to the association, NASW regards policy in this field as well within its sphere of special competence. "We think we can claim to speak from a knowledge of the problem that is more immediate and direct than that of almost any other organized group which has appeared before you," said Eveline Burns—an economist who could not join NASW under the current limitations on membership—to the House Ways and Means Committee in 1958 on behalf of NASW, "for, while we find ourselves in general agreement with the policies proposed to you by the American Public Welfare Association and the AFL-CIO, our understanding of the needs of people stems from the experience of our members in private as well as in public welfare agencies, and our clientele comprises many who are not merely unor-

---

[39]Harold Silver, "Certification: A Look at the Record," *Social Work,* VII (July, 1962), 27-32.
[40]Nathan E. Cohen, "A Changing Profession in a Changing World," *Social Work,* I (October, 1956), 19.

ganized workers but, in many cases, persons who are not members of the labor market at all."[41]

The claim that experience outside the public field provides a knowledge of public assistance more immediate and direct than that provided by public welfare practice is not easy to understand. In the absence of a challenge to that claim, the social work professional group continues to be regarded as public spokesman for the relief client. In reality, professional social work, NASW style, seems to have neither an immediate nor a direct tie to either public assistance workers or public assistance clients.

[41]U.S. Congress, House, Committee on Ways and Means, Hearings, "Social Security Legislation," 85th Cong., 2d Sess., 1958, p. 986.

CHAPTER VIII

A Case of Nonsupport

IN THE FIRST few months of 1961, public and political acceptance of public assistance in Illinois were probably at their highest point since the program had become effective a quarter of a century earlier. By the middle of 1962, and for more than a full year thereafter, public assistance was the state's most obvious political problem. Over the whole time span, no newspaper exposés of fraud in the program were developed, no public official was caught selling relief for votes, and no sudden outburst of recipient or social worker militancy called special attention to the program. Neither the recipients nor public attitudes suddenly changed. Political leadership at the state level and in Chicago's government remained constant. Nevertheless, in 1962-1963, a Democratic Governor and a Republican legislature took turns in attempting to hold back relief funds, with emergency surplus food stations and hunger marches the eventual result.

What set of circumstances can result in a turning off of welfare funds by public officials who control the appropriations process? We have seen that the matching grant requirement coupled with the open-end authorization of the Social Security Act leaves Congress no practical choice but to pay whatever bills the states present based on the prevailing grant-in-aid formula. State legislatures are under no comparable constraint. At the state level, budgets for individual relief cases are established administratively; the certainty of legislative appropriations adequate to meet those budgets is not present. For example, in 31 states, ceilings on relief payments have been written into the law and thus impose an absolute, prior limit on spending on any one case.

A different kind of appropriations problem occurs when a state legislature or a governor or both renege on public assistance spending patterns previously agreed to. Illinois presented an extreme case of this sort, one involving a large number of recipients. How and why did it happen? Is there any evidence in the Illinois story to portend change in public assistance policy in rich, urbanized, industrial, two-party states of the north like Illinois? Or, to the contrary, is there evidence that the relief program can withstand the indifference and antagonism of either inexperienced, or hostile, or skeptical politicians and still survive, substantially unchanged? New directions in Illinois could mean new directions in New York, California, Pennsylvania, or Ohio. Stability after challenge, on the other hand, would suggest that public assistance policy is not likely to be significantly altered at the state level. The very fact that Illinois money for relief was allowed to give out briefly is unique. But it requires a detailed look at the politics of this case of nonsupport to determine whether it should cheer or dismay those who support present categorical assistance policy.

I. A MATTER OF MONEY

Governor Otto Kerner came to power in January, 1961, unaware of the complexity of issues with which he would have to deal, and without a mechanism for learning about those issues. In a campaign which permitted him to capitalize on personal integrity and sincerity, there had been neither need nor desire to narrow in on specific state problems aside from mental health, a cause that Kerner had chosen to pluck from the bag of issues available. When he quickly named a distinguished professor of psychiatry to direct mental health work, welfare groups were cheered by the indication of a sympathetic governor.

If the will was there, however, the way was unknown and unmarked. Arriving in Springfield, the Governor thought that with his small staff carried over from the campaign, and with the files and records of the Governor's office, he could go to work on state problems. As it developed, the files and records of the Governor's office went out with the outgoing Governor, who felt no obligation to tell his victorious opponent what the job involved. Kerner's small campaign staff had two special talents: the first was to maintain the image of a sincere and dedicated Governor who cheerfully went to meet the people everywhere he was invited; the second was rigorously to enforce the state sales tax law in order that state revenue could be increased without the appearance of new taxation. Important as these talents are, they did not serve to maximize the Governor's information and understanding of state affairs. For three months, Kerner marked time while he and his friends looked for people who could help put together a program to propose to the legislature.

Public assistance was not marked for the spotlight. Throughout most of the 1950's, relief appropriations' procedures were routinely irregular. Underbudgeting of costs and a deficiency appropriation with which to finish out the year were standard practice, taken for granted. This fiction permitted the budget to be balanced—a constitutional requirement—but it inhibited no one. For practical purposes, public assistance expenditures were tied to eligibility conditions and personal allowance standards, rather than to appropriations. The budget put no real limit on spending for relief; it reflected an estimate of convenience about the number of recipients to be benefited. If the estimate was too low, expenditures were later increased. Eligibility and allowances were not expected to be adjusted to fit the money appropriated; it was understood that money would be appropriated later to meet the need. The system was really a kind of open-end authorization accompanied by an automatic appropriation, an adaptation of congressional practice to fit the needs of the state. Although some legislative purists grumbled from time to time about 18- rather than 24-month budgets in public assistance, no serious effort was ever made to upset the practice. When underbudgeting in public assistance was attacked, the accompanying suggestion was not that allowances be made to fit the budgeted funds. It was said, instead, that more money should have been appropriated in the first place, and the budget balanced by cutting funds elsewhere or by raising taxes. Raising taxes, however, was not a popular position when the happy alternative of achieving a balanced budget and avoiding a tax increase was so easily achieved by the deficiency appropriation technique.

In describing an identical practice in New York State, Donald Herzberg and Paul Tillett call a $2.3 million cut in welfare appropriations "a calculated risk that welfare authorities had been 'unduly pessimistic' in their estimates of future needs." The effect of the action in the instance described was "simply to defer recognition of a cost to be incurred in any event in the same year, which would be financed through a deficiency appropriation at the next session."[1] The Illinois practice was not unique.

Complicated as the bookkeeping was, relief expenditures had been

[1]Donald Herzberg and Paul Tillett, *A Budget for New York State 1956-1957* (Inter-University Case Program Case No. 69; University: University of Alabama Press, 1962), p. 25.

high in Illinois for more than a decade. Public assistance represented a larger percentage of total expenditure under Adlai Stevenson (1949-1953) than under William Stratton, his successor (1953-1961), because Stevenson did not spend for other things while Stratton did, not because one was charitable and the other uncharitable. Whatever the differences in spending or other habits, neither of Kerner's immediate predecessors — one Democrat, one Republican — resisted public assistance expenditures, neither complained about the effect on the budget, and neither did much more than accept the judgments of need made by the Illinois Public Aid Commission and its administrative staff.

These were the rules of the game, and they were well understood: underbudgeting and deficiency appropriations in order to make it appear that the state was only spending up to its current income; unquestioning acceptance of the judgment of the commission and its staff about the money needed; acceptance of professional judgments about personal allowances and budgets for recipients; *status quo* in eligibility. They were based, however, on the existence of a bank, of a pot of surplus money accumulated during the war. The surplus could be tapped for all or part of the deficiency appropriation needed, and then revenue and expenditure for the following biennium would not be thrown out of adjustment by borrowing to meet current requirements. If the surplus had been inexhaustible, there would never have been a public assistance crisis in Illinois in 1961-1963. But, when the bank appeared to have run out of capital before the conditions for withdrawing funds had been changed, crisis became inevitable in one of the major spending fields: common schools, higher education, highways, or public assistance.

The latter appeared to be in an unusually good position to withstand trouble. Important credits had accrued to the public assistance program with the submission in December, 1960, of the so-called Greenleigh Report on ADC in Cook County.[2] Commissioned by an *ad hoc* citizens' committee appointed by the County Commissioners, the report had an official flavor by virtue of financing from federal, state, and local governmental agencies. Cook County ADC cases had increased from almost 13,000 families in 1954 to 24,500 families in 1959. To find out why, the *ad hoc* committee hired Greenleigh Associates, described as "a management consulting firm with experience in the health and welfare field."

The Greenleigh Report concluded that Cook County ADC recipients were not newcomers: 90 per cent had lived in the state for five

[2]*Facts, Fallacies and Future,* 2 vols. (New York: Greenleigh Associates, 1960).

years or more, 25 per cent of the mothers and 75 per cent of the children were born in Illinois. Recipients from outside had come to take a job, to be with their husbands, or to join relatives, not to get on public assistance. Racial discrimination in employment was characterized as one of the most serious direct and indirect causes of ADC dependency. One-half of the families were thought to have a high rehabilitation potential which was not being realized. The number of ADC mothers neglecting their maternal responsiblilities was called negligible. Seventy per cent of the families had at least one illegitimate child, while about one-half of all ADC children in Illinois were illegitimate. In most instances, the mother did not want to have the child; in about half the cases, she did not know how to prevent pregnancy. No fraud was found in the sample investigated, while ineligibility or suspicion of ineligibility was found in less than 2 per cent of the cases. The Cook County Public Aid Department was gently reprimanded on only one count: in its efforts to keep ineligibles from the rolls, the department in some cases denied assistance to eligible families. Two additional criticisms beyond the department's control were offered: case loads were too large for efficient operation and for the achievement of rehabilitation goals; and the ADC assistance level was much below the reasonable subsistence standard called for in the state public assistance code.

From the point of view of public assistance public relations, the report was a masterpiece. A comparable document appearing under the sponsorship of the American Public Welfare Association might have gotten some passing attention from a small group. The Greenleigh work achieved widespread and prominent news coverage by the metropolitan press, favorable editorial comment, and respectful attention in the Chicago business community, all surely attributable to the use of the citizens' committee technique, to the importance in Chicago affairs of the chairman of the citizens' committee, C. Virgil Martin, President of Carson Pirie Scott and Company, the large Chicago department store, and to the billing of Greenleigh Associates as a management consulting firm.

The description was technically correct, and, as we shall see, acceptance of Greenleigh Associates as management consultants contributed to the report's favorable reception. Chicago's newspapers either did not know or failed to find it newsworthy that Arthur Greenleigh's lifetime professional career had been in social work. After studying at the New York School of Social Work, he spent seven years in emergency relief and public assistance agencies, and in 1939 began 17 years in a variety of refugee agency jobs. Named first executive director of a new refugee service formed by the merger of two agencies in the field, Greenleigh resigned after two years of internal dispute related to the merger and organized Greenleigh Associates in 1956. There is no question of Greenleigh's integrity, but the selection of his firm kept the orientation of the study of an important public assistance program within the fraternity of social workers.

Press comment on the Greenleigh Report could not have been better if that comment had originated in the Public Aid Commission's own publicity office. Thus, the Chicago *Sun-Times* said editorially (December 7, 1960), that the new factual report would be a good basis on which to build a legislative program built on truths, not myths or old wives' tales. "We wish to underscore the fact," said the editorial, "that this report was made by a New York management consulting firm that came into the Chicago situation 'cold,' with no preconceptions. It was out to get hard facts. The committee that hired the firm consisted of eminent Chicago business and professional people with C. Virgil Martin, president of Carson Pirie Scott and Co. as chairman." The Chicago *Tribune* while expressing concern about ADC costs (December 10, 1960), noted that the report "made by a firm of management consultants . . . disposes of hardy myths about the ADC program." The *Tribune* went on to speak kindly of the possibility of "hiring more and better trained social workers and other specialists." Editorial comment in Paddock Publications, a chain of suburban papers, applauded the work of the "distinguished laymen" comprising the citizens' committee, and observed (December 22, 1960), that the findings "are exactly what welfare specialists and those concerned with public aid problems have been saying for years. The difference is that the committee's conclusions cannot be written off as the mutterings of idealistic social workers." Each of the four Chicago dailies carried numerous stories reporting the findings of the committee as they were released in piecemeal fashion between December 6, 1960, and February 10, 1961. Public assistance in Illinois had not had as good press coverage at least since the depression.

Kerner gave two positive indications of his willingness to go along with the good-will-to-reliefers sentiment that seemed to prevail. First, in a message to an extraordinary joint session of the legislature in March, 1961, the Governor detailed some of the things he was for or against. He was for the relief client. In public assistance, Kerner said that he thought it was time for Illinois "to stop badgering the relatively helpless recipients," a line that, of course, delighted welfare supporters. Standing ready to do his part, he urged that the quasi-independent commission be abandoned in favor of an executive department of public assistance so that the governor could have appropriate responsibility for a program that accounted for a substantial part of state spending. The legislature found the *status quo* preferable, a fact which did not bother Kerner, who was suggesting, not crusading for the change. "I do not welcome the responsibility for the public assistance program," he told an associate while the proposal was under discussion, "but I do not see how I can properly shy away from it."[3]

Republican legislative leaders looked on the proposal as unnecessary. "We've been over that Commission three or four times," the most influential Republican senator told an interviewer, "and it always comes out clean. I can't see any point in killing it."

The Governor's second indication of support for the welfare-oriented position came in June when, given an unexpected opportunity to name a new chairman of the Public Aid Commission, Kerner chose C. Virgil Martin. Governor Kerner thus appeared to place the prestige of his office behind the Martin attitude to public assistance, an attitude about which there could have been no doubt in view of his widely publicized connection with the Greenleigh Report.

Martin took over expecting the usual public aid rules to prevail. In October, the commission implemented a plan, long in the works, to increase relief allowances by about 10 per cent. For the ten-year period beginning July, 1951, and ending September, 1961, changes in personal allowances had been very moderate, so that despite occasional adjustments to meet higher food costs, there had been a decline in the purchasing power of the personal allowances granted a typical ADC family. October increases brought the purchasing power of the personal allowances to a level higher than it had been in July, 1951. In other words, after October, 1961, the ADC family was slightly better off than it had been ten years earlier—if it was not being gouged for rent and putting part of its personal allowance into that item. The Greenleigh study, it will be recalled, had concluded that existing allowances were insufficient to satisfy the statutory requirement of a reasonable subsistence compatible with health and well-being.

While Kerner was calling for an end to "badgering" of public aid clients and the commission staff was planning program improvements, the beginnings of state budget troubles were developing. Although

[3]In this chapter, direct quotations attributed to individuals, but not otherwise documented, are derived either from personal interviews or from newspaper stories appearing in the *Chicago Tribune,* the *Chicago Sun-Times,* or the *Chicago Daily News.* Where the source is one of the latter, I have not considered it either useful or necessary to footnote every quotation. I have not used any newspaper quotation unless it is in accord with my independent understanding of the issues and personalities involved.

some of the Governor's newly recruited advisors urged him to ask for increased taxes in order to meet projected common school, university, and welfare needs for 1961-1963, Kerner held off on any decisions until his friend, campaign manager, and Director of Revenue, Theodore Isaacs, reported on the prospects for increased revenue from tighter administration of the sales tax law. Isaacs was single-minded and nonideological in his concern for avoiding a tax increase; Kerner was single-minded and nonideological in his dependence on Isaacs who was convinced that Democratic governors had to overcome the tax-and-spend image. A tax increase in 1961, Isaacs thought, would kill Kerner's chances for reelection in 1964.

It is common enough for a political executive to face the competing goals of low taxes and high-level public services. The distinguishing feature of the present case is that the Governor was able to separate the goals and keep them from a direct confrontation. Mental health, education, and public assistance were the expensive public services. In dealing with the state university and with mental health needs, Kerner was helped by 1960 referendum approval of two bond issues which made it possible to write off virtually all capital construction in these two fields. University and mental health spokesmen were in a weak position to argue the point in view of what appeared to be a windfall from the bond issues. Operating expense funds might be increased within expected sales tax revenue increases. With common schools, increases in the school population did automatically add to the state's costs, but any addition to the state aid per pupil figure was resisted by emphasizing the desirability of a larger assumption of costs at the local level. In education and in mental health, then, high-level services were to be maintained by borrowing and local taxation so that the state budget would not be strained.

Public assistance was separated from the budget problem by simple noncommunication. The Governor assumed that the commission would live within its budgeted appropriation for 1961-1963, an appropriation about 10 per cent less than the amount requested. It was an assumption made in good faith since Kerner did not know that eligibility provisions and allowance levels had always determined relief expenditures no matter what the budgeted figure was. But there was no one to explain the Governor's inexperience to the Public Aid Commission, and no one to explain the Illinois experience to the Governor. Unaware of the politics of state budgeting, he and Isaacs were adopting as realistic the recommendations of the legislative Budgetary Commission which follows the rule of "the same as last year unless the Governor okays an increase."

The plan of the Public Aid Commission to make cost-of-living increases in clients' allowances was going to cost money. It is not clear whether this fact was especially emphasized to the Governor, or whether he blocked it out of his mind. "The Governor and I did talk about public assistance," Virgil Martin told an interviewer later, "but I realize now that we never really communicated. I believe that public aid is a complicated problem but I think Kerner considers it to be a simple problem. Apparently, we talked past each other." Isaacs was certainly not taking the findings of the Greenleigh Report about inadequate allowances into his fiscal calculations. Preoccupied with sales tax administration, he appeared unaware of the report as late as the spring of 1962 when it became important in connection with a tentative plan discussed in Isaacs' office to send the Governor to Washington to ask for emergency federal funds.

In the final reckoning, bond issue funds and legislation to close some of the so-called loopholes in the sales tax could not stretch far enough to meet school, university, and welfare needs. Education interests were satisfied when, at what was almost the last possible minute, Isaacs conceded that there was no alternative to an increase in the sales tax. Kerner's liberal supporters, who had dreamed of an income tax, a corporation tax, or anything except an increase in the regressive sales tax, were dismayed. Appropriations for public aid were not increased beyond the original budget plan. That would have required a larger sales tax boost than seemed palatable. After the small increase was voted — with Republican help — Kerner was led to believe that he was out of the woods. Further work extending the base of the sales tax and improving its administration would become priority items for the 1963 legislative session so that the 1964 election would be untainted by a state tax rate increase more recent than 1961.

By the beginning of 1962, the watchdogs of state finance found that, even with the added sales tax revenue, the budget would not work. Public assistance spending was proceeding by the unwritten rules. Projecting its spending rate through the biennium would leave the commission short more than $160 million, of which 55 per cent would be state funds. The state didn't have $90 million.

Suddenly, the Governor's troubles were so complex that it was trouble just to sort them out. Even if the state had $90 million, the problem could not be solved because there was no authority for the commission to spend more than the sum appropriated to it. In past years, this had presented no difficulty because a short special session of the legislature would increase the appropriation; the Governor would then find the needed deficiency funds by dipping into the surplus and by juggling cash until the next regular session when the situation could be straightened out. This time, assuming a special session would increase the appropriation, it did not look as if cash would actually be available to spend. If public aid costs were to be met, both new spending authority and new money would be required. An additional complexity was posed by the peculiarities of the Illinois Constitution which makes legislation, including appropriations items, effective on the July 1 following passage unless enacted by a two-thirds vote of all members elected to each house. It would not be easy to accomplish legislative results before July 1; it would be practically impossible after that date. Illinois' primary would take place in April, however, and legislators were not disposed to favor a special money-raising session before then. Kerner accommodated them by avoiding the special-session question prior to the primary, only to face unexpected consequences as that particular primary produced unthinkable results. A series of bond issues proposed by Mayor Daley for public works improvements in Chicago were voted down in what appeared to be a display of taxpayer impatience with governmental costs. Did the Governor now dare to ask for $90 million for public assistance? Did he dare not to? The soap opera began.

The Governor hesitated. Kerner's initial hope was to achieve a nonpartisan special session so that responsibility for added taxing and spending could be shared and thus cancelled out. Viewing the results of the Chicago bond issues, the Republicans would have none of it. Viewing those same results and the Republican warning that tax increases would be on Democratic legislators' heads, the latter wanted no part of a special session either.

Isaacs and other political counselors insisted that a special session would be a disaster resulting in major losses in the November election. Two, perhaps three, marginal Senate seats held by Democrats would be endangered. Mayor Daley, looking ahead to his own reelection campaign in April, 1963, would benefit from having the issue put over until after that time. If, however, money actually gave out after July 1, 1962, but before the 1963 session was well under way, the Governor would be in an untenable position, faced with the need to make whatever concessions the Republicans demanded in order to get the two-thirds vote necessary for quick action.

Out of this unhappiness, all at once it seemed logical enough to the administration to ask: how did the Public Aid Commission get us into this mess, and why doesn't it get us out? Putting the issue in those terms made it possible to transfer guilt. Now, it was no longer an immense, virtually insoluble problem of state finance that the inexperienced administration found difficult to understand and impossible to

214

solve. The dilemma of the special session could also be put aside. By behaving as if the unwritten rules of public assistance expenditures did not exist, the Governor could turn a stern face to the commission and demand an explanation. What he got was an orthodox short course in public assistance, spiced with the new gospel that was then being pushed before Congress as Secretary Ribicoff's revolutionary new approach. It seemed to be a revelation. Kerner was sufficiently impressed to direct a barnstorming tour in which he and his Lieutenant-Governor explained programs to "come to grips with the causes" of public assistance. These programs included job retraining, securing new industry, trade expansion, better high school vocational training, and equal job opportunities for Negroes.

To show its vigor, the commission voted to report cases of ADC illegitimate births to state's attorneys for possible prosecution under adultery or fornication statutes and to remove children from such unsuitable homes. Critical votes for the resolution came from two *ex officio* members: the appointed State Director of Finance who was also Democratic State Chairman, and the elected State Treasurer, a Democrat who faced a reelection campaign in 1962. Virgil Martin was absent from the meeting because of illness. "Social workers," reported one Chicago paper, "were appalled by the action — although unwilling to go on record."

Other fronts were opened to prove that if costs were to exceed appropriations by $160 million, the causes were either in faulty administration by the welfare bureaucracy or in totally new circumstances beyond the control of the state's political leaders. Administrative inadequacies were to be attacked vigorously. State Treasurer Francis Lorenz proposed to his fellow commissioners that the agency hire a management consulting firm to survey commission purchasing and personnel practices, estimating that $200,000 could be trimmed annually from relief administration costs. Buying filing cabinets in small lots at $108 rather than identical cabinets for $87 each in large lots, and buying standing ash trays for $30 each rather than dime store glass ash trays for 15¢ were illustrations of purchasing malpractices offered. No cutback in the number of employees was anticipated, but doubt was expressed that employees were being put to the best possible use. Other examples of dubious adminstrative wisdom were brought to the Governor's attention. He was sufficiently bothered by a $3 expense-account luncheon claimed by the commission's executive secretary to contrast it with his own practice of a 75¢ bowl of soup paid for personally. A management survey won everyone's enthusiastic approval except perhaps that of the commission administrative staff.

While prosecution of mothers of illegitimates and the cost of ash trays and lunches were receiving attention on one level, the revenue experts realized that it would take quite a few ash trays to have real bearing on the deficit in state funds. Isaacs and some others con- cluded that a massive injection of federal funds was required and was legitimate. Illinois' problem, they said, was a consequence of an unanticipated influx of migrants from Mississippi who flocked to Chicago via the Illinois Central Railroad but were unable to find employ- ment. Newspaper accounts of southern Negroes being offered one-way transportation to northern centers were used to buttress the analysis. If this position could be sustained, it could be argued that because the emergency fiscal problem was traceable to a public assistance problem that was interstate, the costs should be federally met. Statistical data, graphs, and charts in support were solicited from diverse sources in hopes that a compelling case could be developed which the Governor might take to Washington and lay before President Kennedy. When it became evident that the only available data on migration of aid recipi- ents were in the Greenleigh Report—which had held that most recipi- ents were long-time residents—the plan to send the Governor to Washington with a briefcase full of support died for want of anything to put in the briefcase.

The plan to crack down on illegitimacy was having its troubles, too. Raymond Hilliard, Cook County's outspoken Public Aid Direc- tor, said it would not work, that if implemented it would place a moun- tain of work on his department and that of the state's attorney, and would result in futile attempts to prosecute. The Cook County state's attorney said adultery cases were simply too difficult to prosecute. Virgil Martin wanted no part of it. An advisory opinion from the Health, Education, and Welfare regional representative held that the plan would be out of conformity with the federal act. Governor Kerner who was depressed over the possibility of losing rather than gaining federal funds declared his opposition to the commission resolution, with the comment "It's utterly ridiculous." This judgment did not cheer the two Democratic state officials who had voted for the proposal because they considered it necessary to give every possible impression that the Kerner administration was actively pursuing economy in public assist- ance.

No one knew what the Governor wanted, including the Governor himself. It was clear that he was outraged by the failure of the commission staff to practice small economies. Martin, sharing Kerner's reservations about the executive secretary but for different reasons, favored a reorganization that would bring in as chief administrative officer a highly paid and highly talented executive who would not

216

necessarily have a professional welfare background. The retired president of the Illinois Bell Telephone Company was his first choice for the job. While the public assistance crisis was developing in the spring of 1962, Martin was quietly conducting a nationwide search for a new executive secretary.

What was not clear was whether the Governor was restricting his unhappiness to the administrative staff, or whether he was planning or could be pushed to take at least a tentative crack at the relief recipients. All of Kerner's earlier behavior — exemplified by the Martin appointment itself, the "stop badgering the reliefer" phrase, and his barnstorming explanation of the causes and cures for public assistance — suggested a negative answer. But the money problem remained and there was no plan advanced to meet it. Special-session talk had run into almost unanimous political opposition. In April, Kerner was speaking hopefully of the work of the Commission on Revenue, created to study the state's financial needs and ways to meet them. Now it was the beginning of June, the Commission on Revenue was quiet, and the Governor had still given no sign that he would follow the unwritten rules of public assistance budgeting and recommend additional funds.

Sometime in this period, Kerner discussed his money troubles with Martin, telling him that economies were necessary. The Governor was under the impression that at that time Martin told him "I think we can save you 10 per cent." Ten per cent would not have made the program solvent through the biennium. Kerner had been led to believe, however, that with some fund juggling and some borrowing of cash from earmarked accounts, a saving of 10 per cent would make it possible to hold out until the regular legislative session convened in January, 1963. Although the state's cash balance might be very low indeed by that date, he thought necessary new taxes might be achieved then on a bipartisan basis as a result of the work of the Revenue Commission. (In hopes of capturing the opposition, Kerner had appointed as its chairman a Republican lawyer whose tax views were notoriously conservative.) On June 11, after telephoning the news to Martin, the Governor announced that he would not "take the risk of an unproductive special session." Instead, to bolster the state's cash position, idle money allocated to "other sovereign areas" would be withheld until absolutely needed, and cuts in public assistance payments would be required:

Since expenditures of the Illinois Public Aid Commission have increased, rather than decreased, I have asked the IPAC to review their estimates of needed revenue during the next 12 months and within reason to reduce payments. Certainly the area of public aid has been causing a drain on our

General Revenue funds. Because of this, a reduction in payments to recipients, as well as stringent administrative economies are called for. I hesitate taking anything from the subsistence payments which we provide through IPAC to those less fortunate than the majority of Illinois citizens, but we must preserve the financial integrity of Illinois.

Since substantial savings already have been accomplished in the code departments, further savings can only be accomplished by curtailment of IPAC expenditures.[4]

Kerner was astonished by the reaction. No voice was raised in support of his proposition that preserving the fiscal integrity of Illinois and adequately feeding Illinois' relief clients were incompatible objectives. The Republican Cook County Commissioner who had triggered the Greenleigh study said Kerner's plan was "absolutely ridiculous" and would "take bread out of the mouths of deserving people," while the Republican leader of the State House of Representatives said that "if people go hungry" as a result of the relief cuts, Kerner must "assume the blame." Raymond Hilliard called it indefensible to single out public aid as the goat in the state's financial crisis. The Chicago chapter of the National Association of Social Workers termed the announcement by Kerner "the most shocking statement made in recent Illinois history by a responsible official." Editorial comment was in the form of disbelief. After all, said the Chicago *Daily News,* the Governor can really borrow money from special funds and put it into the relief program without asking the legislature, so it must be assumed that he is just trying to "extract a little political profit." The *Tribune* thought it "possible that Mr. Kerner called for lower relief payments as a publicity gimmick, knowing that a great cry of protest would arise and that the cuts would not be placed into effect." Unwelcome praise came from the downstate Republican chairman of the legislative Budgetary Commission. Reduced allowances for relief recipients, he was quoted as saying, "won't hurt them at all."

Democratic politicians ran for cover. Those who were *ex officio* members of the commission let the word get out that they had not been consulted. No one else would say anything except Mayor Daley of Chicago who blamed Republicans for failure to appropriate enough money for relief in the 1961 legislative session. Two weeks later, Raymond Hilliard told the American Public Welfare Association that the Kerner administration had short-changed public aid. Daley and Hilliard were both right. The Governor had concurred in the decision to cut $110 million from the public aid request in 1961, but no Republicans had independently insisted on appropriating the additional

[4]Illinois Information Service, News Release (Chicago, June 11, 1962), p. 2.

amount. Daley tried to make sure that whatever happened the Democrats were not going to be tagged as the party of relief cuts. "Anyone who makes relief a political issue had better be pretty careful," he said. "It has never been done in the state, and I hope to God it never will."

Five of the nine Public Aid Commission members made it plain that they considered relief allowances already to be at a bare minimum. Declining to order a cut, a unanimous commission at a special meeting restricted itself to passage of a resolution naming a three-member subcommittee to confer with the Governor to get his views in greater detail.

It dawned on Virgil Martin that he was being asked to preside over a Kerner-ordered cut-back in relief allowances after having been willing front-man for the Greenleigh Report which had contrary implications. Moreover, the phrase in the Governor's statement calling for "stringent administrative economies" implied to Martin that Kerner was suggesting inefficiency and waste of taxpayers' money by the Public Aid Commission. In short, Kerner appeared to have stumbled into a mess and seemed to expect Martin to pull him out. Since it was obvious when he first became chairman that the commission was headed for serious financial trouble, Martin did not like the present turn of events at all. He quit. In a letter written exactly one week after Kerner's economy announcement, Martin said that he would preside over the special meeting to consider relief cuts and over a regular July commission meeting without being "either obstructive or critical of the situation in which the state of Illinois finds itself," but that he wanted out since it was now "certain that the sorry plight of Illinois' financial condition is to be placed on the Illinois Public Aid Commission." A telephone call from Daley to Martin to urge him to reconsider provided a signal to Democratic state officials serving on the Public Aid Commission that they were not obliged to line up behind the Governor. They didn't. What happened instead was an embarrassing lesson to Kerner of the consequences of breaking the rules without warning.

Martin led his subcommittee to a meeting with Kerner and explained that a 50 per cent cut in allowances would keep the public assistance program solvent until June 30, 1963, that a 24 per cent reduction would provide enough funds to run until the end of February, and that a 10 per cent reduction in all public aid grants across the board, effective August 1, would enable the commission to operate until January 31, 1963. Having initiated the move for a cut in allowances, Kerner was expected to choose the particular formula. No serious attention was given to the possibility of a 50 per cent cut. Entirely aside from the humanitarian considerations involved in halving budgets that were already supposed to be at the minimum level compatible with health and decency, a reduction of that magnitude would have brought the Illinois allowances below the point at which maximum federal grants were available. Between an obviously severe slash of one-quarter and a slash of 10 per cent which might be considered marginal, Kerner chose the smaller cut. It would avoid a special session, although the legislature would have to act almost immediately after it convened in January, 1963.

That was six months off, however, and the Governor was an optimist. He was so much of an optimist, in fact, that he regarded the 55-minute meeting with the subcommittee of the Public Aid Commission as the beginning of peace. Perhaps things could even be worked out with Martin. "I have not accepted his resignation," said Kerner; "I only announced that I received it." The plan to cut 10 per cent from clients' budgets was subject to ratification of the full commission, of course, at its meeting scheduled for July 6, but that was assumed to be only a formality because the Governor wanted it. Kerner went about his business without considering the limitations on gubernatorial power, on the one hand, and the totality of gubernatorial responsibility, on the other hand. At first, the commission members themselves seemed equally unaware of these facts of political life, but within a week more than a majority of members came to the same conclusion Martin had obviously reached earlier in the month, *i.e.,* that the Governor might change the rules but that he could not compel others to play by the new rules.

The decision to noncomply might never have been made if Kerner had not played the commissioners for fools at a press conference the day before the scheduled ratification session. It had been one thing to accept a mandate from the Governor when it was presumably a matter of maintaining the state's fiscal integrity. This was patriotism. But now Kerner justified the cut in different terms. The commission, he said in effect, was not frugal. Relief recipients should not be buying food at stores giving trading stamps; milk and groceries should be purchased wholesale, in bulk, and doled out to clients; rentals should be forced down although public aid officials seemed to consider high rents "inviolate." With these ideas on the record, the Governor added that "It's too bad if we can't make suggestions without some people feeling insulted," a public utterance that did not persuade Virgil Martin to reconsider his resignation.

Ratification of the 10 per cent cut at this point would have been tantamount to a public confession that the state was on the verge of payless paydays because the commission had allowed relief clients to collect green stamps. It would also have put the commission in the position of apparently agreeing with Kerner that the "numerous" For Rent signs he stated he had seen in Chicago meant that clients could be moved to cheaper apartments — as if Chicago's tight residential segregation did not exist and the large Negro relief population could really live anywhere in the city.

After listening to spokesmen for Catholic Charities of Chicago and ten other private groups, all of whom opposed any cut, the commission voted unanimously to defer action. One by one, the six gubernatorial appointees had come to realize that they were not legally obliged to support the Governor, while the three *ex officio* members had had unmistakable signs from Mayor Daley that they were not politically obliged to support the Governor. In addition to his telephone call to Martin, Daley had permitted the Chicago City Council to adopt a resolution urging Kerner not to cut relief payments until the state's welfare problem was reexamined. Sponsored by aldermen from the city's seven Negro wards, it was a reminder that these wards provided a Democratic plurality of almost 115,000 votes. Daley himself made no statement indicating acceptance of the relief cuts; he kept insisting that the problem could be worked out. "I hope it will be amicably settled," said Daley blandly, asserting confidence in everybody involved.

There was still no kind word for Kerner. "The relief problem is a difficult one," editorialized the Chicago *Tribune* a few days later, "and it isn't made any easier by impractical suggestions, no matter how exalted the office occupied by the man who puts them forward. Mr. Kerner may profitably reflect that if there were a simple way of stretching the appropriations to cover the needs, someone would have thought of it long before Mr. Kerner took over the governor's mansion." The *Daily News* noted that the commission's estimate of its needs had been cut by $110 million on Kerner's own request, and offered a reminder that the accepted practice had been to spend as needed and seek supplemental appropriations. Governor Kerner, said the paper, should now take the straightforward course and call a special session for that purpose.

With the cut dead, Kerner saved what he could by issuing a statesmanlike announcement that he had been convinced that it "would unduly penalize many helpless people and hundreds of private agencies and their supporters." A special session would be called after the November election. Ever charitable, Martin explained that the Governor at first had not been fully informed of the dilemma facing the commission. Daley was delighted, characterizing the outcome as an indication of the great leadership of Kerner, Martin, and the commission. Among those not delighted was Isaacs—in any of his roles as Kerner's campaign manager, principal policy adviser, or Director of Revenue. Out of the state on military duty during the critical period of indecision, Isaacs suspected that Mayor Daley was responsible, later described himself as "sick" to read that Kerner had reneged.

Whoever played supreme commander, the old unwritten rules were now reestablished. Relief payments would continue at existing levels, including the October, 1961, increase. The commission would run out of funds around Christmas; the special session would either appropriate more money, or if there was no free money it would authorize the use of a trust fund to tide the program over to February or March. The public assistance crisis seemed over at that point with no change in policy and with signs that policy could not change. The latter would have been an unwarranted conclusion, as subsequent events disclosed.

II. BIRTH CONTROL

Governors have ordinary human emotions and reactions. Having been publicly humiliated by the commission, and hounded by the press for comment, Kerner thrashed out at what he termed "empire building" within the Public Aid Commission. Less understandably, he turned his attack for the first and only time on public aid recipients, claiming that it was being made so attractive for people to stay on relief that they had no desire to get off. Republicans later made Kerner pay a high price for this bit of self-indulgence. Martin, in his last days as chairman, would not be teased into a response, saying only that the Governor could proceed to fill the chairmanship with a man more in accord with his ideas of administration of the welfare program.

The man chosen for the job—Arnold Maremont—had two ideas of his own about the welfare program but they did not firm up until after he had been appointed. Both ideas—tax-supported birth control and charging the Illinois Senate with discrimination against Negroes—were in violation of the rules of Illinois politics. Like the Governor's cut in allowances, however, they were expressed before their author learned the game.

Maremont, Chicago industrialist and would-be politician, had first been rewarded for his active support of Democrats with an appointment to the Board of Trustees of Southern Illinois University—with the Carbondale campus 300 miles from Chicago, Maremont's political ambition was not likely to be a problem. Subsequently, he was given an additional title as Chairman of a Council of Economic Advisers which was neither a council, nor composed of economists, nor expected to advise. It had been created to fill out Kerner's 1961 legislative proposals. The council had no money either, but Maremont, uncomplaining about his appointments, worked at inventing a role for the council. When the Governor needed a Chicago business or industrial figure to chair the Public Aid Commission, it was natural for him to turn to Maremont whose loyalty had been flattering. One of the latter's great advantages was that the Maremont Corporation, which manufactured automotive replacement parts, did no advertising in the Chicago papers and did not sell retail. Both Kerner and some of his executive staff privately suspected that Virgil Martin's good press was related to Carson Pirie Scott's advertising budget.

When Maremont took over in mid-August, Kerner and the commission had just concluded a new skirmish and a new peace meeting which livened the short post-Martin, pre-Maremont period. A request from the Governor's press secretary for a list of ADC and general assistance recipients in Cook County was rejected by the executive secretary of the commission who pleaded the confidentiality feature of the law but did invite the Governor or his people to come around and copy the list from the public records — after executing an affidavit that the names would not be used for political or commercial purposes. Kerner complained to the newspapers that information was being withheld from him, a complaint which provided a commission aide an opportunity to remark that he was "confident that we have given the Governor everything he has requested and some things he did not request." The peace meeting ten days later found Kerner still furious at the public aid bureaucracy. A few hours after the meeting, Kerner told a caller that he had indicated to the commission his conviction that its executive secretary was ineffective and must go, that he was impatient about lack of action in hiring a management survey organization to review purchasing and personnel operations, that there was a failure in communication between the commission and its staff. Kerner claimed to have evidence that both administrative heads and caseworkers were extending less than maximum energies. Caseworkers were given home visit quotas sometimes too low for a full day's work, he felt, but they considered the quota a ceiling. During the closed session, commission members proposed that the Governor designate one of his administrative assistants as special liaison with the commission. Kerner declined, saying that he did not wish to appear to have a spy in the group.

A formal release issued after the meeting suggested that a new understanding had been reached. The commission agreed to provide the Governor with a monthly progress report of activities as well as the agenda and minutes of its meetings. Kerner announced himself as highly satisfied with these arrangements. Apparently he did not know that his legal assistant had been receiving minutes for several months. No instructions were issued for any member of Kerner's staff to read and analyze the progress reports to be provided. In the judgment of the commission's acting chairman, an experienced, highly respected leader of Chicago social work, Kerner was now determined to have an executive Department of Public Aid in lieu of the commission. Kerner's staff had no such impression, however, and it is probable that the Governor was then ambivalent on that subject. He needed a period of peace.

Arnold Maremont's first major contribution to establishing tranquility was to propose that public aid funds be used to pay for birth control information and devices desired by clients. The immediate effect was somewhat akin to the likely effect of a suggestion that Mayor Daley resign in favor of George Wallace. Although a legislative advisory group had recommended that welfare workers be instructed to refer clients to family planning agencies if birth control information was requested, this was several steps away from authorizing the use of public funds for private medical advice on birth control and for the cost of birth control materials. With a crusader's naive disregard for the niceties of political timing, Maremont permitted the birth control issue to develop during the month before the November, 1962, election. The scheduling was bad, whether the proposal was "intelligent, humanitarian, and economic" as Maremont claimed or whether it was "the opening wedge for related, far-reaching and frightening assaults on the human person." Two Chicago influentials who held the latter view were the supervisor of charities for the Catholic archdiocese and the director of the Cana Conference, the marriage and family life department of the archdiocese. They visited the Governor early in October to explain their objection to a deviation from the policy of governmental neutrality in the birth control dispute. Maremont delayed making his formal proposal until November, but at that monthly meeting a few days after the election, several members of the commission were clearly astonished to see television lights and cameras rolled into the meeting room to record the chairman's statement in favor of immediate adoption of the proposed birth control policy. When Kerner appointed Maremont to run the Public Aid Commission, the Governor's instructions had been to get public aid off the front pages of the newspapers. Nothing was less likely to accomplish that than to open the birth control question in public meetings of the commission.

Birth control is a sensitive political question anywhere. The Democratic politicians who lead the Chicago organization are, almost without exception, practicing Catholics who appeal for votes in a heavily Catholic community. These politicians were distributed in positions of prime importance in the state. Three of them — Michael Howlett, Auditor of Public Accounts, James Ronan, Director of Finance and Democratic State Chairman, and Francis Lorenz, State Treasurer — were *ex officio* members of the Public Aid Commission. A fourth, William G. Clark, Attorney-General, was watching Maremont uneasily. Although these men recognized the need for a Protestant, suburban, blue-ribbon figure like Kerner, their primary allegiance was to the Chicago organization. If a choice had to be made, for example, between losing a hold on the Governor's office and losing the office of state's attorney of Cook County, the Cook County post would be saved and the state position sacrificed.

By personal religious conviction and by political expediency, then, it was to be expected that the three commission members with the best ties to the legislature and to the Democratic statewide party organization would fight Maremont on birth control. For the same reasons, the state's chief legal officer and the Mayor of Chicago could also be expected to be in opposition. Despite all this formidable resistance, Maremont's legacy is a policy of publicly supported birth control for relief recipients. He pushed too hard, too fast, denying the politicians a chance to develop the needed "cover," a rationale that would serve as an explanation to themselves and to their constituents of unexpected political behavior. Still, Maremont's subsequent ouster was for other reasons; it did not stop the birth control policy. It did result in a temporary delay because he picked a public fight at a time when the political leadership of the state was seeking less, rather than more, publicity about problems of race and illegitimacy in public assistance.

Communication between Maremont and Kerner was more frequent but not any better than between Kerner and Martin. In the face of the Governor's interest in getting public aid off the front pages, Maremont adopted a general line that could not possibly achieve that result. "The only attack on the public aid question that is worth anything," he told an interviewer, "is the attack that shoves the problem of public aid into the face of the public and rubs the public's nose in it." While Kerner's public relations people were in agony, Maremont rubbed the public nose with birth control, an abrasive action that made marvelous copy. The noisier it got and the more column inches that were devoted to the question, the less likely it seemed that Maremont could institute a birth control program.

With reporters goading Chicago Catholic politicians, a noncommittal policy could not be maintained indefinitely; yet the political professionals were reluctant to be firmly committed either way. Stalling for time in which to decide on a position that would reconcile city politics, state politics, religious conviction, and moral judgments, the Chicago group insisted on public hearings. "I don't understand the rush to push through this proposal," said one of the commission members. "It is a moral problem," he went on, "and I don't see why we should pay for subsidizing the illegal activities of women on relief." Public assistance dominated the news columns without interruption as more than 40 witnesses testified at two public hearings. Ironically, the hearings were held only a few days after adjournment of that special legislative session Kerner had announced in July to close off the earlier controversy about across-the-board relief cuts.

The hearings produced no surprises; they did provide time for members to find a tenable position. Catholic groups and individuals argued that publicly supported birth control services would foster promiscuity. In view of the high percentage of unmarried, divorced, separated, or deserted recipients, they said, the proposal meant that Illinois would not only condone and support but actually facilitate premarital and extra-marital sexual intercourse. Planned parenthood supporters spoke of the importance of the child and the need to insure against the tragic consequences of unwanted children. Questions by Catholic members of the commission made it plain that they had resolved the conflicting pressures on them: the issue would turn eventually on providing birth control information and materials for women not living with a lawfully wedded spouse. At its December meeting, the Public Aid Commission split on religious lines; by a vote of six non-Catholics to four Catholics, it approved a resolution to provide financial assistance "for family planning for any recipient with a spouse or a child who requests such assistance, including payment for services and prescriptions of physicians." Auditor Howlett assured his colleagues that the opposition fight was just beginning and would resume in the legislature.

Within 24 hours, displaying what he later acknowledged was bad timing, the commission's new executive secretary announced that he would request authority to pay for divorces for relief recipients. Every commission member promptly denounced that idea. Maremont added a denunciation of Howlett for "malicious attempts to tear the commission asunder." Howlett played the statesman, replied that name-calling would not dissuade him from speaking out in matters where he felt responsibility, including the distribution of contraceptives to unmarried mothers. He drew support from the acting head of the Chicago Catholic archdiocese who said commissioners voting for birth control must assume responsibility for any resultant breakdown in public morality.

When the one appointed commission member who opposed the birth control policy resigned, charging that the Governor tried to wreck the commission by promoting the plan, Kerner was smoked out to a formal noncommittal position. "I am not interested directly or indirectly in the matter of birth control," said Kerner, "nor have I voiced an opinion on it." As to Maremont, "he is a man who is well based in public welfare, not an expert, but well grounded." Later Kerner said of the birth control plan, "it can still land in the ash can," and "I may disagree—I may agree." Chicago Democrats who would have had to provide the votes to support birth control in any legislative test could relax. Mayor Daley, of course, was maintaining his usual public silence. If Kerner would not voice an opinion, it meant that neither leader could be embarrassed by whatever might happen on the subject in the regular legislative session beginning in January, 1963.

The regular session could not be worse than November's special session which had been a Democratic disaster. Seemingly contradictory testimony had come from the Public Aid Commission and from the state Budget Director about commission needs and projected expenses. Republican leaders replied that in the face of such administration confusion, it was impossible to tell whether there was really any emergency. Kerner asked for a transfer of money from special earmarked gasoline tax funds and was promptly buried by the highway lobby. He asked for a deficiency appropriation for public aid to carry the program through the biennium and was buried deeper by Republicans who voted only a fifth of the amount requested. That action insured that public aid would have another legislative go-round before the April mayoral election in Chicago. If Maremont alienated enough Catholics by continuing to push birth control, and if enough middle-class voters were alienated by the high costs of relief for Chicago Negroes, some Republicans thought there could be an April political miracle in Chicago. Democrats gave in without a fight, discouraged by the administration's ineptitude, eager to end the special session even on Republican senators' terms.

Kerner now had a new focus: Republicans, especially Republican senators. It was no longer necessary to displace all of his fiscal frustration on the chairman or on the executive secretary of the Public Aid Commission or on the relief recipients. The first two had been replaced, in any event, so that that line was closed. As for the recipients, the Governor never really had his heart in the charge he had been stung into making months earlier that clients were so well provided for that they lacked incentive to get off the rolls. Republican State senators made it possible for him to turn on them as the stumbling block to the civic betterment he so earnestly desired but seemed to be unable to achieve. After the special session, at his first press conference in three-and-a-half months, Kerner referred to "legislative obstructionists who look to another tomorrow to practice their inaction....They threaten to kill all programs if we do this or that, and indicate they will continue their sadistic game of making political pawns of the poor."

But as soon as the legislature assembled in January, it was the Democratic floor leader and all but three of the other 14 Chicago Democratic senators who offered a bill to prohibit expenditure of public funds for birth control devices. Chief sponsor of the bill was a Daley protégé, the senator from the Mayor's home ward. Given Auditor Howlett's earlier statement about keeping contraceptives from unmarried women, it seemed obvious that the desired compromise was an amendment to that effect. Maremont, however, began to give evidence that he really had abandoned hope for a political career in Illinois. He decided to try to show that public opinion favored his position on birth control rather than the position now publicly adopted by the Chicago Democratic organization. First, Maremont told an interviewer for publication that he thought it strange that some of his Catholic friends had only one or two children in view of the unreliability of the rhythm method. Many of them, he said, must be using birth control devices.[5] After all, a 1962 national Gallup Poll showed that 57 to 58 per cent of Catholics interviewed said they were in favor of birth control. Next, Maremont quietly moved to sponsor an Illinois poll which would show popular support for the program approved by the commission, a program not yet implemented and obviously in danger of a legislative veto. To conduct the poll, he personally offered $1,000 to a market research group with which he had had previous business contacts.

For whatever reason, no results were publicized. Actually, Maremont's belief that favorable results would influence legislative behavior was naive because politicians would have had no difficulty in ridiculing the size of the sample if it suited their interests to do so. Precisely this occurred a year later—after Kerner and Maremont had fallen out—when the same survey research organization mysteriously reported poll results showing Kerner to be a weaker potential candidate for

[5]*Chicago Sun-Times,* January 11, 1963, pp. 5, 18.

reelection than Sargent Shriver. The Governor brushed off the results by passing over percentages and focusing on the fact that only 582 persons were sampled. "I think I could find 582 people right here in Chicago who would prefer Khrushchev," he said.

For all his confidence in the results of a poll, Maremont was willing to limit the program to married women; he would not consider a further limitation to married women living with their husbands. Opposition legislators were finding it hard to attract support. Maremont's public utterances were directed to the importance of rigorous enforcement of eligibility provisions, while national and international concern about population increases generated fresh support for birth control. The commission's new administrative leadership gave the appearance of a businesslike, no-nonsense approach. Legislators without religious scruples on the birth control issue saw no reason to intrude on commission policy-making. Daley had not authorized any logrolling to pick up Republican votes, was not pressuring reluctant Democrats. It is not likely that the prohibition resolution could have achieved a majority vote in the House of Representatives if put directly. There was always the possibility, however, that it would be offered as an amendment to the public assistance appropriation bill and slip through on a voice vote, while birth control supporters were engaged in other matters. In terms of intensity of feeling and of control of the legislative machinery, if not in total votes, birth control opponents were in the lead.

When he learned that a legislative prohibition could be tacked on to his appropriation, Maremont explored the possibility of negotiation with the opposition. A possible deal involving voluntary commission restriction of the program to married women (but not just those living with their husbands) in return for dropping all legislative action was proposed to Kerner, a logical middleman to arrange it. According to Maremont, the Governor decided that such a deal would not appeal to the opposition; he discouraged Maremont who then decided to go ahead with implementation of the birth control program. Again showing an exquisite sense of mistiming, he instructed the staff to work for an April 1 effective date; the Chicago election date was April 2. In mid-March, after Daley's mayoral opponent charged that the Mayor was secretly supporting the birth control program, Daley announced himself in favor of the prohibition resolution. Describing it as a forward step, he said he hoped it would pass; in any event, Daley said, neither the city health department nor any other city agency would be an instrumentality by which the birth control plan would be "foisted" on anyone. Promptly, the Senate Public Welfare Committee amended the bill to permit birth control payments only in the case of a married person living with his or her spouse and reported it favorably to the Senate. Kerner still declined to declare his position. Although there was no evidence that he had any cause to be so concerned, the Governor explained that he felt that his opinion "might affect the judgment of this independent commission."

April was the cruelest month. On April 1, a temporary injunction was issued against implementation of the birth control program. On the fourth, Attorney-General Clark—a young Catholic product of the Chicago organization who had narrowly missed being slated for Governor in 1960 and who figured as a possible ultimate successor to Daley as Mayor—declined to oppose the injunction on behalf of the Public Aid Commission and instead intervened in support of the the plaintiff. The commission's own legal counsel thus joined the opposition in as forthright and clear-cut a demonstration of the political underpinnings of legal reasoning as one is ever likely to find. Claiming that the program "would make the State of Illinois a sovereign accessory to sexual promiscuity and prostitution," the Attorney-General instructed the Auditor and the Treasurer not to sign or pay state warrants issued for birth control materials. They needed no urging. That same day, the Senate overwhelmingly approved the bill that would accomplish the same purpose as the injunction.

On top of all this, there were money troubles, and Maremont's confirmation by the Senate was still pending. The former was a serious problem, the latter was not. In February, the legislature had parceled out only enough money to keep the relief program going through April so that a further deficiency appropriation was required before April 20 to maintain a solvent operation. A confirmation hearing had been several times delayed; nevertheless, there was general agreement that Maremont would be approved. In all of the attacks on the birth control proposal, there had been no public attack on Maremont personally. He had achieved a kind of fame as a man who had a proposed solution to one of the state's great problems. Acceptable or not, it was an effort, and there was no call for his scalp by Republicans. If Maremont had not been a Democratic appointee, however, Democratic senators might have opposed him. Some of Kerner's close advisers were appalled by Maremont's ability to provoke embarrassing issues at the worst possible times. In this group, there was some growing suspicion that Maremont did not want to take public assistance—and Maremont —off the front pages.

The money crisis was again very serious. Claiming that he derived the idea from Kerner's abortive effort to impose a 10 per cent cut in allowances, a Republican senator had offered legislation to impose ceilings on public assistance payments. The ceilings would supersede budgets based on minimum health and decency standards. Kerner, who was at the same time agreeing to a cut of 9 per cent in the commission's proposed budget for 1963-1965, denounced the ceiling plan. Senate Republicans made ceilings a condition of support for the May-June deficiency appropriation, while one of them pointed out that only ceilings could accomplish the 9 per cent saving in the forthcoming biennium. The Governor was fighting Republicans this year, however, rather than chairmen and members of the Public Aid Commission or relief recipients. It is pretty hard to find a place to live in Chicago for $75 a month, said Kerner in opposing a rental ceiling, although a year before he had accused Virgil Martin's commission of considering high rents "inviolate" and of ignoring the "numerous" For Rent signs Kerner said he had seen in the city. Because House Republicans were more amenable to vote-trading with Democrats than were Senate Republicans, House approval of a no-ceilings deficiency was achieved. When the legislature recessed for Daley's inauguration, the Senate was unmoved; when it returned, the only progress was to move from deadlocked informal conferences to the formality of a deadlocked legislative conference committee. Each house approved appropriating $47 million for May and June, but the Senate had ceilings attached while the House did not. After one conference session, the Chairman of the Budgetary Commission was quoted by the Chicago *Daily News* as saying "if these people [reliefers] don't get their checks, they can go to Mayor Daley. They elected him."

Against this background, Maremont came to Springfield for his confirmation hearing before the Senate Executive Committee. It was a model performance on both sides. Presented to the committee by the Republican senator from his home suburban district as a man of many talents and interests and of great ability, Maremont forthrightly answered all questions put to him. An expert observer of the Illinois legislature considers that Maremont achieved legislative immortality by actually changing the votes of some members who had come prepared to vote against him. Without giving ground on his opposition to ceilings, Maremont stated that if the legislature imposed ceilings he would accept its judgment or resign if he could not. There were no threats or lost tempers in the course of the 75-minute interrogation. Four votes were cast against confirmation, 17 in favor of confirmation. In voting "No," the Republican leader and the Republican whip—both Catholic—noted that the vote was not a reflection on Maremont personally but on the birth control proposal. The sponsor of the prohibition legislation voted to confirm. It was clear that while

Maremont might eventually have to compromise on the birth control issue, his six-month probationary period as commission chairman was judged a success by a majority of the Senate where the opposition was likely to be concentrated. Confirmation by a strong bipartisan vote came when the committee recommendation reached the Senate floor two days later.

On the mistaken assumption that he was home free, Maremont held a press conference in Chicago the morning after his confirmation. He kept a hammer lock on the front pages by smearing the Republicans who had just approved him. Republican senators, said Maremont, were delaying the deficiency appropriation because 70 per cent of reliefers were Negro. "Republican Senators are getting even with the Negroes on ADC because the Negroes helped to elect Mayor Daley and are generally Democratic," he went on. "Republican Senators are anti-Negro and have set out on a program to injure Negroes.... It is cruel and inhuman and smacks of Hitlerism."[6]

What the legislature hath given, the legislature can take away: this bit of wisdom unknown to Maremont was now demonstrated. The storm on the Senate floor was unparalleled. Members on both sides rushed to defend the integrity of the Senate. Illinois' primary Red hunter, who had characterized Maremont as a fine gentleman in voting to recommend confirmation a few days earlier, now read off the names of a series of Maremont "affiliations" with groups calling for an end to nuclear testing and found him unfit "mentally" and "morally." Kerner was staggered. After confirming that the statement was not a misquotation, he acknowledged publicly that Maremont had impaired his usefulness. Outraged by Kerner's desertion, Maremont refused to resign or even to speak to the Governor. Daley, who had blasted birth control, became Maremont's apologist by suggesting that a man could make a mistake and be forgiven. "That is why we have erasers on pencils," said the Mayor, in offering a word of compassion for the businessman who lost his head in politics. As it turned out, Maremont was erased. It took an *ex post facto* amendment to the Senate rules, but he was deconfirmed by unanimous vote of the Republicans while the Democrats all sat silent.

Birth control subsequently followed a curious legislative path. The prohibition bill was stopped in the House when it became clear that the Speaker would not call it up for a vote. A Republican, elected Speaker with the consent of the Chicago Democrats, he had been generally considerate of legislation favored by that group. On the other hand,

[6]*Chicago Tribune,* April 26, 1963, pp. 1, 2.

that very consideration had resulted in antagonisms between House and Senate Republican leaders. At the end of the session, with the Speaker still surprisingly firm, a compromise evolved which provided that the birth control program would be restricted to married women living with their spouses while an interim commission, chaired by the sponsor of the prohibition proposal, would study the question and report back to a later General Assembly.

In the summer of 1964, Mayor Daley said that the city would seriously consider establishing a birth control program for indigent mothers, thus amending his position of the previous year. Early in 1965, the Chicago Board of Health started the most far-reaching birth control program in any major city—free, open to all residents regardless of marital status or income. Daley embraced it as a public health measure. Thereafter, the legislative interim commission virtually endorsed the Maremont program, insisting only that clients be mothers—married or unmarried—over 15, before birth control services be made available. The General Assembly adopted an appropriate resolution. A Senate that was not much different in membership from the Senate that had deposed Maremont voted 41-8 in favor of birth control services for welfare recipients.

It was mouth control, not birth control, that killed Maremont politically. Whether he could quickly have overcome antipathy to providing contraceptives to unmarried women at public expense is not certain; it is certain that his imaginative attack on the public aid problem was winning more admirers than detractors. Republicans had no quarrel with Maremont. If the dispute over ceilings was to be mediated, Maremont was the logical man to do it. Republican senators had cut themselves off from their Democratic colleagues. "Things around here are different," one Democratic leader told a friend. "I used to be able to walk over and talk to them. Now, they just don't want to deal with me at all." Kerner had never developed any contacts with opposition legislative leaders—and very few with Democratic legislative leaders—so that he had no chips to cash. In addition, of course, the Governor was hard put to reconcile his cut-back of public aid budgetary requests and his proposal for an across-the-board reduction in allowances with an opposition to ceilings. Daley was anathema to Republican senators who correctly suspected him of controlling House Republican votes with Chicago and Cook County patronage jobs. Maremont was the swing man in a situation that was getting out of hand. Kerner had not expected to cut off all relief money when he tried for a cut of 10 per cent, and neither had Republican senators when they came up with ceilings. Maremont was indispensable to a reasonable solution which involved no loss of face for either the proponents or opponents of ceilings. He was in a strong enough position to ignore Kerner's wishes for less publicity, to challenge plans for inadequate appropriations, to push the Chicago politicians on the birth control issue, to reexamine ADC without alienating the Negro population. Misusing his strength, Maremont publicly questioned the motivation of a legislative majority, an act outside the pale.

The consequences could hardly have been more catastrophic. Concentrating on the parliamentary problems involved in deconfirmation, the Senate was in no mood to negotiate on ceilings. Deadlock persisted, appropriations for ADC purposes gave out. In lieu of checks, federal surplus food cards were mailed to 16,405 families in Cook County. Disorganization was understandably dominant. Semitrailer trucks of food came to warehouses without available floor space and were rerouted; laborers to do the unloading were not. Thirty settlement houses were established as distribution points; only ten small delivery trucks were available to move food from the warehouse to the settlements. "Let it be thoroughly understood," said Mayor Daley, "that no one in Chicago will go hungry." Kerner said nothing.

A belated compromise was born out of bipartisan shame at the nationwide publicity accorded the depression-day soup kitchens in 1963. Emergency money to finish out the 1961-1963 biennium was approved without ceilings. While ceilings were established for the 1963-1965 appropriation, they were to be made flexible by a provision allowing a bipartisan legislative committee to authorize deviations from fixed limits. But after opponents of ceilings put the question, the obliging Regional Office of the Department of Health, Education, and Welfare objected to the involvement of a legislative commission in fixing budgets. This arrangement was said to be a violation of the federal requirement that the program be administered by a single state agency.

Without time to research the problem of federal bluff, and fearful of being responsible for the loss of federal funds if it turned out not to be bluff, Republican senators gave in this time. Ceilings were written into the law, but the administrator rather than a legislative group could permit deviations. In his decisions, the administrator would give "substantial" consideration to the views of a legislative advisory committee. Five months after the legislative session ended, new standards which cut back on allowances were established, ADC family ceilings eliminated. Over the opposition of Chicago Democrats, a majority of the legislative advisory committee gave its advisory approval to the lowered standards developed by Kerner's Director of Public Aid. That job had been awarded to the executive secretary of the Public Aid Commission when the legislature—as an incidental reaction to the Maremont affair —finally dissolved the commission, replacing it with an executive department.

After public assistance "hunger marchers" paraded to the State Office Building in Chicago to protest the new relief standards, Daley announced a plan to ease hunger and lack of clothing among hardship cases. Although the Director of Public Aid insisted that relief allowances were adequate if managed right, the mayor was less certain. "I don't think there's anyone hungry in Chicago," said Daley. "At least I hope to God there isn't." Among those expressing doubts about the adequacy of the new public assistance allowances were the Welfare Council of Metropolitan Chicago ("a picture of stark, threadbare existence"); the Chicago Chapter of the National Association of Social Workers ("a systematically imposed program of grinding want"); Arnold Maremont ("The President of the United States has declared war on poverty and the State of Illinois has declared war on the poor"); and the Chicago *Daily News* ("Illinois values: whole milk for convicts, powdered milk for children on relief").

III. THE CASE EVALUATED

What is the significance of the story? Illinois was on the verge of a major breakthrough in public assistance policy when Maremont made his critical mistake. As a compassionate skeptic, challenging the shibboleths of the professionals without ignoring the politicians' concerns with costs, he was forcing reexamination of aspects of relief policy that had come to be taken for granted. It cannot be emphasized too strongly that that reexamination was not the cause of his undoing. Maremont brought about his own downfall; no legislative body is likely to sit quietly when it is slapped in the face with a swastika. What is impressive and significant is that Maremont could open the birth control question and carry it to the point of success. With that opening wedge, he was prepared to and could have provoked a major review of the adequacy of allowances, of recruitment and training of workers, of the housing of clients. Anachronistic policies were in danger. Resistance to change turned out to be surprisingly weak when the effort to achieve change was made directly.

The point is underscored by Kerner's experience in changing the old pattern of relief spending unrelated to appropriations. Campaigning for reelection in 1964, Governor Kerner told a downstate party rally that Illinois had been overwhelmingly successful in counteracting the nationwide trend of increasing public assistance rolls. Expenditures were squarely in line with appropriations. The turning point, he said, had come with creation of the executive department to replace the commission. Kerner's estimate of when Illinois began to hold the line on relief expenses was correct; his explanation of why was not correct. Coincident with the creation of the executive department, the new rules for public assistance expenditures were made clear. Underbudgeting would no longer be accompanied by the certainty of later deficiency appropriations. If this had been made clear to the old commission in 1961 before the biennium started, the turning point, so-called, could have come two years earlier although the protests would have been loud. Two years earlier, however, the Governor had not yet learned the name of the game, let alone promulgated the rules.

Maremont might have effected other changes in relief policy if he had not made an unforgivable charge. As it is, not enough changed in public assistance in Illinois in view of the "deviant behavior" of the policy-makers. The actions of the Governor, of the General Assembly, of Maremont, and of some of the other administrative officials were all out of keeping with the patterns of official behavior in the model of a stable program we have come to expect. If money runs out, governors are supposed to ask for more and legislators are supposed to vote more — but for a while, these did not. If there is opposition to providing birth control materials to clients, administrators and legislators are supposed to back away — but those in Illinois only backed away momentarily. Official debates in northern states about ADC costs and issues are supposed to avoid injecting race as a special political problem — but Maremont stated the question explicitly. Challenging the wisdom and values of the welfare bureaucracy is more common with northern Republicans than with northern Democrats — but the liberal, Democratic Governor of Illinois led the challenge.

For all these deviations, public assistance in Illinois is reestablished now on substantially the same terms as before: allowances are still appallingly low (some lower now than ever); illegitimacy is still not especially singled out for official attention, except through birth control arrangements; an overt, direct inquiry into and an attack on the causes of disproportionately high numbers of relief cases among Negroes has not been undertaken; Illinois schools of social work have not been pushed to revamp their curricula to give any added emphasis to public assistance policy and problems; with the elimination of the Public Aid Commission, the program is less than ever exposed to the attention of individuals and groups without a direct interest in public assistance.

The chances for change in Illinois may have been lost, then, not because policy was examined and sustained, but because the challenger carelessly fouled out. Important aspects of public assistance policy on the state level can be changed. Maremont concluded that a dialogue on relief policy was a prelude to change. He was right. Such a dialogue, however, requires a mastery of the subject. It also produces short-run political discomforts: the dangers of Negroes feeling threatened, of Catholics charging state-supported immorality, and of the economy-minded running wild. For these reasons, there is a tendency to pay the bills without raising questions about fundamentals.

Kerner was reelected in the Johnson landslide. Peace has again settled over the Illinois public aid program. That management survey of public aid administration once considered so vital by everyone concerned never did come off.

CHAPTER IX

Relief Policy Reconsidered

AFTER 30 YEARS of a federal-state public assistance program designed to deal principally with problems of the indigent aged, dependent children have become the more vexing problem; in many states benefits for adults and for children are inadequate to meet even minimum standards of health and decency;[1] state money sufficient to provide these inadequate benefits is uncertain; trained personnel to administer the program are hard to find. Social workers continue to believe politicians to be hostile; politicians continue to believe social workers to be unrealistic. Information about the program comes chiefly from those who invented it and admire their own handiwork. The constitutional rights of recipients are subject to abuse even while the problems of fraud and "cheating" are again on page one.[2] Public assistance grows in costs and, in the ADC category, in number of recipients through good times as well as bad.

Notwithstanding all of this, relief policy is not a matter of persistent concern and attention. Why has there not been more in the way of consideration of alternatives to a policy that clearly satisfies no one? The discussion in previous chapters makes it possible to conclude now that three characteristics of the welfare policy-making process are of

[1]U.S. Department of Health, Education, and Welfare, Welfare Administration, "Old Age Assistance" (Washington, February, 1963, process duplicated), p. 5, and "Aid to Families with Dependent Children" (Washington, February, 1963, process duplicated), p. 6; Ellen J. Perkins, "Unmet Need in Public Assistance," *Social Security Bulletin,* XXIII (April, 1960), 3-11; for a detailed analysis of unmet needs in Pennsylvania, see Pennsylvania Department of Public Welfare, *Public Assistance Allowances Compared With the Cost of Living at a Minimum Standard of Health and Decency* (Harrisburg, Penna., January, 1964), 8 pp.

[2]" 'Cheating' — welfare's trial," *Christian Science Monitor,* March 5, 1965, p. 1.

special importance in understanding why the product is as it is. These characteristics are the automated nature of congressional action, the absence of presidential leadership, and the absence of strong interest group participation. This chapter first reviews these features of the policy-making process, then considers the effects on present policy of some old assumptions about federalism, social insurance, political influence, and program goals.

I. MAKING WELFARE POLICY

The policy-making process in any field is likely to have one or more characteristics to distinguish it from the way policy is made in any other field. For example, one important feature of the civil rights policy-making process in recent years has been discussion, negotiation, and prior agreement among the Attorney-General, the Minority Leader of the Senate, and sometimes the ranking minority member of the House Judiciary Committee. This procedure developed out of the practical necessity of securing Republican support for cloture votes in the Senate. The Minority Leader, whatever his participation in policy-making in other fields, is unlikely to have as direct a role when cloture is not a problem. Another example of a distinctive characteristic associated with one area is seen in the making of agricultural policy. The process there has frequently included submission of a price support and acreage allotment proposal to referendum vote of one or another group of farmers. Direct participation of a clientele group by referendum is not part of the ordinary policy-making process in other fields. In foreign policy-making, few people would dispute that plenary power resides in the President, a characteristic certainly unique to policy-making in that delicate field. Like the distinctive features of policy-making in civil rights, agriculture, and foreign relations, those associated with public assistance also have an important bearing on the end product.

1. Public welfare policy-making is automated. The machine is programmed to sort the indigent into fixed categories, to test for formal eligibility within those categories, to apply the standards established by the separate states, to figure the costs, to fractionalize the bill between governments, and to repeat the process endlessly. The latter is the most important of the instructions in the program because it means that production of benefits will go on even if no further congressional attention is paid to the instructions regarding categories, eligibility, standards, or costs. If the program was written to halt the production of benefits until a separate appropriations program was completed, pe-

riodic evaluation would be built into the system. By establishing an open-end authorization to appropriate for an indefinite period and by making the federal share of relief costs an obligation of the United States, morally if not legally beyond congressional control, the Social Security Act's public assistance titles make periodic congressional appraisal of policy most unlikely.

Of all the formal and informal mechanisms through which Congress participates in making policy, its constitutional power over the public purse usually provides the most effective insurance that at some stage Congress will have an opportunity to exercise a control, or at least to influence the character of a program. The open-end authorization and the obligatory appropriation provide little incentive, however, for inquiry into the workings of public assistance policy. For all of its self-perceived role as guardian of the Federal Treasury and critic of budget estimates,[3] the House Appropriations Committee implicitly and explicitly acknowledges its impotence in public assistance. Lest this impotence becloud its ferocious reputation, the committee usually skips lightly and quickly over the public assistance budget. Since no authorization action is required from the legislative committees, there must be a positive decision to hold hearings to bring public assistance into the purview of the House Ways and Means or Senate Finance Committees.

The difference between an indefinite, open-end authorization and an authorization for a fixed period of time only should not be assumed to mean the same thing as the difference between providing adequate funds for public assistance and not providing adequate funds. The difference rather is between making public assistance policy widely visible and keeping it automated and largely invisible. Congressional hearings held in 1965 in connection with authorization of funds for the second year of the poverty program gave a visibility to policy development, successes, and failures in that activity that public assistance has had only three or four times in 30 years. There is no evidence that Congress would fail to provide whatever money is needed in an annual or biennial authorization; in being forced to attend to the authorization, it would also give to public assistance policy a public airing which is now absent from the policy-making process. The policy-making process in foreign aid provides an appropriate comparison.

2. Most welfare policy-making does not involve a clash between strong groups with antagonistic interests. The American political system

[3]Richard F. Fenno, Jr., "The House Appropriations Committee as a Political System: The Problem of Integration," *American Political Science Review,* LVI (June, 1962), 310-24.

works best, as Edward Banfield has written, when there is a clash of concrete interests rather than of abstract principles.[4] It is hard to generate attention for a program that lacks the raw materials for such a clash: organized groups, each with something to gain or lose from whatever turn policy takes. Where there are such groups, they can be expected to articulate goals and to find flaws in the position taken by the opposition. But welfare interests are supported in the public assistance policy-making process by organizations that are only tangentially involved through a devotion to principle. This is true of the National Association of Social Workers, the overwhelming majority of whose members do not work in public assistance and who would be largely unaffected by public assistance policy changes. Participating groups with a direct interest in welfare policy — the National Federation of the Blind is an example — speak for only a very limited part of the welfare clientele. Organized outright opposition to policy is similarly absent. No multiplicity of competing interests contributes to maximizing the visibility of policy-making. Intensity is low; those who can be heard do not have a great deal to gain or lose. Those with a great deal to gain or lose cannot be heard.

An exception to the generalization is the periodic clash between state and national interests over distribution of costs. Senate policy-making leadership is the key characteristic here. Acting as spokesmen for state government interests, a succession of senators — McFarland, Kerr, Long — have moved to increase the federal share of relief funds. The antagonistic federal government interest has been represented by a succession of Presidents — Truman, Eisenhower, Kennedy — who supported that interest intensely enough to avoid taking the lead to improve welfare benefits, but not intensely enough to make all-out war on this issue against the Senate sponsors. The result has been a formula change whenever the Senate is stimulated to act.

3. Presidential leadership in welfare policy-making is uncommon; when exercised, such leadership is highly effective. The transformation in the respective roles of President and Congress that has taken place over the last 30 years is a well-known phenomenon. Congress and the country expect the policy agenda to be established by the President. The problem that does not command presidential comment and recommendation has little chance of receiving formal consideration. Proposals for legislation included in the State of the Union address and proposals that are the subjects of special messages fix the practical boundaries of congressional and popular attention. But when President

[4]"American Foreign Aid Doctrines," in Robert Goldwin (ed.), *Why Foreign Aid?* (Chicago: Rand McNally, 1962), p. 28.

Kennedy sent his special message on public welfare to Congress in 1962, it was the first time any President had given that kind of emphasis to the subject. Congressional response was prompt and it was friendly. Almost every aspect of the program embodied in the draft bill accompanying the Kennedy message was enacted into law. In this unique test case, involving policy proposals outside of the financing of public assistance, receptivity to presidential initiative in welfare policy-making was high.

One explanation of the absence of presidential initiative in making welfare policy is the relatively depressed position of public assistance in the federal administrative hierarchy. When the old Social Security Board had independent status, Arthur Altmeyer could go directly to President Roosevelt with policy proposals in social insurance and in public assistance. Now the way is a great deal less direct and the competition for presidential interest is much greater. At present, problems of public relief are most likely to come to presidential attention as money problems because a significant budget item is involved. Aside from the cost issue, public assistance has no easy route to the top. Until 1963, the administrative organization of the Department of Health, Education, and Welfare gave public assistance only bureau status within the Social Security Administration. The latter was itself forced to compete with the Office of Education, the Food and Drug Administration, the Public Health Service, and the Vocational Rehabilitation Administration for attention within the Department of Health, Education, and Welfare. Even elevation to separate Welfare Administration status in 1963 has left public assistance in the midst of the hundreds of Health, Education, and Welfare clientele groups. In a political world in which the already independent Housing and Home Finance Agency was said to be disadvantaged because it lacked formal Cabinet rank, and in which interest groups are urging that there be Cabinet departments for education, transportation, science, consumer affairs, and the arts in order that attention may be focused on them, the Welfare Administration has no pipeline to the center of power.

In what respects do these features of welfare policy-making—absence of presidential leadership, absence of effective interest group organization and participation, and the automated character of congressional spending—bear on welfare policy itself? Certainly, they help to account for the fact that policy has changed so little. The policy-making process has protected from challenge some old assumptions on which continuing policy is based. These old assumptions about the nature of American federalism, about the insurance-assistance relationship, about the probability of political influence and favoritism in relief administration, and about the goals of a public assistance program are not likely to survive a permanent change in one or another aspect of the welfare policy-making process. Even the single shot of presidential leadership in 1962 shook the existing assumptions about program goals. The point, of course, is that most of the assumptions are grounded in the politics and power relationships of the mid 1930's rather than those of the mid 1960's.

II. FEDERALISM AND RELIEF STANDARDS

As an illustration of some of the classic justifications for American federalism—experimentation, diversity within unity, flexibility—the federal-state public assistance program is tailor-made. Lien laws, relative responsibility provisions, suitable home requirements, residence standards are permissible subjects of state statutes. Federal influence is obvious, extensive, and constant, but it is not irresistible nor is it exerted in every aspect of categorical assistance. One recent official look at the role of the states in the program—that taken by the Advisory Commission on Intergovernmental Relations—confirms earlier conclusions: the states "have had a much greater voice in shaping their public assistance programs than frequently has been assumed by critics of the Federal role... the actions of the States have had significant impact on the program." Previous sections of this book illustrate the special potency of the states once a state plan has been approved and the program is in operation. Federal funds have not been withheld for noncompliance since the 1951 dispute over confidentiality in Indiana, but the federal agency has by no means won all the disputes since that case. Indeed, it did not even win that one. Cooperative federalism is evidenced in public assistance by the federal-state sharing of costs, of responsibility for personnel, and of eligibility determination.

Other American social legislation does not involve federal-state sharing that is equally extensive. Old age insurance would be unaffected if the states were legally abolished tomorrow. With a few minor adjustments, housing and urban renewal programs could survive the demise of state government, and so could both veterans' benefits and agricultural subsidies. Of all the important programs involving money payments to individuals, public assistance is most illustrative of cooperative federalism, most dependent on interaction between governmental levels. If the goal of public relief in America were to show how federalism operates, the goal would be achieved.

For the welfare recipients and their sympathizers who are less concerned with how relief policy is made in a federal system than with the substance of that policy, the federal-state public assistance program is a conspicuous failure. Its very dependence on federal-state interaction is both one reason for the failure and a major impediment to change for the better. The need for interaction has contributed to appallingly low assistance payments, has made possible such inequities as Arizona's $85 limit on monthly money payments in OAA compared to the limit of $190 in neighboring New Mexico, and has produced an irrational pattern of lien laws and relative responsibility requirements. It would be absurd, of course, to argue that the relief problem would not exist if the program were federalized, but it is quite realistic to argue that many public assistance clients would gain from conditional federalization of benefits and eligibility conditions.

There are several hundred public assistance standards in the United States now. They range from failure to provide public assistance of any kind for able-bodied, childless persons between 18 and 65 in half a dozen states and failure to provide aid to the disabled in Nevada to the separate categorical assistance plans enacted and the benefit schedules developed in each of the states. Every state program has a distinctive explanation to account for its level of support as well as for legal and extra-legal eligibility conditions. Variations between categories and between states are a reflection of local history, political and social attitudes, and economic circumstances. That there is not a national relief standard is evident from the range of OAA payments between, for example, Mississippi's recent monthly average of $40 and Minnesota's of $110. Variations between categories as a result of local history are clear from a comparison of Louisiana's average OAA payment of $84 per month – 10 per cent over the national average – with Louisiana's $23 average ADC payment – 25 per cent below the national average. Huey Long expected to make every man a king, and his program included "adequate" pensions for the aged. Even where there is no Huey Long in a state's history, current political circumstances result in different policies between categories within a single state. The Illinois case detailed in a previous chapter showed a critical preoccupation with ADC, but a willingness to abide OAA. Some states value ADC more highly than OAA. Idaho is an example: money payments there in the adult category are about 5 per cent below the national average, but ADC payments are a full one-fourth over the national average.

Relief clients gained significantly from creation of the federal-state program to replace state and local responsibility when the states could not meet the costs during the depression period. Many states still can't or won't meet current relief costs. Were it not for the budget surpluses acquired during World War II (because of the combination of anti-inflationary high tax rates and the necessary moratorium on many ordinary domestic activities), a public assistance money crisis would have confronted several states — Illinois is an example — ten years before it did. Surpluses are gone now, spent in part on public assistance that did not wither away. As far as the comparative economics of the situation is concerned, 1965 is like 1935: states are in a fiscal squeeze and are seemingly incapable of raising the kind of money needed to finance their major responsibilities in health, education, and welfare; but the federal government is in no such difficulty. Federal tax yields and the absence of constitutional inhibitions on federal spending put Washington in an excellent fiscal position which may be even further improved by reductions in defense costs over the next several years. If availability of money were the sole criterion for fixing responsibility for welfare activities, the program would surely be federalized. But availability of money is not the sole criterion; economics is tempered by politics in the formulation of policy. The appropriate question, then, is whether the politics of federalism continues to demand a federal-state system in public assistance.

It was a daring thing, in 1935, to commit the federal government to a permanent involvement in public relief. The theory of dual federalism then still dominant left poor relief a problem for the states. Operations of the Federal Emergency Relief Administration (FERA) had not been reassuring to those who deplored federal action in this field and who assumed it meant unconscionable federal control. Restrictions on federal authority inserted in the Social Security Act, according to Josephine Brown, resulted from adverse reaction to the authoritarian nature of the FERA, an agency that was authoritarian not only in the exercise of its power to assume control of funds, but in its ordinary relations with the states with which it dealt.[5] That history, President Roosevelt's disinclination to involve the federal government in direct relief, and the then prevailing view of federalism as a system of independent rather than shared powers combined to produce a program which allowed the federal government to exercise its constitutional authority to tax, but which preserved major relief policy authority for the states. Some of that policy authority was conspicuously misused and consequently whittled down by the 1939 amendments to the law. After passage of those amendments, it will be recalled, the national administrator claimed the federal agency had all the power it needed.

[5]Josephine Brown, *Public Relief 1929-1939* (New York: Henry Holt, 1940), p. 211.

Actually, the national agency still lacks a power of fundamental importance to the program, the power to insist on minimum standards, but it has been assumed that federal authority to establish a floor under public assistance payments cannot be secured. Such a provision had been part of and then deleted from the original Social Security draft bill. It appears never to have had serious consideration since. Justification for its absence supposedly lies in the argument that, in a federal system, each state should be free to fix its own allowances based on local conditions and on the predilections of its own elected authorities. New York and Massachusetts old age assistance laws were the models for the provision in the draft bill that states must furnish assistance sufficient to provide, "when added to the income of the aged recipient, a reasonable subsistence compatible with decency and health." The provision was objectionable to southern members of Congress who were reluctant to provide any opening wedge for federal intrusion on the handling of the Negro question.[6] Elimination of the requirement for a reasonable subsistence left the states free to pay pensions of any amount, however small, and yet recover 50 per cent of their costs from federal funds. Southern congressmen were also successful in their argument that conditions for the approval of a state plan should be stated negatively rather than positively. States thus became free to impose conditions for assistance other than those dealt with in the federal statute. Administration of these state-imposed conditions could be depended upon to be disadvantageous to the Negro in the South. The southerners were accommodated as the price of peace because, as always, they were in strategic positions in the Congress and because the permissible range of federal authority was still very much in doubt.

Improvements in the formula have brought the federal share of relief allowances well above the 50 per cent originally established in OAA and above the one-third originally established in ADC. Dominant views of the range of federal power have also altered. Nothing, however, yet precludes the use of federal money to sustain allowances at levels below reasonable subsistence. Average monthly OAA payments (including direct vendor payments for medical care) were below $70 in 15 states in March, 1965, which means that the federal share was at least two-thirds of the total payment in those states. In Mississippi, where the average monthly payment that month was $40, the federal share was $33. For ADC, the federal share of the Mississippi average payment of $10 was $8.20.

Relief compatible with minimum standards of decency and health

[6]Edwin E. Witte, *The Development of the Social Security Act* (Madison: University of Wisconsin Press, 1962), p. 144.

is clearly not being provided by many states that, nevertheless, derive most of their relief money from federal grants. Neither the law nor the politics of federalism now requires that the situation be perpetuated. Unfortunately, however, none of the advisory council or social work studies have turned their attention to the insertion of a requirement that relief allowances be compatible with minimum standards. Inadequate personal allowances is the least publicized problem in public assistance, and the problem area most beyond the reach of the federal government under present statutes.

The politics of federalism does not mandate the degree of state independence that is possible in public assistance. More recent grant-in-aid programs in other fields are far less permissive. Indeed, the most exacting federal standards have become commonplace. Not only has the old dual federalism given way to a cooperative federalism, but cooperative federalism is itself giving way to acceptance of national control. Provided two major formal opportunities by the Eisenhower administration to blueprint a shift of responsibility to the states, spokesmen for the latter struck out in both the Kestnbaum Commission (1954) and the Joint Federal-State Action Committee (1957). Federal control may be deplored, but it is accepted. There is no difficulty in illustrating cases of ready acceptance of federal control. When it became apparent a decade ago that a network of highways to facilitate automobile travel had to be constructed, President Eisenhower proposed a 90-10 federal-state division of costs. States happily joined the program and there are few complaints about federally established specifications. More recently, President Johnson, squarely asserting that the carrot treatment was a failure in securing state legislation against billboards along federally aided highways, asked the Congress to write such a prohibition into federal law as a condition of the grant-in-aid. Even closer to home, Johnson's proposal for minimum federal standards in state unemployment insurance programs was received peacefully. The "seven promises" required of local units by the 1954 Housing Act make federal aid for urban renewal contingent on federal approval of such peculiarly local matters as participation of local community organizations. Significantly, federal approval of locally established building standards is also required as a condition of support. Thus, federal money for highways or for urban renewal can be withheld until there is state or local compliance with minimum standards. Yet, funds that may not be provided to support the cost of a highway that is too narrow or a building that is inadequately wired may be provided to support relief benefits below minimum standards of health and decency.

The practical danger in demanding compliance with minimum standards is that a state or states will choose to withdraw from a program completely rather than commit a large enough sum to the program to meet such standards. So be it. Public assistance can be federalized in any such state and the federal costs need not exceed costs for which the national government is already committed. Moreover, the decision to federalize can be made in a totally objective way. Mississippi, the extreme case, serves as a ready illustration, although there are 19 states where ADC benefits recently were so low that the state did not qualify for full federal sharing. Under legislation effective January 1, 1966, there is a federal obligation to pay, in the ADC category, about $24 of a $32 monthly average allowance, ($15 of the first $18 plus, for the poorest states, 65 per cent of the next $14). In other words, if Mississippi were to escalate its ADC allowances to reach the $32 average, the current federal obligation and payment — under the statutory direction to the Treasurer of the United States — would be $24. With the actual Mississippi average at about $10, an average standard fixed at $24 would mean a 140 per cent increase to the state's dependent children. The entire amount could be paid by the federal government without adding to the charges that the Treasury is already legally liable to pay if Mississippi were to act independently to improve benefits. Federalization need not be permanent. Under this arrangement, a state should be able to resume responsibility for its indigent and resume control over its categorical program by participating at the minimum level necessary to assure full federal grants. Mississippi, in the illustration used here, could resume control by establishing a $32 average payment for its ADC recipients and contributing $8 of that amount from state funds. (Current maximum payments in Mississippi are $25 for the first child and $90 for a family.)

Other categories involve comparable problems. In OAA, establishment of a floor fixed at the point of present federal responsibility would result in modest enough average benefits of about $56 in the poorest states ($31 of the first $37, plus 65 per cent of the next $38). Benefits would be increased to that level in the states not now reaching it, or the program would be federalized. The states paying between $56 and $75 would be unaffected by the minimum standard as long as the formula for computing the federal grant is unchanged.

Federalism is less a current barrier to minimum standards in public assistance than is the inability of the clientele group to organize in support of such standards and the absence of a system to publicize present inadequate standards. Economic reality and political practicality are not incompatible. Like the first caretaker grant provision for

ADC in 1950, and the addition of a second parent in 1961, a minimum standard provision in all categorical assistance is now overdue and is waiting for someone to nudge it along.

Only a relatively few states would be faced with the choice between federalization and benefit increase that a minimum standard of the kind proposed here would demand. In some states, not all categories would be involved. It would be a modest first step toward a realistic federalism that recognizes the right of a state to be niggardly toward its indigent, or the plight of a state that is itself indigent. Assumption of responsibility for public assistance by the federal government is the appropriate remedy in either of those situations. When the state is willing or able to resume responsibility, the way for it to resume its responsibility is open. Since staff must already be employed under a merit system presumably approved by the Department of Health, Education, and Welfare, there should be no problems of personnel meeting different standards. Clearly, the questions to be resolved by an affected state are: can it afford independence? how much is independence in public assistance policy worth? No great dangers to the democratic system are inherent in federalizing public assistance where there are negative answers. Federalism, as it has been understood since the New Deal, is not meant to preclude feeding the poor.

III. OBSOLESCENCE OF OLD AGE ASSISTANCE

Old age assistance is a perfectly sensible category of public aid if it is necessary to classify needy people in order to facilitate relief administration. When the goal of public assistance was expressed in simple terms as relief of the very poor, old people who were very poor could be assumed to have some characteristics in common, especially in connection with minimum subsistence levels. This assumption led to the creation of separate categories and has sustained separate rates of federal participation in programs for the aged and for children. Considered more likely to be comparable to the very old than to the very young, the blind and the disabled, to their benefit, have been grouped with the old for purposes of federal financial contributions. Since 1962, legislation exists to permit states to merge all three adult categories in a combined state plan that can also include medical assistance for the aged. Some minor additional federal payments become possible for a state filing a combined plan.

Rather than grouping OAA with other categories, it would be more consistent with presently accepted goals of public assistance to eliminate OAA in favor of a contrived universal old age insurance. In the words of Secretary Ribicoff, "The keynote of all our efforts is prevention of dependency in this and future generations, and the rehabilitation of those who now find themselves on the welfare rolls." Of the four basic categories, OAA recipients are surely least likely to be amenable to prevention of dependency and least likely to be candidates for rehabilitation. It is possible to envisage programs designed to prevent dependency among the blind and disabled and even in some young, fatherless households. Rehabilitation efforts through education that can, in due time, lead to self-help and self-care for these same groups are similarly understandable. But time works against the old age client who cannot be expected to learn a marketable skill after the age of 65 — and who probably could not market it even if he did learn it. Once economic relief became incidental to rehabilitation, OAA became illogical in public assistance.

It now appears especially timely to eliminate the distinction between old age insurance and OAA cases. This process can be started by crediting OAA recipients with minimum old age insurance coverage, appropriate contributions to the trust fund being made from general revenue. (Exactly this technique is being used to bring all the aged under Medicare.) For some present OAA clients, further benefits would be unnecessary. Others, including the one-third of the OAA case load already drawing old age insurance, would require a supplementary benefit that could take the form of an "insurance dividend." Since 1950, OAA has been withering away, however slowly: the number of recipients has declined from 2.8 million to 2.2 million in 1964, a total coinciding with that of 1943. To pay "back premiums" for this group and shore up the trust fund, if necessary, would have several advantages: concentrating available social welfare personnel in the stickiest of current welfare problems, ADC; relieving the states of what is still their single costliest assistance category; and, thus, allowing more realistic support levels in ADC, as well as more adequate spending for mental health, common schools, and universities. Further, the action would be logical in light of the explicit and implicit changes in categorical assistance and social insurance policy already made.

Two of the three components of the Social Security Act — unemployment insurance and old age insurance — involved benefits to be available only to those or the families of those who were both employable and at some time employed. The third component — public assistance — was conditioned on old age, infancy, or blindness, on practical unemployability. Whatever the merits of this original conception, it has been eroded through the years so that, on the one hand, for some lucky people the merest shadow of employment can bring a windfall of so-called insurance benefits. On the other hand, unemployability is no longer a prerequisite for categorical assistance.

Characteristics usually attributed to social insurance and public assistance respectively are really not inherent and indispensable aspects of each. Since tenBroek and Wilson first made that point in 1954,[7] its validity has become increasingly obvious. For example, payment of social insurance as a matter of right in a contributory system is surely inconsistent with a limit on the income of social security recipients, but such income limits continue to obtain for persons below the age of 72. The legal right of eligible persons to receive public assistance, stemming from the prohibition on waiting lists, is more of an insurance characteristic than a characteristic of charity. Protective payments of benefits to a third person on behalf of an incompetent beneficiary were part of the social insurance apparatus years before they became allowable in 1962 as a reluctantly agreed-to experiment in public assistance. Since the advent of the unemployed parent phase of ADC, simultaneous technical eligibility may exist for unemployment insurance and ADC-U. Simultaneous benefits under old age insurance and OAA have long been common, and, as has been noted, are now paid to a third of the total OAA caseload. Extension of unemployment compensation by federal action in 1961 (and proposed by President Johnson as a permanent program in 1965), may be viewed as a dividend to those involved in the insurance program, but it is equally realistic to view it as public assistance. Federal general revenue funds were provided to the states in a manner more comparable to the provision of public assistance grants than to the unemployment insurance program. No other insurance program has been known to provide additional months of benefits because jobs were scarce. Finally, the existence of a minimum benefit schedule and periodic increases in benefits voted by Congress in old age and survivors' insurance is another deviation from the payment-benefit relationship ordinarily associated with an insurance plan. In short, however much it pleases us to believe that social insurance is not public charity, it sometimes is.

Where charity is involved in social insurance, as in extended unemployment benefits, it is a perfectly rational reflection of dominant interests. Great numbers of unemployed are a potential cause of unrest unless money is provided for their support. Extended benefits from federal revenues relieve the burden from the employer-financed state

---

[7]Jacobus tenBroek and Richard B. Wilson, "Public Assistance and Social Insurance – A Normative Evaluation," *UCLA Law Review,* I (April, 1954), 237, 246; see also Frieda Wunderlich, "Social Insurance versus Poor Relief," *Social Research,* XIV (March, 1947), 75.

trust funds. But adding the symbolic effect achieved by asserting the primacy of the insurance concept provides that "mix" that, as Murray Edelman has shown, contributes to political quiescence.[8]

Recognition of the obsolescence of the OAA category would be rational in the present circumstances, just as recognizing the inadequacy of unemployment insurance arrangements was rational in 1961. If OAA lacks the insurance symbol that would make rational change consistent with political reality, an appropriate symbol can be provided. Federal payment of "back premiums" may be acceptable, or an authorization for states to pay old age insurance contributions on behalf of their OAA clients may be even more palatable. Current arrangements provide neither the security of insurance nor the advantage of social services. An OAA recipient receives a monthly check on the basis of need, but he is rarely visited by a case worker. The demands of ADC make home visits to the aged a matter of low priority. Public assistance is officially committed to providing social services, but the OAA client gets comparatively few, perhaps because he can use so few of the services now available. He cannot be counseled to retrain; birth control is not a problem; he is past needing help with child adjustment difficulties; his most compelling need may be companionship and physical assistance, services that public assistance is not well equipped to provide. Public assistance does very little for its OAA cases other than provide money. When it does more, the effort is stolen from ADC. Social insurance provides money, too, and many of its recipients are no less in need of companionship and physical aid than are OAA clients. Having chipped away through the years at the requirements for admission to the select "insured" class and having shown steady concern with the problems of the aged, Congress may now be quite ready to adopt "the aged who seek service" as a more sensible category than the present one which divides the lucky aged with a few quarters of old age insurance coverage from the unlucky aged without a few quarters of coverage at the right time in their lives.

IV. POLITICAL INFLUENCE

It would be naive to assume that a well-organized political machine would not make such use of the public assistance rules as it can. When a hard line to relief recipients happens to coincide with a hard-fought political campaign, some precinct captains on Chicago's South Side, for example, leave the impression with some clients that an

[8]Murray Edelman, *The Symbolic Uses of Politics* (Urbana: University of Illinois Press, 1964), p. 41.

incumbent's defeat could result in information about the client's hidden treasures reaching the public aid authorities. Political influence can't put an ineligible person on the rolls, however, and it can't strike an otherwise eligible person from the rolls. Politicians can provide an assist to an eligible case by alerting him to his rights under the law and they can blackmail ineligible recipients. But so can policemen, doctors, grocers, social workers, and others who frequently come in contact with welfare clients.

To deplore political favoritism in public relief is an admirable enough thing, but it has been largely irrelevant for 25 years. The relief scandals of the Federal Emergency Relief Administration period have had no counterpart since 1938 in the administration of public assistance under the Social Security Act. For all the attention generated by occasional exposés of assertedly mink-coated, Cadillac-driving relief recipients, there has been no demonstration that political connivance was involved in keeping ineligible clients on the rolls. Senator Robert Byrd's agitation in connection with the District of Columbia ineligibility rate did not extend to a suggestion by him or by any of his colleagues that the presence of ineligibles had anything to do with partisan political activity. When Governor Jimmie Davis provoked the Louisiana suitable home controversy, it was not because the group involved had voted wrong but because they were colored wrong.

Relief of the poor, together with public education and public health, is a domestic policy issue that politicians often insist should be kept out of politics. Having made the assertion, politicians check on each other. They will look for opportunities publicly to deplore opposition deviation from this nonpartisan high standard. No charge is made to sound more shocking than the charge that there is politics in relief, that the opposition has permitted politics to intrude on a supposedly roped-off area. If the charge can be made to stick, it represents an important victory. "Anyone who makes relief a political issue had better be pretty careful. It has never been done in the State, and I hope to God it never will," had been Mayor Daley's solemn word in 1962. Beyond the loss of support from interested professional groups, there is a wider electoral jeopardy involved in being caught tampering with the relief values the political organization had claimed to hold sacred. This was the jeopardy in which Governor Davey and the Ohio Democratic organization were placed in 1938, with exposure by the professionals in the Social Security Administration of Davey's politicking in OAA. It probably cost Davey renomination and it cost the party the election. Arthur Schlesinger, Jr., notes that the probable negative electoral effects of politicking with relief were acknowledged by such different political types as Harry Hopkins and Arthur H. Vandenberg, the Michigan Republican Senator who was no New Deal sympathizer.[9]

Democrats tried to sting the Eisenhower administration by accusing it of mixing politics and relief when Jane Hoey was fired as Director of the Bureau of Public Assistance in 1953. "There is nothing political about poverty," insisted Miss Hoey by way of suggesting that the Republicans thought the contrary. "The loyal civil servant has nothing to fear but firing itself," quipped the *Democratic Digest* in trying to show that Miss Hoey's dismissal was a contradiction of lofty Republican platform statements. The Council on Social Work Education wrote Health, Education, and Welfare Secretary Oveta Hobby that the Hoey incident "must undermine public confidence in the nonpolitical administration of the [public assistance] service,"[10] while a spokesman for the New York City chapter of the American Association of Social Workers protested that one of the top public assistance jobs in the country was now opened to political pressures.[11] Democratic Mayor-Elect Robert Wagner underscored the presumed difference between Democratic and Republican approaches to relief by publicly offering Miss Hoey the job of New York City Welfare Commissioner. Without much of a case, Democrats were seeking to suggest that hypocritical Republicans had been caught, so to speak, with their political hands in the nonpolitical poor box.

Politicking in relief is viewed differently from politicking in highways, rivers and harbors, public buildings, and even in defense contracts. In these latter activities, it is expected that public funds will be spent where the need is evident and also where partisan gain is possible. Edward Kennedy's subtle claim that "He can do more for Massachusetts" was a kind of subliminal reminder of how some decisions are made, as was Pierre Salinger's California campaign literature stating "All doors are open to Salinger." Robert Kennedy's promise in 1964 that, if elected Democratic Senator from New York, he would wait upon the Secretary of Defense in a Democratic administration and insist that the Brooklyn Navy Yard be kept open was less subtle. Because it dealt with the award of a contract for public business, however, it fell within the usually accepted permissible limits for exerting political influence. Kennedy's appearance in the Secretary's office a day or two after election was widely publicized and generally approved. So was the Secretary's decision to close the Yard.

[9]Arthur M. Schlesinger, Jr., *The Politics of Upheaval* (Boston: Houghton Mifflin, 1960), p. 355.
[10]"Open Letter," *Social Service Review,* XXVII (December, 1953), 429.
[11]*New York Times,* December 11, 1953, p. 41.

But efforts to keep a marginal case on the public assistance rolls through political intervention would be universally deplored.

Public assistance does not get caught up in politics as a consequence of machinations by one party or another to exchange bread for votes. No one accused Davey of withholding relief from political opponents. Providing the bread was not the partisan issue. It was Davey's effort to publicize it by unorthodox means that brought trouble. Miss Hoey was not fired in order that the Republicans might discriminate against Democratic recipients of public assistance. Along with a good many other bureau chiefs, she was fired because Republicans had been out of power for 20 years and needed some high-level jobs. The confidentiality repealer achieved through the Jenner amendment, it will be recalled, was not pursued to punish Democrats and reward Republicans or vice versa. The Newburgh affair was not a partisan political matter; supported by Republican city councilmen, the program was snuffed out by a Republican state administration. Illinois' 1963 crisis provoked an accusation from the Chairman of the Public Aid Commission that Republican senators were indifferent to providing relief funds for Negroes in Chicago who habitually vote Democratic; it should also be noted that the origins of the crisis were in a Democratic Governor's efforts to cut relief budgets. In sum, whatever the nature of the political involvement of public assistance, it is not an involvement that can be explained as the crude exchange of votes for welfare favors. Written rules now reenforce a widely held antipathy to that kind of trade.

The importance of recognizing that there are now no Tammany Halls, no Frank Hagues, and no Martin Luther Daveys waiting their opportunity to make public assistance administration a tool of the machine lies in the chance to reexamine the question of what constitutes appropriate training for public assistance workers. At the beginning of the program, there was a determination to equate social work training with effective administration of public assistance law because the alternative was unbridled patronage and possible favoritism, evils that Harry Hopkins fought in the FERA operation. The changed character of politics in America, and the changed character of politics in relief since the 1939 merit system amendment, the prohibition on waiting lists, and the early show of strength by the national administrative agency, weaken the case for professional social work methods as a barrier to partisan politics in public assistance. If professional social work training cannot be justified as a deterrent to undesirable partisan influence in relief administration, it must be justified on other grounds. Up to now, however, other justifications are not persuasive. Public assistance rolls do not decline on any steady basis as the number of trained workers increases, although short-run changes are occasionally dramatic. More important, public assistance is certainly not a superior program to either OASDI or unemployment insurance, yet in neither of the latter is the methodology of professional social work utilized to aid dependent clients.

It is comforting, perhaps, to all of the groups who deplore the growth of public assistance to be able to attribute it partly to the shortage of trained social workers. Similarly, the support of appropriations for training social workers seems like a positive attack on public assistance. But the training problem in public assistance is not the shortage of trained social workers as much as the shortage of sure knowledge about the kind of training best suited for welfare workers. The only useful professional skill is that which is a specific remedy for the problem at hand, but it has yet to be demonstrated that professional training in social work is a specific for the relief problem. If a new breed of professionals must be trained to cope with public assistance, this is neither an invitation to patronage nor an insurmountable difficulty. An adaptation of present training in sociology or in economics or in psychology might produce people no less capable of helping public assistance clients than does the graduate social work curriculum which steers so clear of most aspects of public relief issues.

The social worker's process-style interview and his relationship with the client have not been shown to have an advantage in today's public assistance situation over the skills of the home economist, or the child psychologist, or the paid companion. Persons suffering from poverty, discrimination, and a disorganized family life — characteristics associated with many public assistance cases — cannot be expected to respond to individual therapy with any major character changes, a Russell Sage Foundation study of potentially delinquent girls found recently.[12] And the poverty program is busy stressing social work without professionalism, the "deprofessionalization" of social welfare implicit in its efforts to involve the poor themselves in program planning. Public assistance is susceptible to controlled study by staffing otherwise comparable local agencies with workers of different backgrounds utilizing different methods, maintaining a control group, and measuring the results against agreed-upon goals. But all the measuring up to now has been done by those with a commitment to existing ways. The independent audit has yet to replace the friendly audit.

[12]Henry J. Meyer, Edgar F. Borgatta, Wyatt C. Jones, *et al., Girls at Vocational High: An Experiment in Social Work Intervention* (New York: Russell Sage Foundation, 1965).

Social workers are admirable people, full of understanding for the client and his situation, anxious to provide help to the emotionally troubled, disturbed by the presence of want, and fiercely nonpolitical. In a nationwide program that employs over 35,000 workers and spends $5 billion on eight million people, however, the stakes are too great to assume the appropriateness of professional training in social work just because social workers are good people, and because making the assumption in another era helped prevent political control of relief. Yet the present policy-making process makes no arrangements for inquiring into the current validity of that assumption or of many other assumptions that seem to control public relief policy.

V. GOALS

The evolution of public assistance policy reflects changing attitudes about the function of relief in American domestic affairs. Both that attitude and present policy are characterized by an ambivalence between economic aid to the destitute and steps toward elimination of technical destitution. But there is no agreement on either the causes of destitution or how the success or failure of relief policy should be judged. The economic crisis of the 1930's gave rise to emergency adjustments suitable for the moment. When 17 per cent of the national population was in need of some kind of relief at the lowest point of the Great Depression, it was enough to provide that relief. With states incapable of doing the job, it was enough to arrange a way to put federal funds into OAA and into relief of orphans. Frank Bane, first Executive Director of the Social Security Board, remembers that the original ADC concern was only with the widows and orphans. "The ADC example we always thought about," he told an interviewer, "was the poor lady in West Virginia whose husband was killed in a mining accident, and the problem of how she could feed those kids." If people did not freeze or starve, the relief program was a formal success.

Success is not still measured in those terms. President Kennedy's 1962 State of the Union message described a new public welfare program "stressing services instead of support, rehabilitation instead of relief, and training for useful work instead of prolonged dependency." This language was repeated by Secretary Ribicoff in his communication to Congress transmitting the draft of the Public Welfare Amendments of 1962. It is not clear, however, whether a program that "stresses services instead of support" fails if the costs of support continue to increase. Nor is it clear whether a program stressing "rehabilitation instead of relief" fails if relief needs remain dominant and rehabilitation remains undefined. Public assistance policy is not readily evaluated in terms of failure or success of rehabilitation and service. These objectives cannot be measured like the provision of food and clothing. The hazy nature of the newly stated objectives obscures evaluation of policy.

Even while the President was describing the proposed new program, Ribicoff paid a visit to Senator Harry Byrd, whose Finance Committee had jurisdiction over public assistance, and delivered a memorandum which reported administrative changes in the welfare program designed to "promote rehabilitation services and develop a family-centered approach" and to "provide children with adequate protection, support, and a maximum opportunity to become responsible citizens." These are admirable objectives. They recognize that the public assistance problem is principally an ADC problem, but they introduce a perplexing note. Is the public policy enunciated by President Kennedy of training adults for useful work instead of prolonged dependency consistent with the public policy enunciated by Ribicoff of providing children with adequate protection, support, and a maximum opportunity to become responsible citizens? Is the focus on child welfare or on adult rehabilitation? Specifically, has the idea of protecting a fatherless child by keeping the mother in the home been abandoned in favor of training for useful work?

However well the cause of alliteration is served by pushing rehabilitation instead of relief and services instead of support, the cause of clarity of policy is injured. "Born of depression, the original pioneering welfare legislation well met the problems of that time," said the Ribicoff memorandum for Byrd, "but the quarter of a century that has passed has taught us many new things."[13] In the list of lessons learned that followed, however, there was no mention of the great new ADC dilemma: whether the program should be preoccupied with the economic needs of dependent children and their families or whether its preoccupation should be with transforming adults into breadwinners. Ribicoff later described to the House Committee the case of a deserted mother of six children who "couldn't work now because of the daily demands of the children, the oldest age 13." Within a year after a welfare worker — professional, skilled — took a serious and friendly interest in the problem, the family was on even keel, the mother was planning to go to work, there was "no question" but that she would become self-supporting.[14] The case was offered as a success story in

[13]U.S. Congress, Senate, Committee on Finance, Hearings, "Public Assistance Act of 1962," 87th Cong., 2d Sess., 1962, p. 54.
[14]U.S. Congress, House, Committee on Ways and Means, Hearings, "Public Welfare Amendments of 1962," 87th Cong., 2d Sess., 1962, p. 167.

rehabilitation; emphasis on services instead of support apparently included sending out to work the mother of six children under the age of 14.

In fact, there is a fortunate confusion between expressed official goals, private judgments, and actual practices. The official commitment is to reduction of dependency, to self-support, and to looking ahead to the end of the need for public assistance as a result of the grand new welfare program of our times. Yet the private judgment of a high-ranking official in Health, Education, and Welfare is that the ADC problem is "insoluble." Actual practice in the field, judging from the steady increase in ADC cases and costs, is to carry on as always in the manner of the first days of the program when the West Virginia miner's widow was provided money to support her children and as much in the way of understanding and nonfiscal therapy as a dedicated social worker was capable of providing. Outside the legislative hearing room, rehabilitation, self-help, and self-care are not practical alternatives to providing relief adequate for minimum standards of health and decency to persons unable to provide for themselves.

The choice is not properly stated between services and support, or between rehabilitation and relief. Rehabilitation of the moral standards of an unwed mother may be a separate thing from relief for her children and for herself. Home economist services for an uneducated rural mother adrift in an urban center may be virtually independent of her continued need for financial assistance. Emphasis on rehabilitation and on services instead of support has made it appear that these are real alternatives, that it is a realistic goal to look ahead to the point where people become self-sufficient so that they no longer need assistance. It is not a realistic goal. There are fewer needy miners' widows now than there are deserted or unwed mothers. But the likelihood of self-support isn't much different. In an economy that demands an ever higher level of skill for employment, how much chance is there for the undereducated late starter? The official case was made in 1962 in terms of relief and rehabilitation as alternatives, either as a matter of strategy to secure support for services or as a matter of accident, as the proponents of services got carried away with their own case. In either event, it was a disservice to the cause of public assistance because it obscured the need for officially separating the old image from the new, of separating the cases for which ADC is a specific remedy from those for which some new techniques may be in order. In the latter group are the families where moral rehabilitation of the mother may be as important a social goal as money support for the family. This is the case, for example, in 37 per cent of the Illinois ADC cases where there are two or more illegitimate children. The purpose of ADC there must be both rehabilitation and relief, and both objectives will be advanced if the duality of the purpose is squarely acknowledged.

On the other hand, for the modern version of the miner's widow, for the victim of discrimination in education or in employment or in housing, for the helpless aged, for the chronically unemployed, unskilled worker, some of whom are caught in what John Fischer harshly but accurately calls "the stupidity problem," the primary goal of public welfare is a reasonable subsistence. It is a goal that has yet to be achieved.

INDEX

INDEX

Abbott, Grace, 44
Academy of Certified Social Workers (ACSW), 202
Ad Hoc Committee on Public Welfare (1961), 37f., 121, 130, 145, 172ff.
ADC. *See* Children, aid to dependent
ADC-U. *See* Unemployment, aid to dependent children of
Advisory bodies, 169ff.
Advisory Commission on Intergovernmental Relations, 243
Advisory Council on Economic Security (1934), 19, 169
Advisory Council on Public Assistance (1958-1960), 169, 171f.
Advisory Council on Social Security (1947), 138f., 169
Age qualification, 85, 108, 155
Agency goals in welfare, 117
Alabama, 29, 94
Alaska, 81
Alinsky, Saul, 157
Allen, Byron T., 86n.
Allott, Gordon, 65
Altmeyer, Arthur J., 20, 34, 72, 88ff., 95, 130, 163, 242
Amend, Myles, 111
American Association of Public Welfare Officials, 149
American Association of Social Workers, 197f.; New York City chapter, 254. *See also* Social work, professionalization effort; National Association of Social Workers
American Legion, 25
American Public Welfare Association, 13, 14, 40, 42, 73, 110, 116, 130, 139, 144, 157, 203; compared with other

associations in Public Administration Clearing House, 149f.; formation, 148f.; membership, 149f.; public understanding project, 151f.; statement of basic principles, 152
American Society of Planning Officials, 150
Annual reports of federal agency, 167f.
Appropriations Committee, U.S. House of Representatives, 47, 62, 78, 240
Appropriations Committee, U.S. Senate, 66, 68, 72, 77, 120, 172
Appropriations process in public assistance, 60ff., 239f.
Appropriations subcommittee, Departments of Labor and Health, Education, and Welfare appropriations, U.S. House of Representatives, 39, 63, 70ff., 78
Appropriations subcommittee on Labor—Health, Education, and Welfare appropriations, U.S. Senate, 26, 63
Arizona, 81, 95, 133, 244
Arizona v. *Hobby*, 83n.
Arne, R. E., 198n.
Audit exceptions, 87, 90, 163

Bane, Frank, 257
Banfield, Edward, 241
Barkley, Alben, 52
Bell, Winifred, 145n.
Berman, Jules, 95n.
Birth Control and Public Policy (St. John-Stevas), 124
Birth control services, 117, 123ff., 233; Illinois controversy, 222ff.
Blackwell, Gordon, 152n.

263

PRINTED IN U.S.A.